PREFACE

Within the pages of this book lies a tale of a singular dam and park that bore the brunt of Hurricane Matthew's fury in October 2016. Situated just outside the charming town of Zebulon, North Carolina, this park once cradled a striking dam, crafted over a century ago with robust concrete blocks as its foundation. In its prime, it served as the beating heart of a mill, harnessing the flowing waters to grind cornmeal.

As you peruse the contents of this book, you'll embark on a journey to cultivate an enduring fondness for the dam's original architecture. My odyssey with this subject commenced in 2015 when I began capturing the essence of the dam and its surroundings through the lens. Standing at the water's edge, beholding the cascade that follows a torrential downpour is a mesmerizing and tranquil experience. The rhythmic flow of water possesses the capacity to instill serenity within your body and mind, offering solace as each wave adheres to the same captivating patterns.

This book stands as a testament to my profound adoration for this dam, from its transformation into a glittering spectacle adorned with massive icicles in the winter to the grandeur of its vigorous, unrelenting flow, rendering it a thing of sheer beauty, until its splendor was marred almost beyond recognition. Yet, at its core, a glimmer of its former glory remains, even at the site of its breach. I continue to capture its essence, especially after a deluge, hoping for the eventual creation of a splendid, enhanced park.

Notably, this site still draws numerous families who come to its edge, sharing meals while immersing themselves in the captivating spectacle of the water's flow.

I extend my heartfelt hope that you will appreciate the culmination of years of dedicated work within these pages. Should this book find success, two more volumes await their time, filled with thousands of photographs awaiting their own story. May your venture through these images be a source of genuine delight, allowing you to envision the graceful dance of flowing water. For those seeking to delve into the history of The Little River Dam and Griss Mill, a wealth of information can be found by simply searching "Little River Dam, Zebulon, NC" online.

Timothy K Smith

DEDICATION

Now to the most important person in my life besides my children Jennifer and Marc. She is my sweet loving wife who has put up with me for forty-nine years. We have been married March 3, 2024 for Fifty-years. I have loved this woman so much for all of these years and continue to. We support each other One hundred percent. Thank God she is in very good health. She has watched my health deteriate for almost thirty-years. First it was my Heart, then Severe Diabetes, then my Lungs and the other deceases just keep adding up. She drives me everywhere I need to go like the Veteran's Clinic and I know some places she doesn't want to go, but she does with no complaints. Becky just cares so deeply for me as I do for her. Thank you my love!

I want to thank my children Jennifer and Marc for being so accepting and patient with me all of their lives, with either a video camera or still camera focused on them. I love you all and I hope you enjoy all of the hard work we have done on this book.

ACKNOWLEDGEMENT

As a Father a Grandad and Caring Husband I would like to dedicate this book to my family. If it weren't for my grandkids alot of these photos would not exist in my library. They have helped me with my walker and making sure I stay upright and even helped with some of the shots. I love my grandkids so much. The kids you see through out this book are my helpers. So, thank you so much Jenna, Emily, Nicholas, Jocelyn and Landon. Kids, so there are no misunderstandings, notice I put your names by age not favorites

It was Christmas Eve in 1985 and we had some heavy rains.. I drove down to what was at that time, the abandoned Jaycee Park after the local chapter disbanded. It's hard to believe that it's 37 and a half years ago and yet I still remember the water thundering over the dam. I was by myself and turned into the park... The tall chest high weeds and scrub pines made it difficult... but I got to the edge of the Little River and stood in awe of the power of the waters-vibrating the ground where I stood actually intimidating me to a degree... I still remember that feeling. I looked around at the undergrowth and litter everywhere as far as you could see. I shook my head and wondered "why"?? I remember saying that it was a shame someone hasn't cleaned it up.... and I remember me saying: "Well, what's the matter with you? It was then I began within a few days to begin picking up the litter. Then with a 20 inch wide Sears Roebuck push mower I managed to clear the acreage.... pulling not pushing as I went along. Hand tools like an iron rake, sling, mattock, hoe, axe, and weed cater and two chainsaws. I eventually purchased a total of two riding mowers and branched out to the west bank of the river and the highway right aways on both sides and the ditch banks. There was a lot of hard physical work clearing the vegetation off the dam and boulders by machete and iron rake and pitchfork. Freezing temperatures in winter and sweltering heat in the summer. Poison oak became more of a nemesis than snakes and deer flies! I was allergic to it and often was covered with the trimmings and poison. Dr. Hwang had to give me shots to ease the blistering, Dr Hwang had to give me shots to ease the blistering. People would ask me why I did this restoration...

I told them that I wanted to create a natural area where families could enjoy nature, fishing, paddling canoes or kayaking and exploring... I wanted to see families enjoying picnics... The Mayor (Frank Wall), requested that I come to stand before the town council. He began by asking about how much money did I think that I had spent... I estimated between $3,500 to $5,000 of my family's resources. He said that he and the board wanted to reimburse me for my expenses...... I was left speechless and finally said: "I didn't do it for the money-It was a labor of love... He was left puzzled and asked well, what would you want? I answered back; "Well ~ I would like that one day when I prove it viable as a park - to have it adopted into the Parks and Recreation Department as a Town Park... "What would it be called?" I answered back that the Little River flows through it... Little River Park! And so it began... Dave Privette ran the grist mill down there and the townsfolk who couldn't afford to travel to the coast.. would go down to the river to what was nicknamed "Dave's Beach" according to Eva Liles... she remembered her childhood there. Dave's son Wayne Privette went into WW2 and some time while he was overseas the mill was destroyed. Wayne Privette ran the local TV repair shop... his wife Betty was a cafeteria lunch lady at the school. Many times when I went down to lock the gates at dusk... Wayne and Betty would be down there having a picnic.... I would leave them to their moments of memories... and return later. There are many who have memories of times past.. Unfortunately many have passed on these last years.

John Middleswarth

The following is a newspaper clipping.

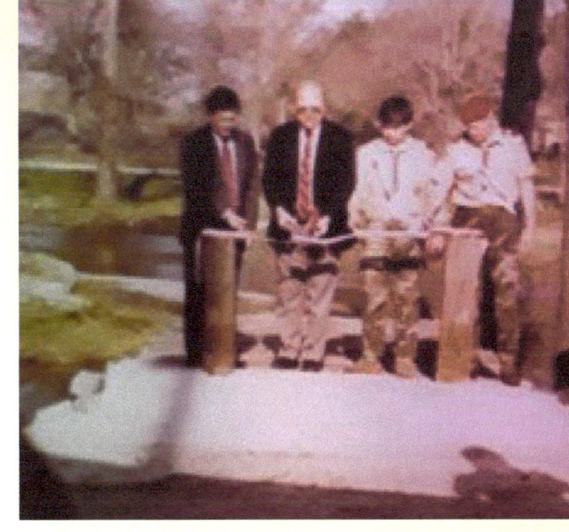

Self-appointed caretaker
Zebulon's John Middleswarth takes pride in the appearance of the Little River Park on N.C. 97. Because of his dedication, this town recreation area now draws families from several different communities.

Photo by Mary Beth Newhart

3 years later Middleswarth still dedicated to park project

By MARY BETH NEWHART
Record staff writer

There still isn't a sign proclaiming it as a town recreation area, but the Little River Park west of Zebulon on N.C. 97 has gone through a great many changes since John Middleswarth appointed himself as its caretaker three years ago.

The park is the property of the Town of Zebulon, and was a project of the Zebulon Jaycees before the group disbanded in 1985.

The appearance of the park has come a long way from the first night Middleswarth became obsessed with its restoration — Christmas Eve 1985.

"There was trash everywhere," he explained. "I started to clean it up Christmas Day and once I got started, I'd just find more. I just kept it up after that."

All the improvements have been made by Middleswarth, along with the help of a few dedicated friends like Lizard Lick "mayor" Charles Wood.

As for financial assistance coming from the town, there has been none. Middleswarth figures that he has spent about $3,500 of his personal monies on the upkeep and maintenance of the park since he began his project.

"Although it's town property, there is no maintenance out there (at the park)," he said.

He used a push lawnmower the first year, and went through a 20-inch blade every month. Middleswarth now uses a riding mower, and he hopes it will last him awhile.

"I can't afford to buy another mower. My wife would kill me."

Ten months ago, the ___

Board of Commissioners voted to accept the park as an official town recreation area. Middleswarth was told by the town manager Donald Horton that an order for a sign had been placed. The sign has yet to appear.

"The park used to be a garbage dump," Middleswarth said. "Now people from all over, not just Zebulon but Middlesex, Bailey, Lizard Lick and Wendell, come to use it. When the weather is nice, there are probably about 12 to 15 people here just out for lunch. And people do just come out when it gets cold, people come out when it gets cold, people come out and just sit in their cars and listen to the water running over the dam."

— A lot of people just sit and listen to the water running over the dam."

Middleswarth estimates that the park dates back to pre-Civil ___

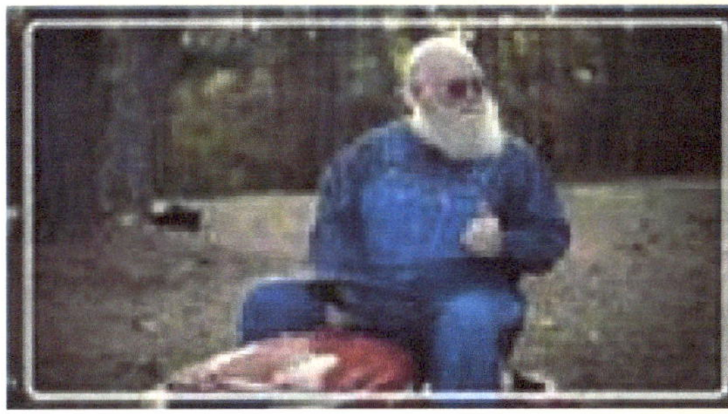

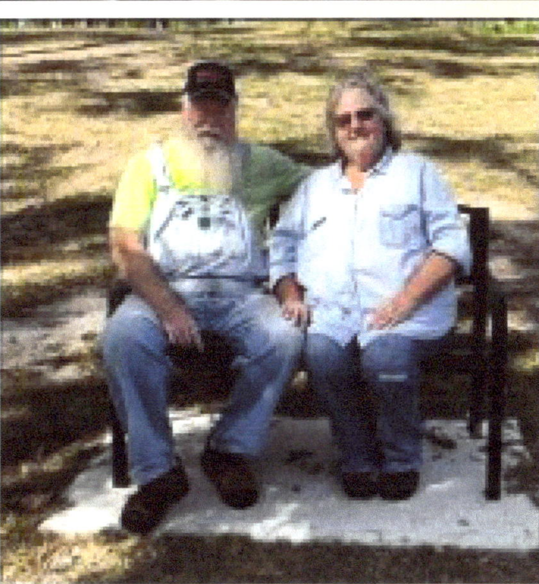

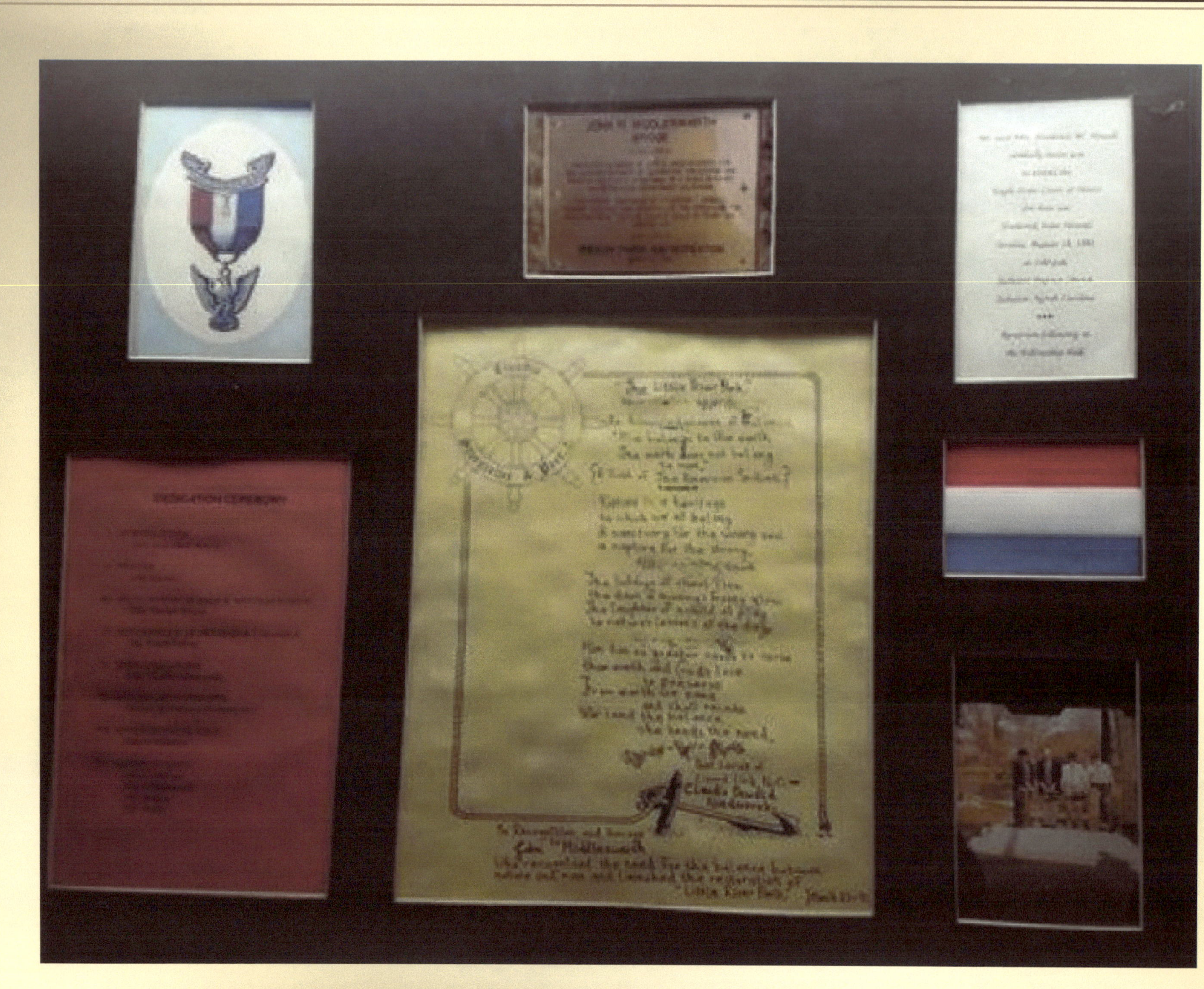

Thank you John Middleswarth for the hard work in caring for the Park and Dam all of these years. It takes a good caring person to do this for the people in your community..

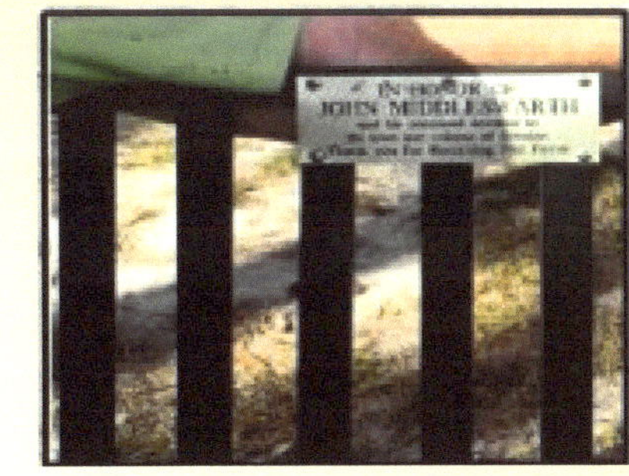

This bench was donated to the Little River Park in honor of John Middleswarth for all of the work and time he has put into the park Unfortunately, the original bench was destroyed by a Tornado..

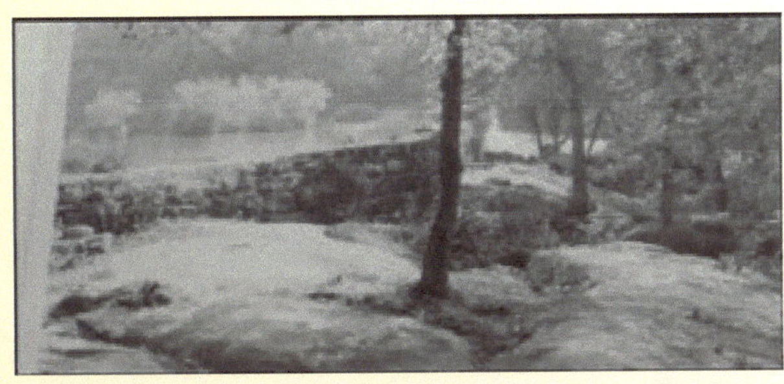

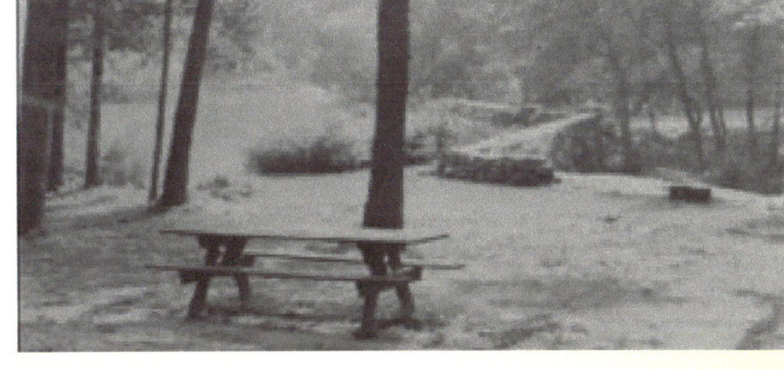

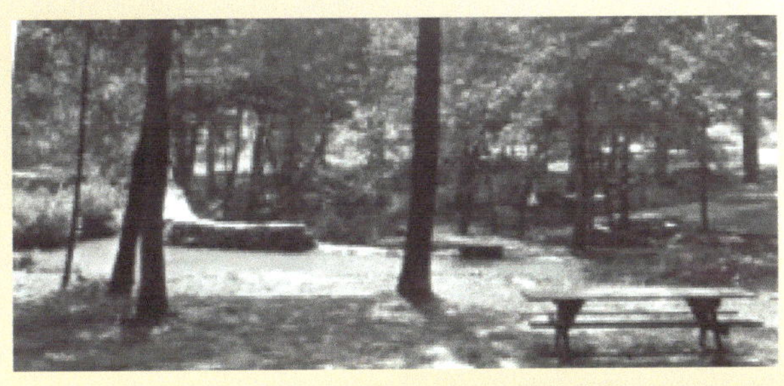

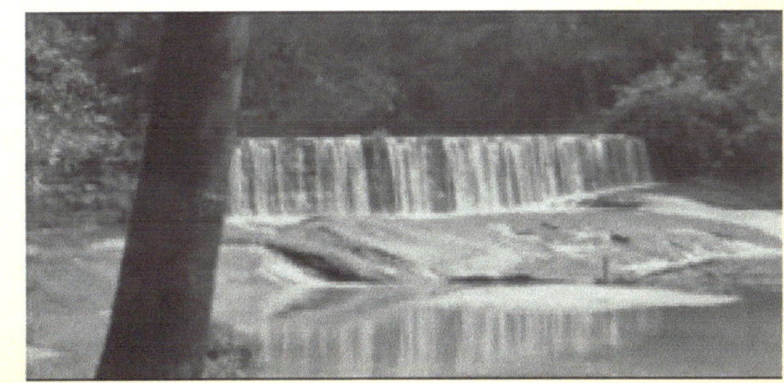

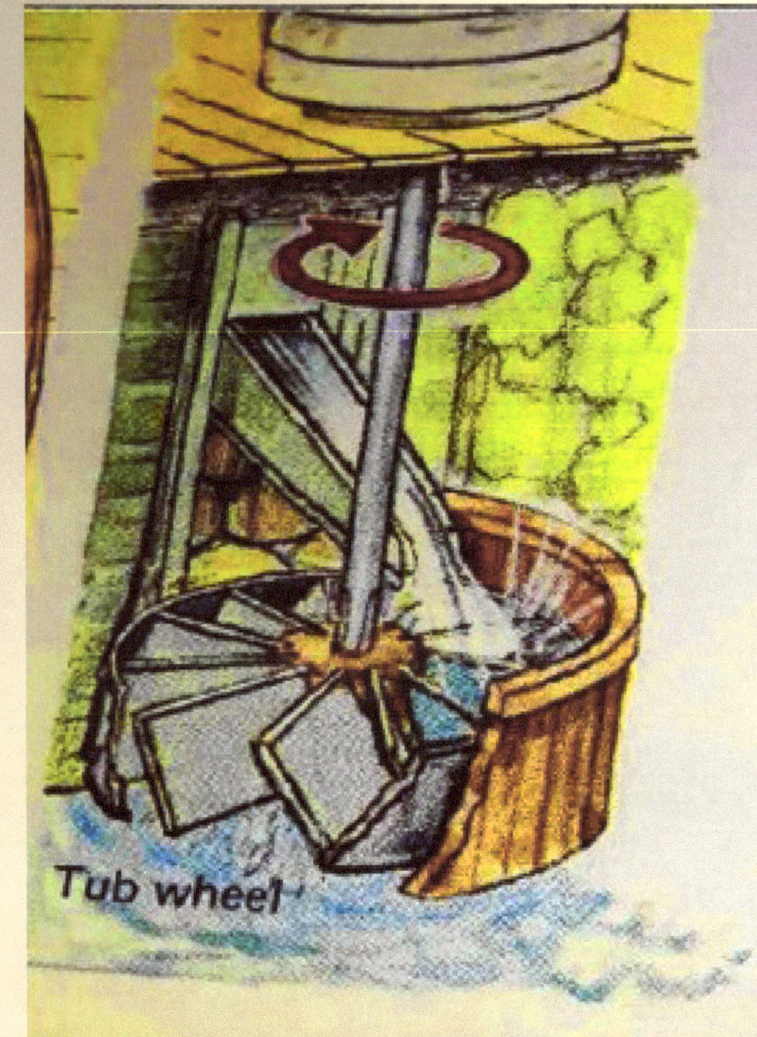

...ility and variety marked the waterwheels of the past. Their diameters ranged from 3 ft. to 20 ft., and they incorporated every conceivable water-flow scheme. The most efficient type was the overshot wheel shown above, but if the water source was not high enough, a breast wheel or undershot wheel was employed. Of low efficiency, but simplest to build because it used no gears, was the tub wheel. A typical large wheel made 10 to 20 revolutions per minute; with wooden gearing this could be stepped up to 10 times the rate. A number of traditional waterwheels are still in operation in America, turning out the stone-ground meal so highly prized by home bakers.

Principles of a Freestanding Dry Wall

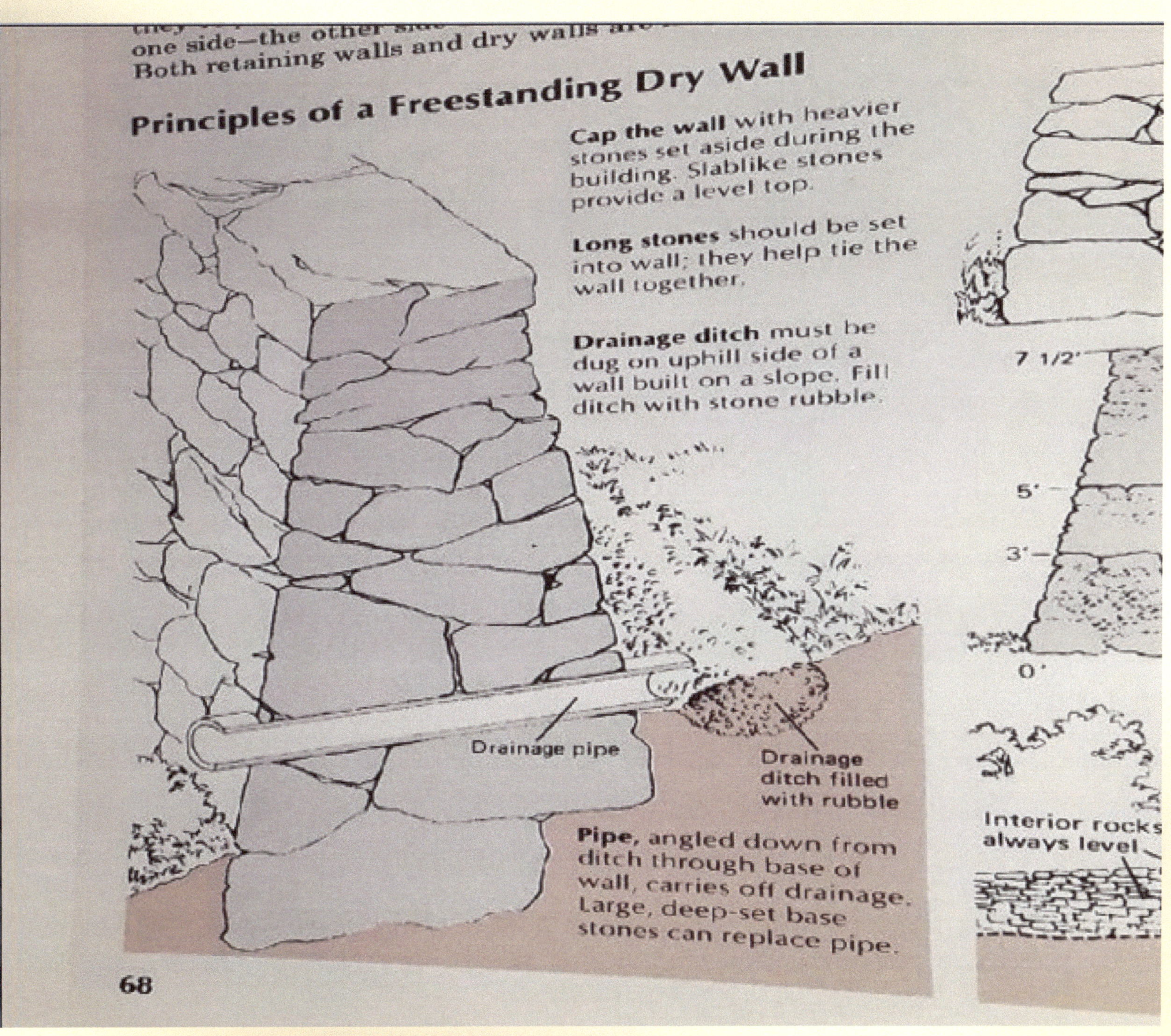

Cap the wall with heavier stones set aside during the building. Slablike stones provide a level top.

Long stones should be set into wall; they help tie the wall together.

Drainage ditch must be dug on uphill side of a wall built on a slope. Fill ditch with stone rubble.

Pipe, angled down from ditch through base of wall, carries off drainage. Large, deep-set base stones can replace pipe.

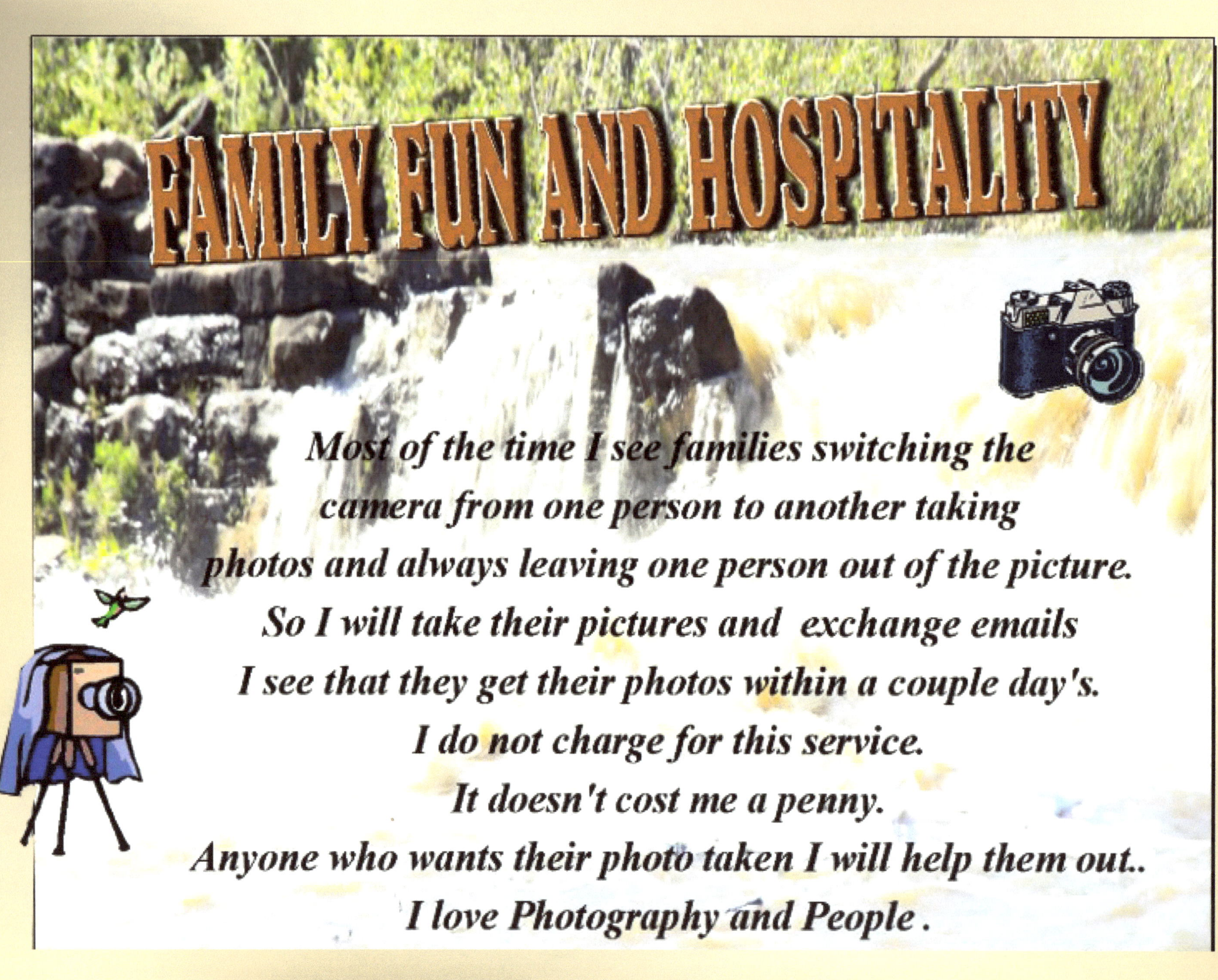

FAMILY FUN AND HOSPITALITY

Most of the time I see families switching the
camera from one person to another taking
photos and always leaving one person out of the picture.
So I will take their pictures and exchange emails
I see that they get their photos within a couple day's.
I do not charge for this service.
It doesn't cost me a penny.
Anyone who wants their photo taken I will help them out..
I love Photography and People .

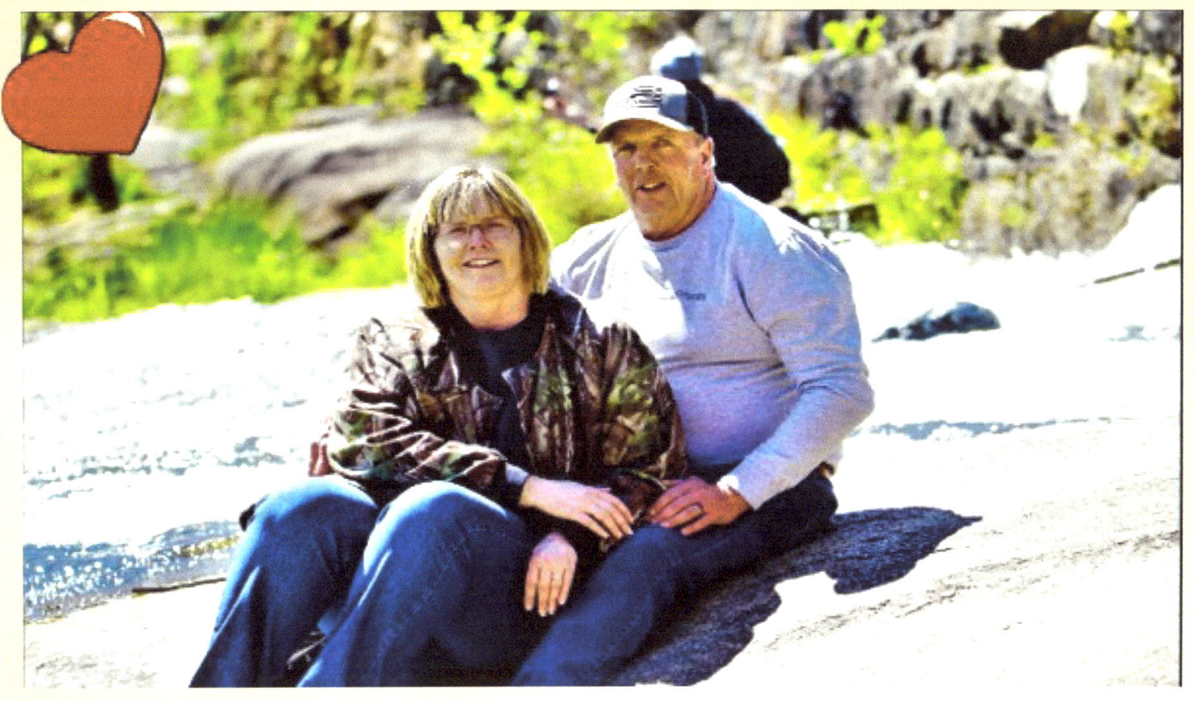

This couple, Lisa and Thomas was very sweet and excited at what I was doing. Shortly after I took their photo's Thomas passed away. Keep this family in your prayers. "Rest in Peace my Friend!"

Thomas "Clay"- everyone knew him as Clay

Born: May 25, 1965

Died: September 10, 2022

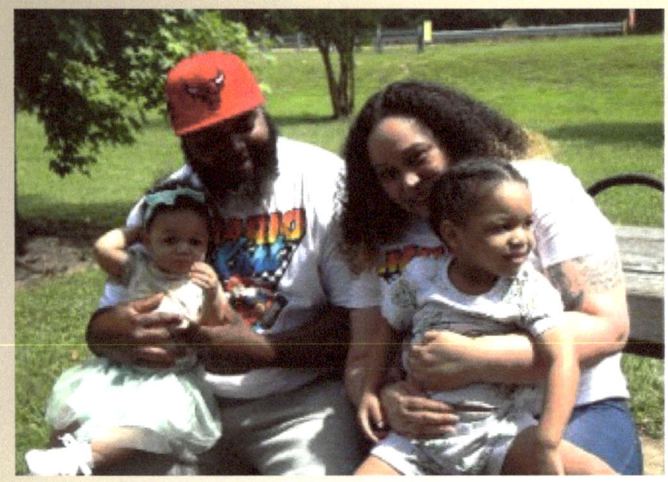

A new addition since I took the bottom photo

Father: Thomas

Daughter: Princess

Son: King

Mom: Faisha

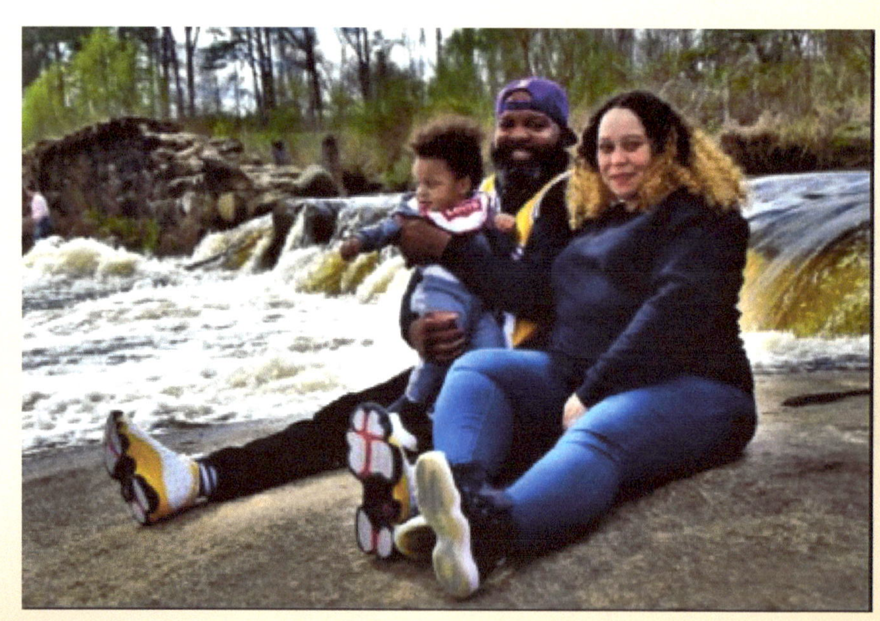

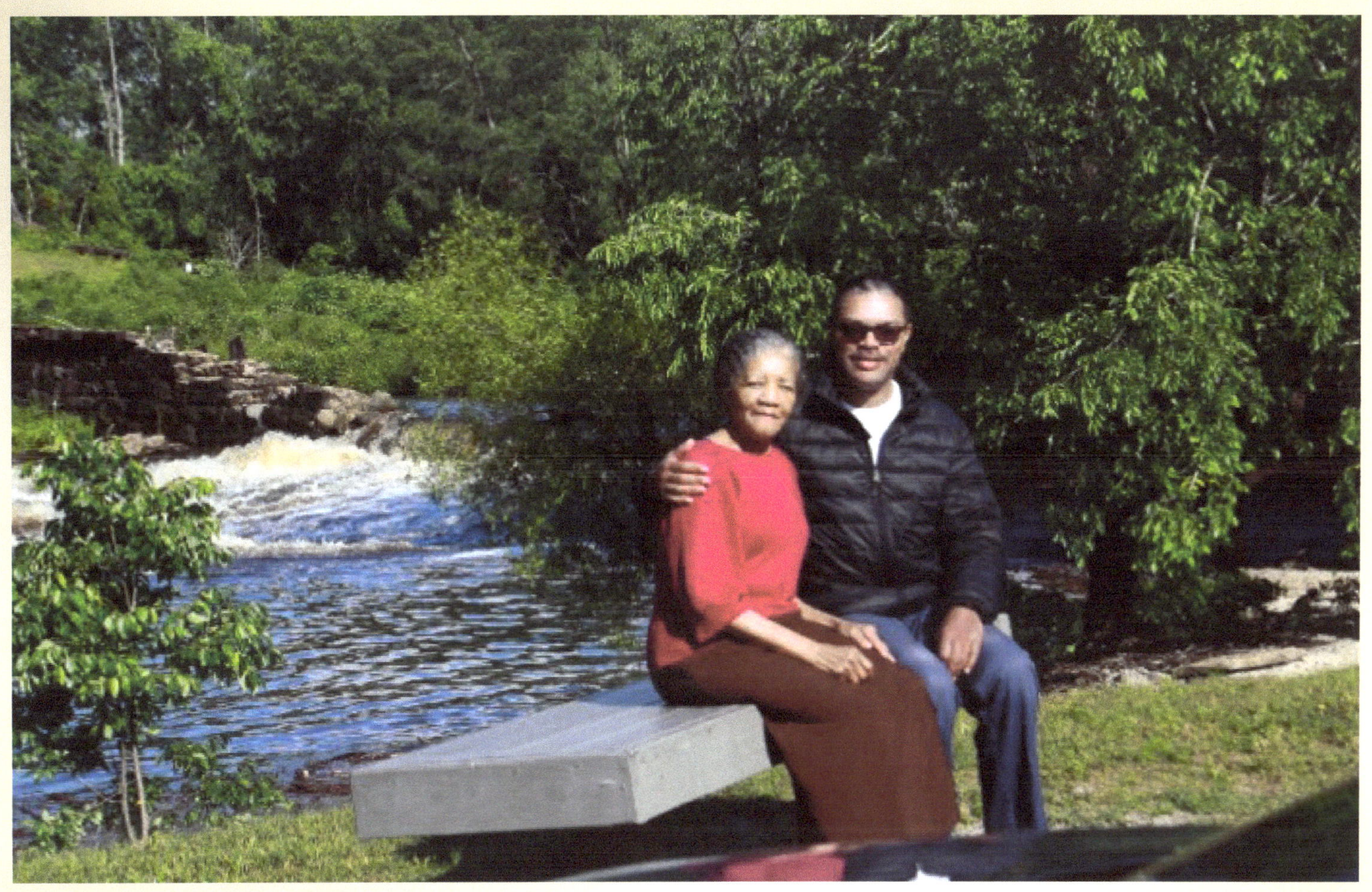

Alexis and his mother Victoria

This section is about the beautiful water flowing over and around the

boulders while making its path down the hills behind the dam when

there's an overflow..Plus, during the Winter the Ice that hangs from the

top of the walls of the dam and the wild vines.

Then there's the original dám that was described in the beginning of

the book before Hurricane Matthew,

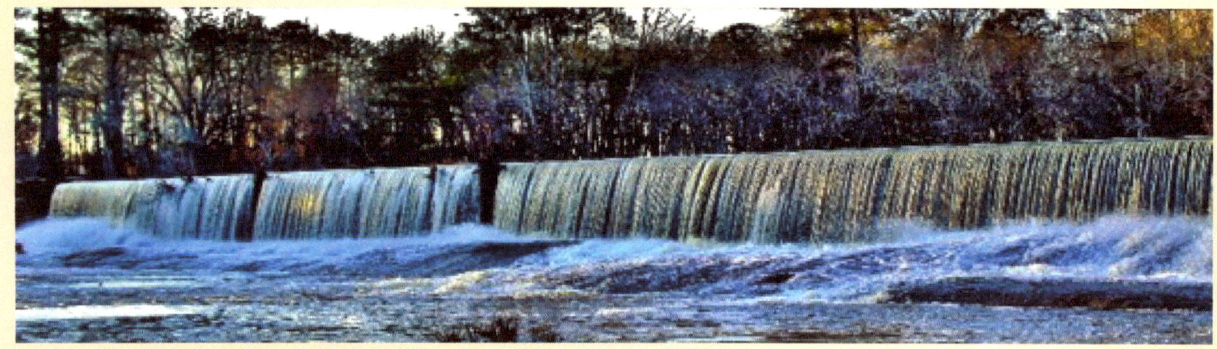

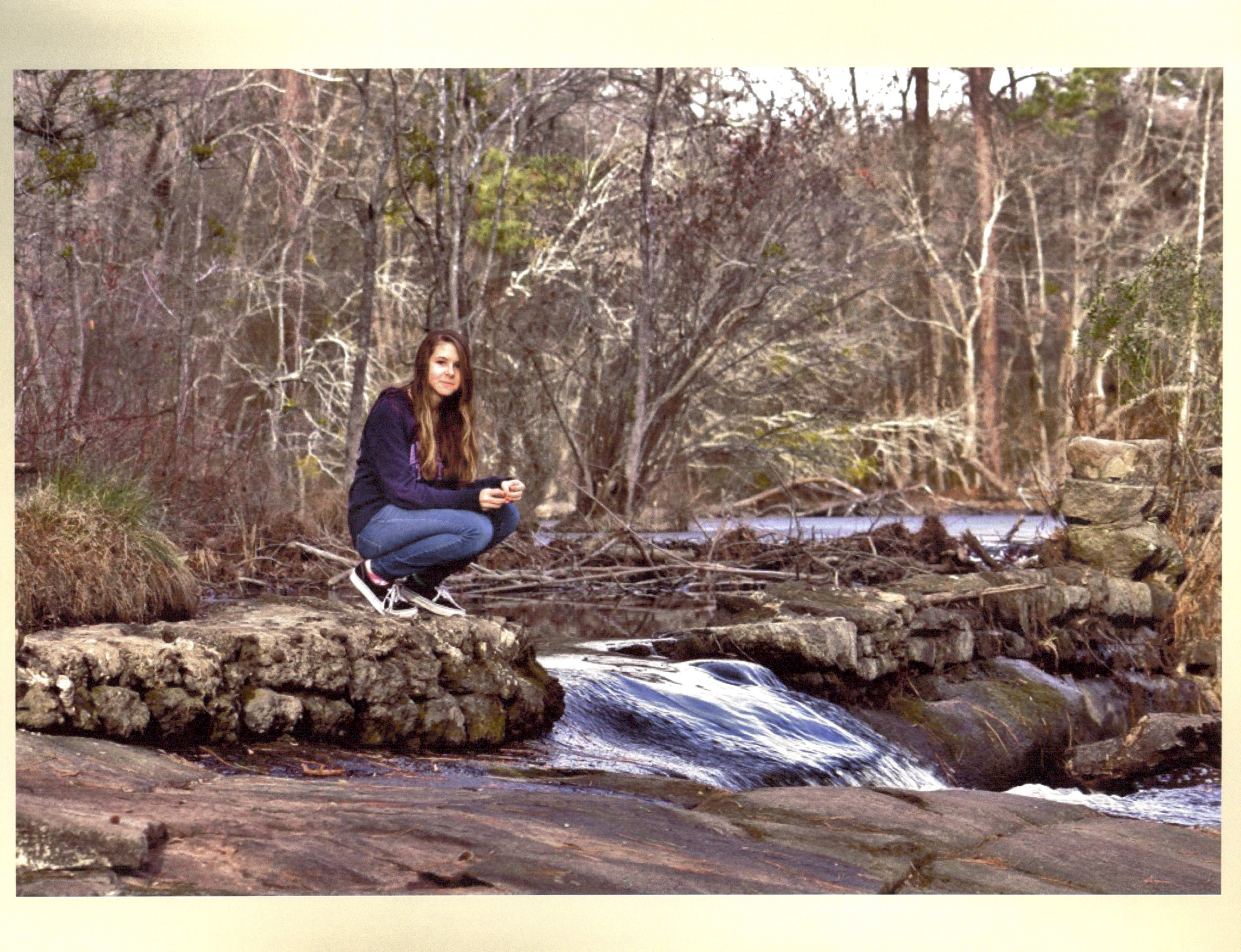

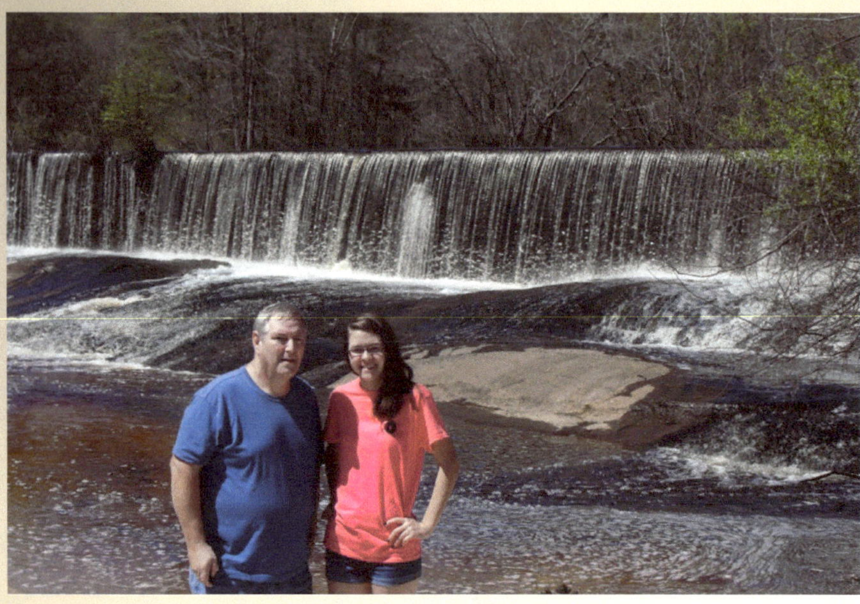

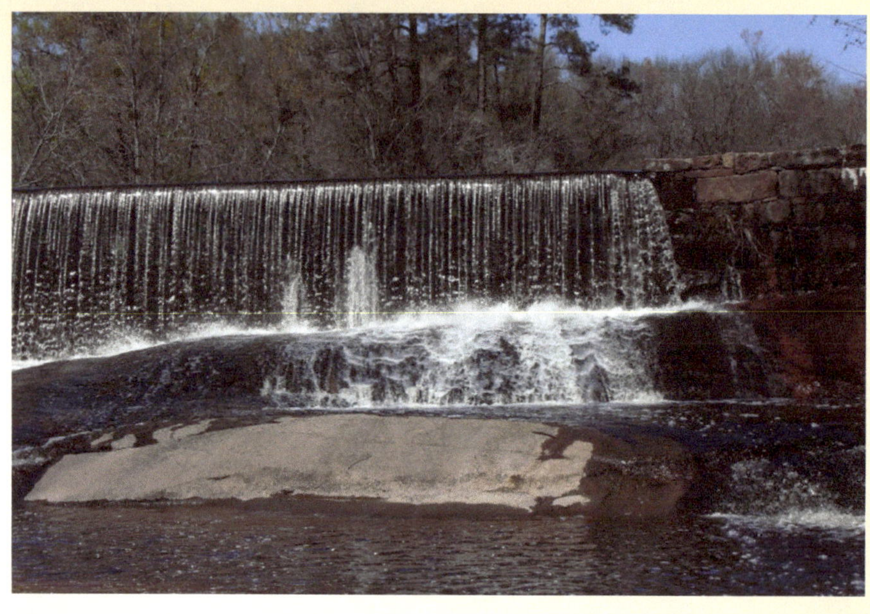

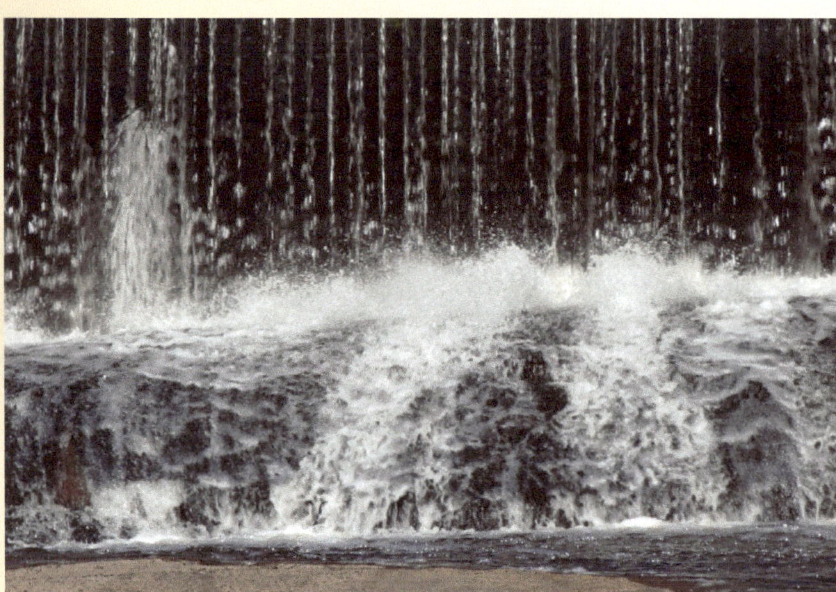

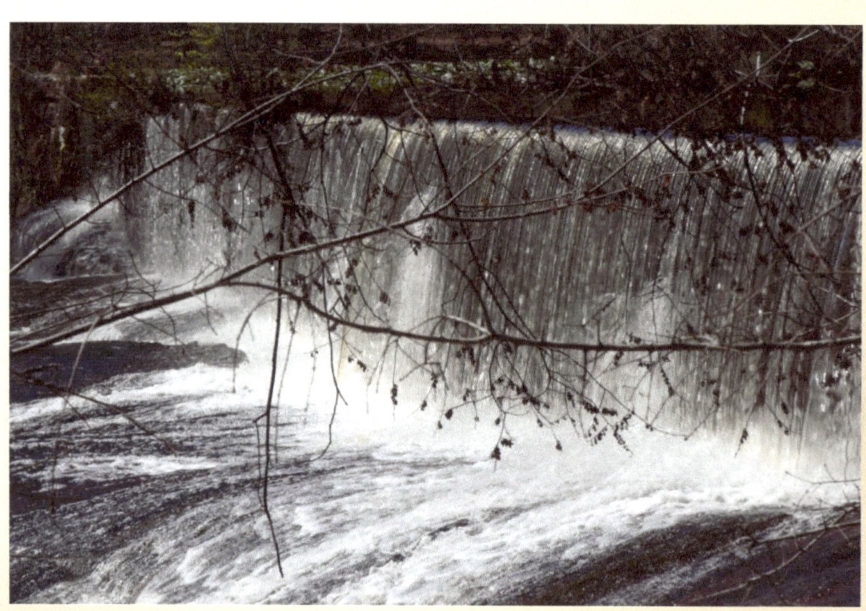

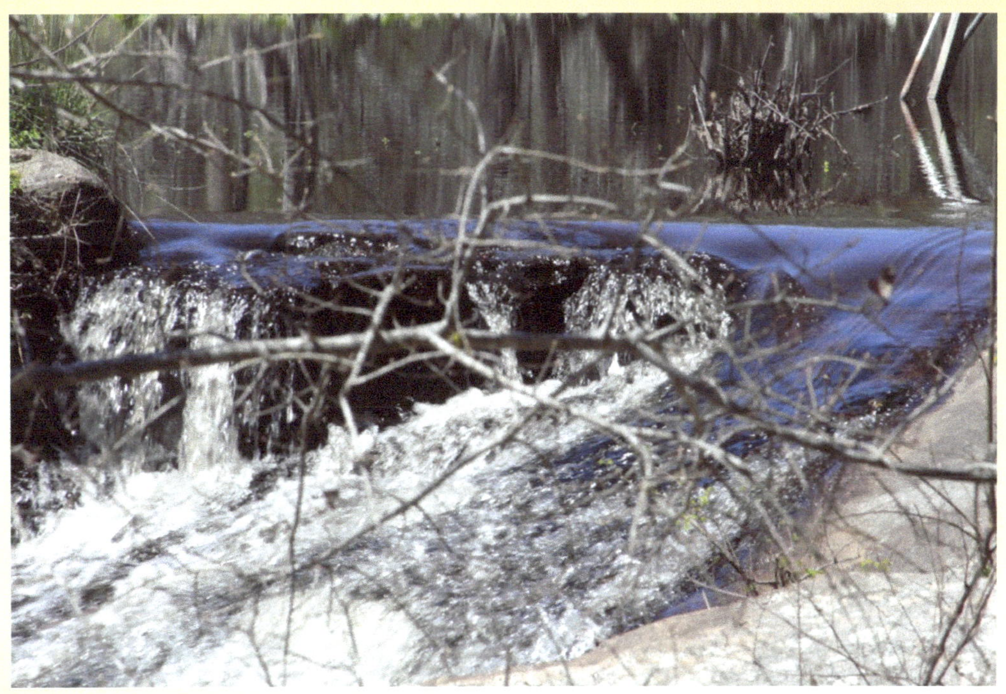

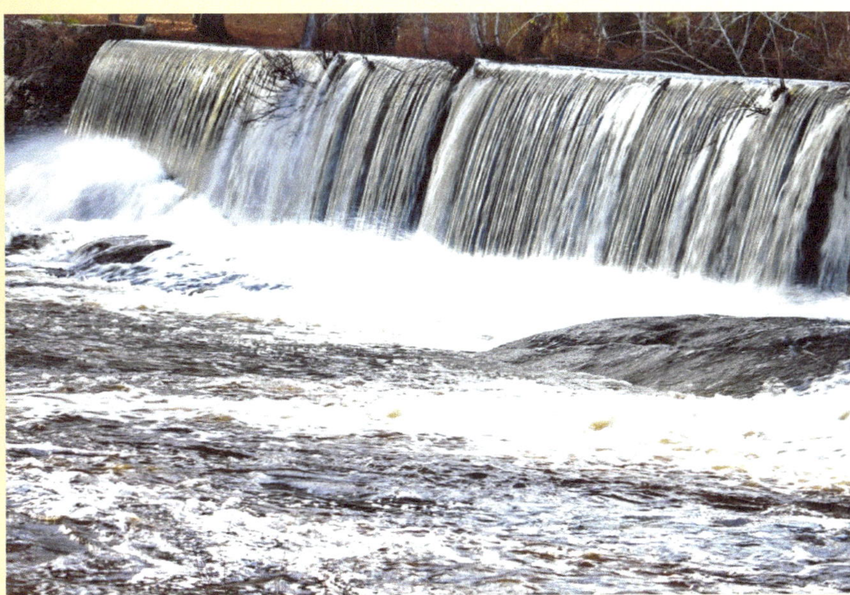

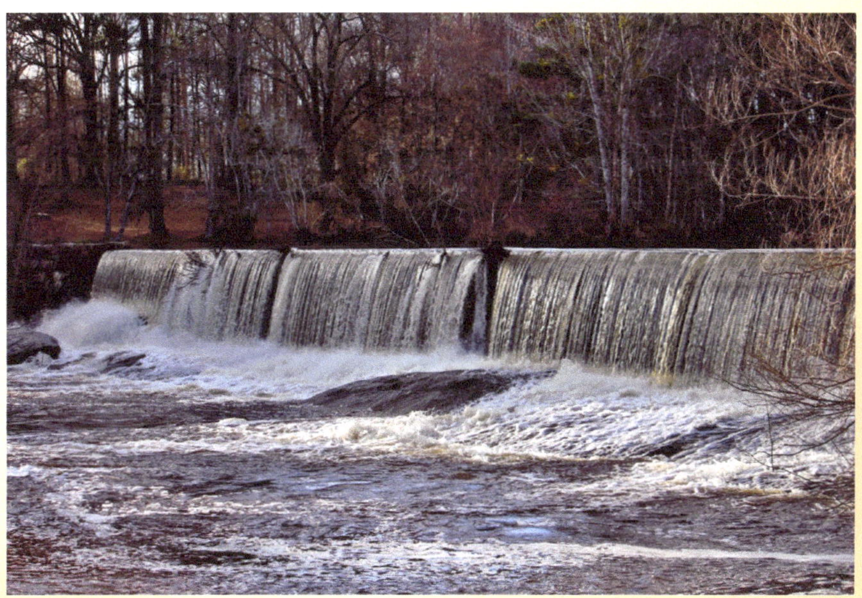

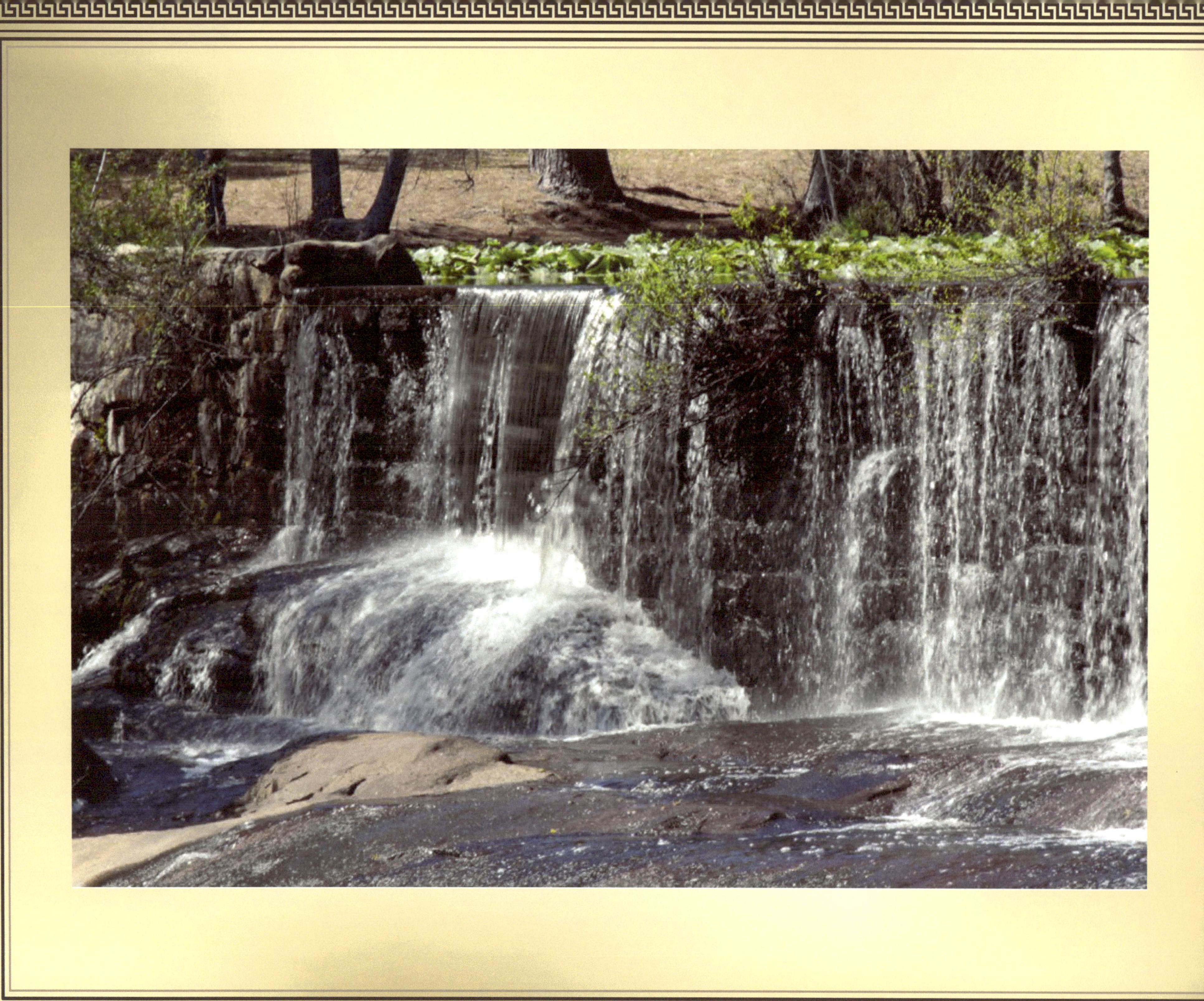

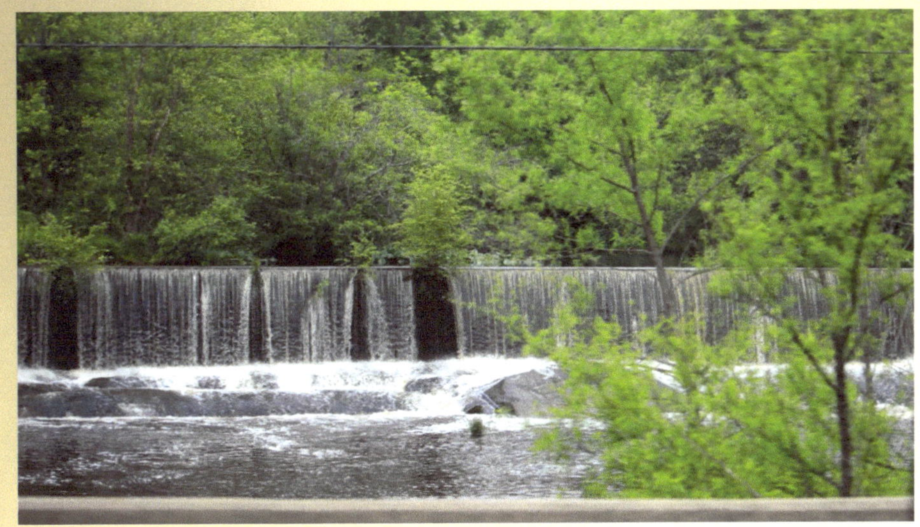
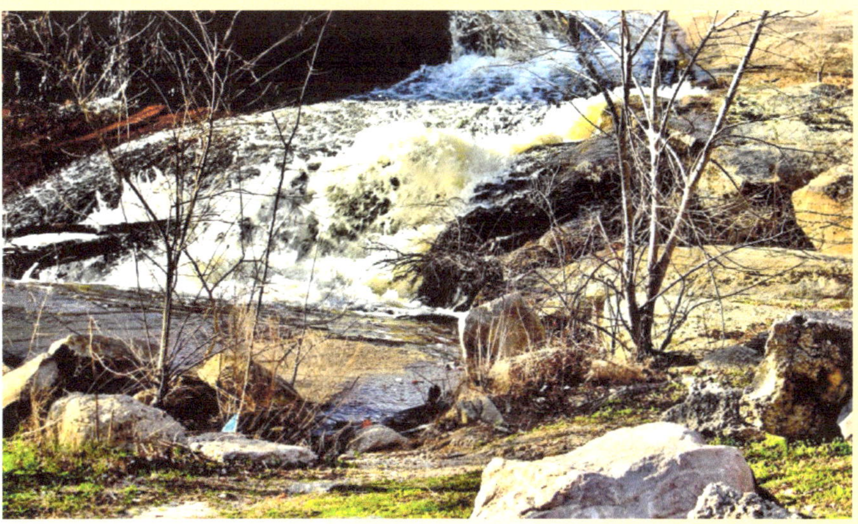
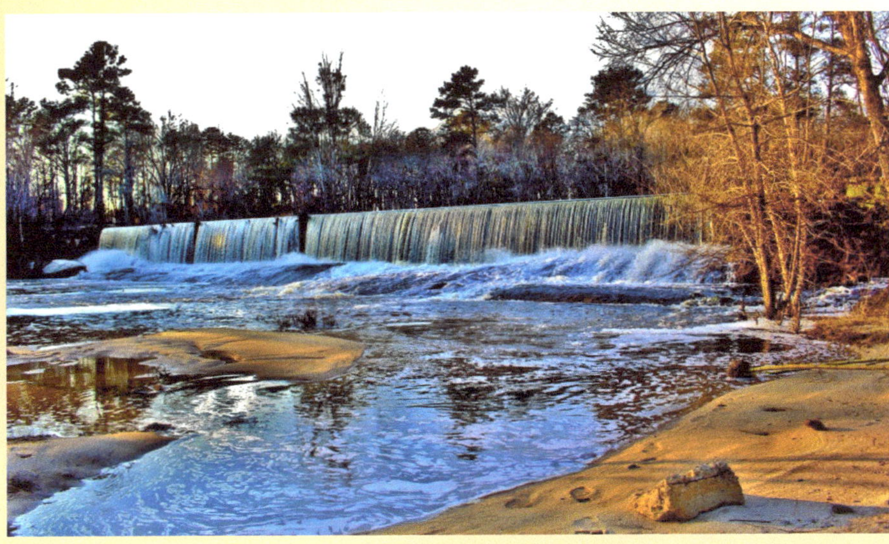
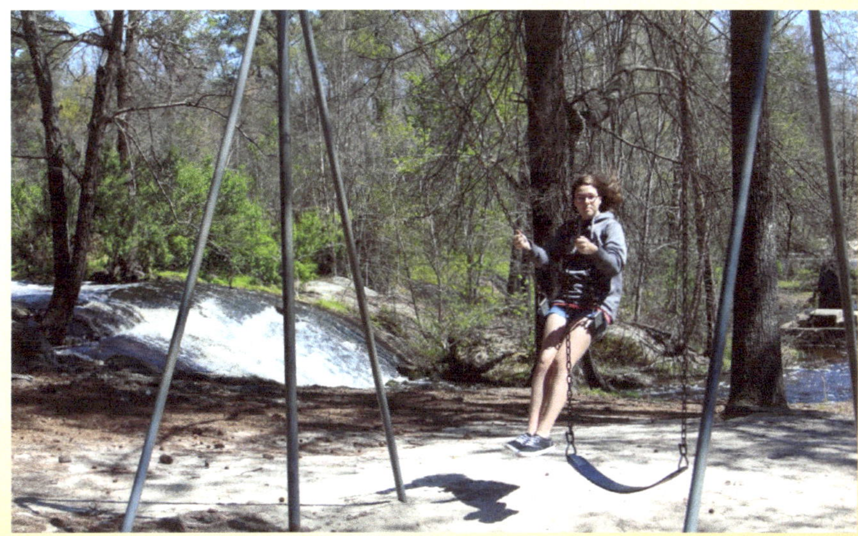

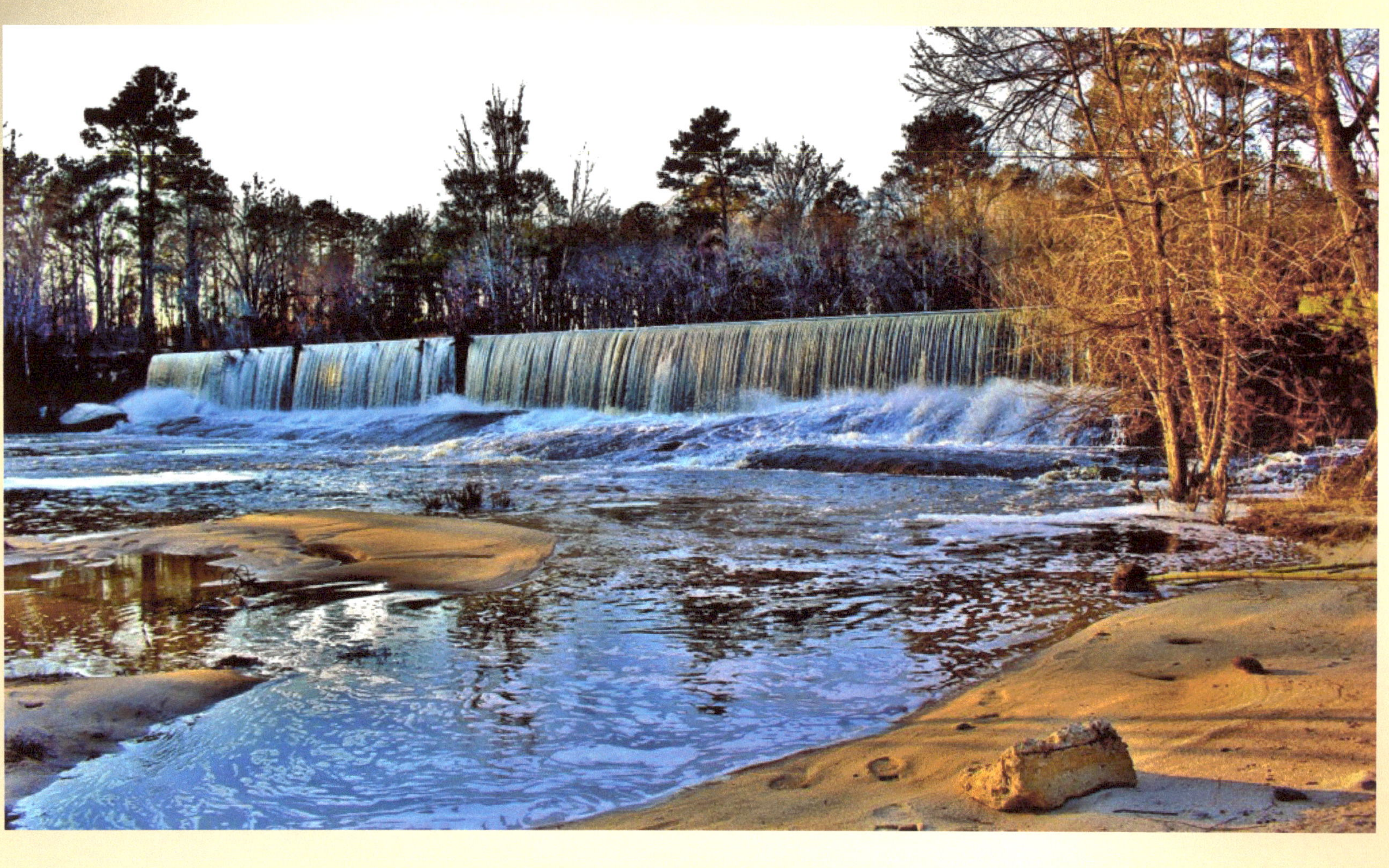

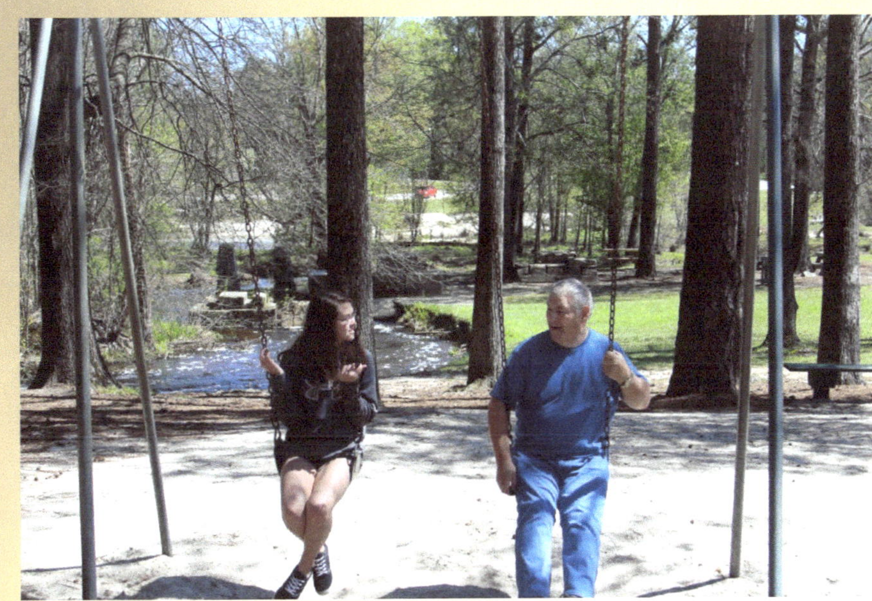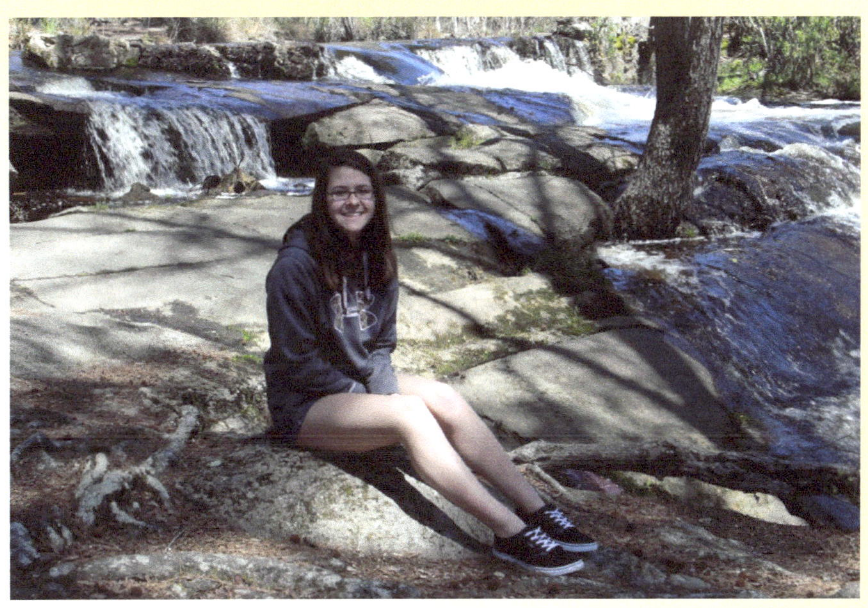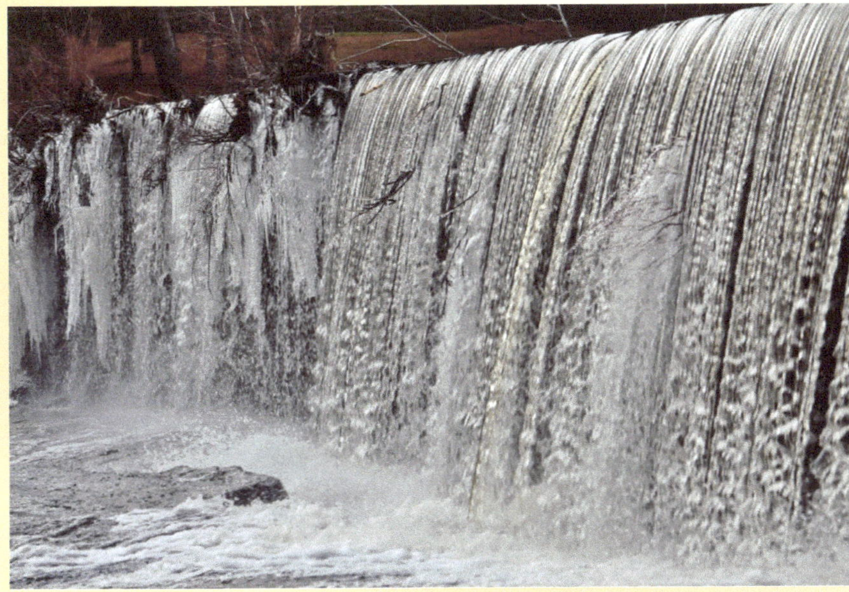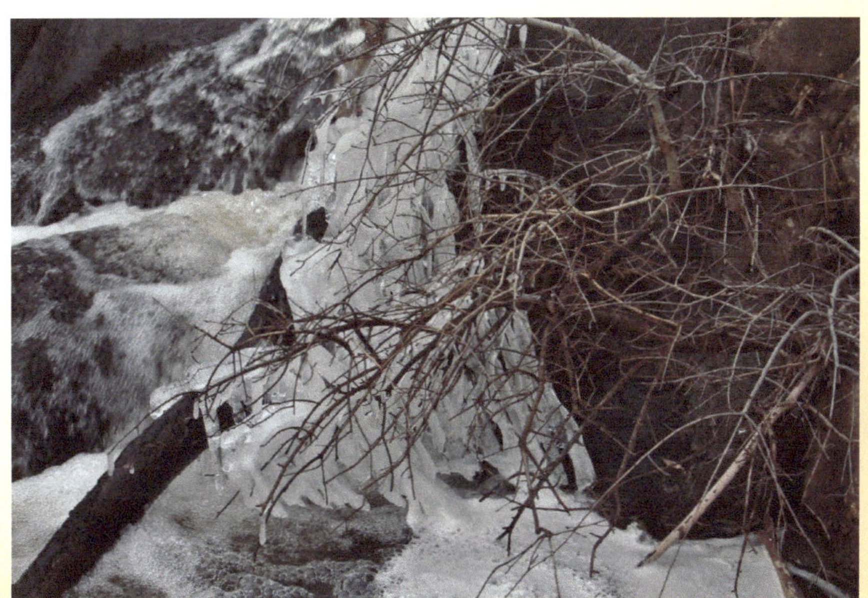

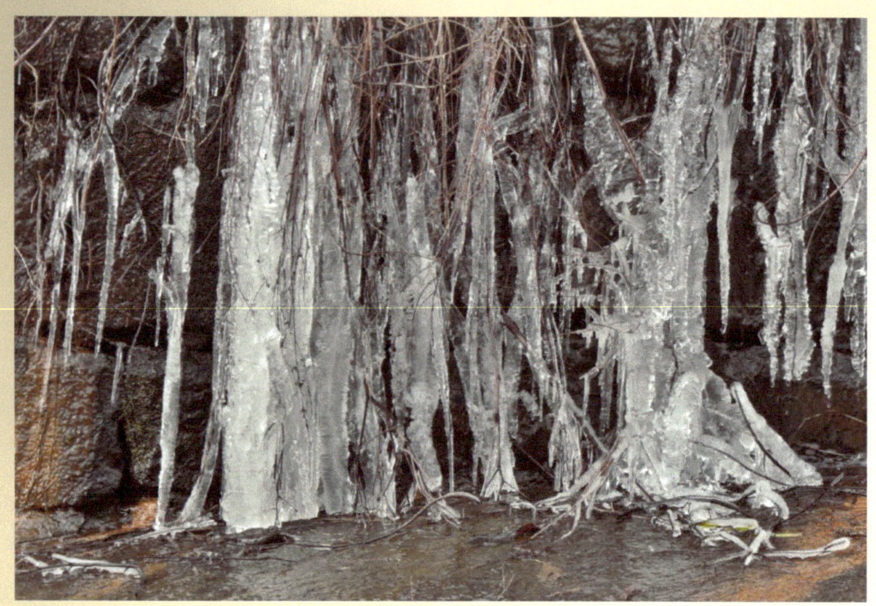
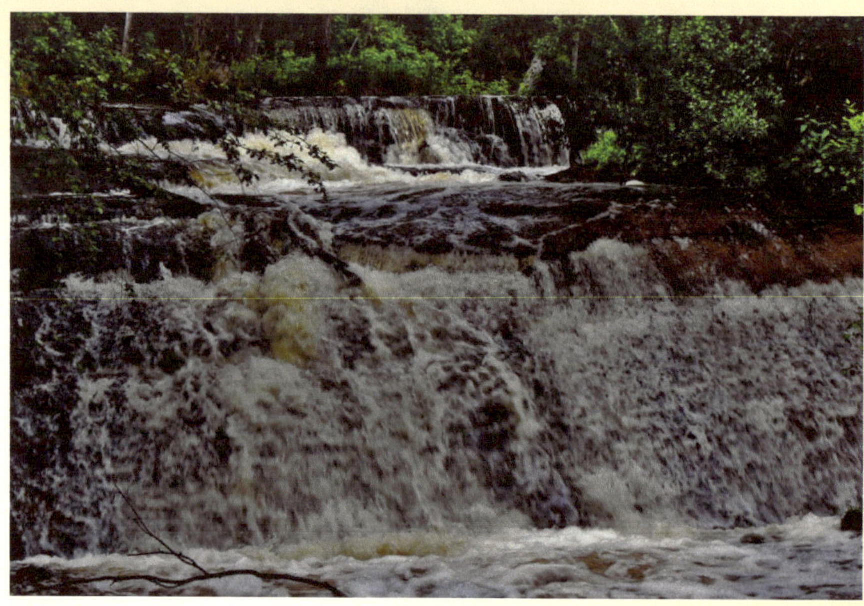
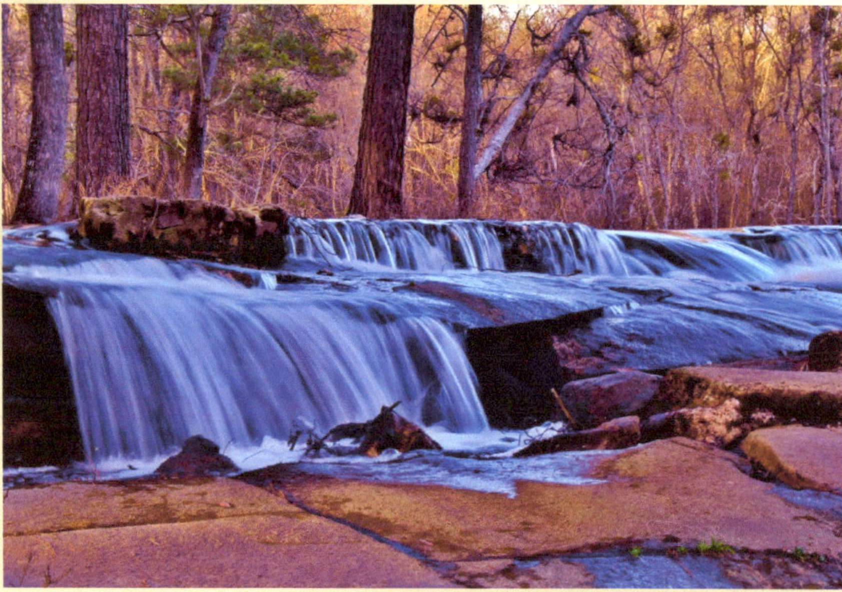
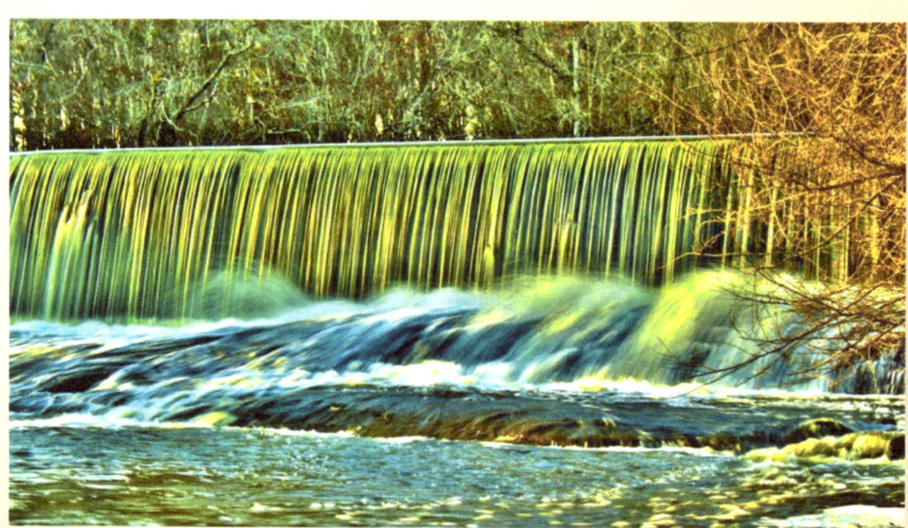

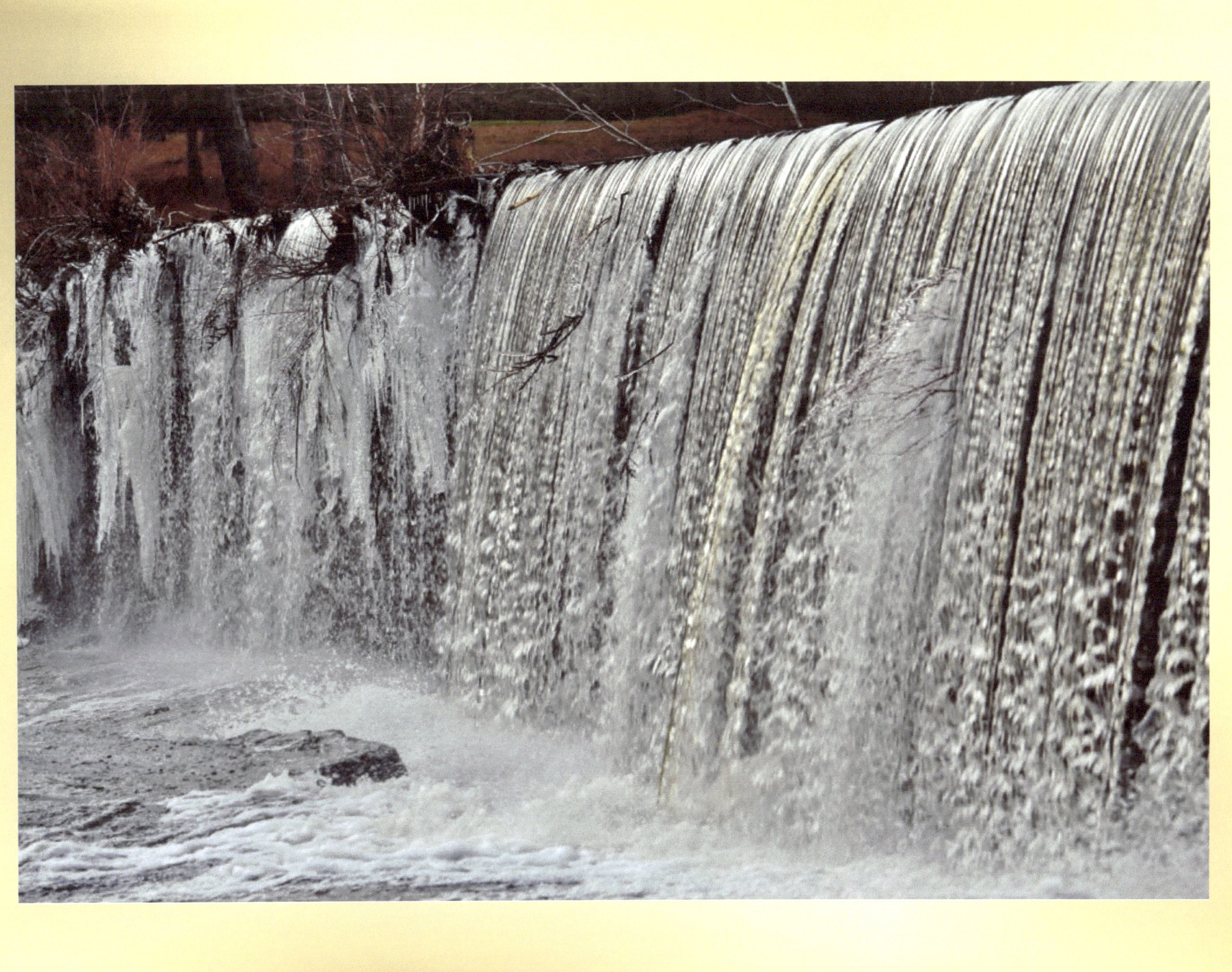

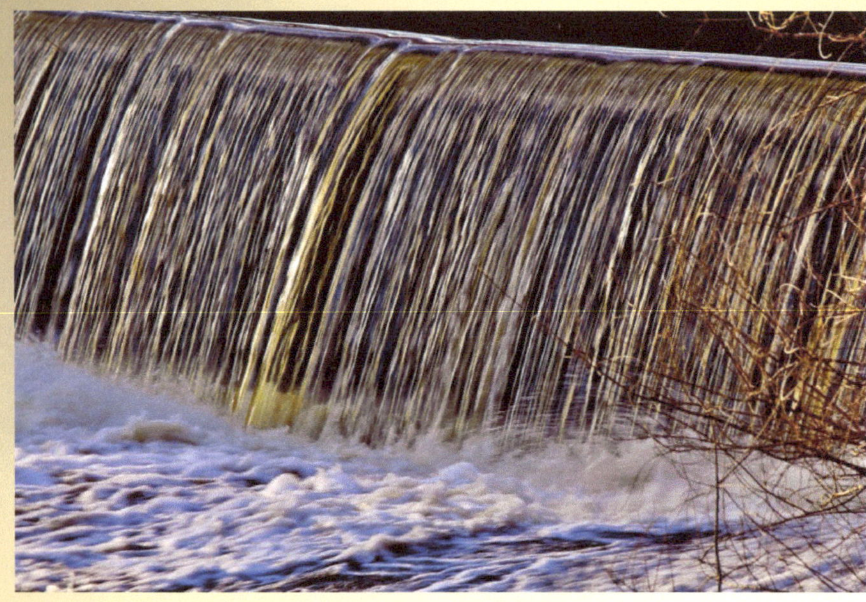
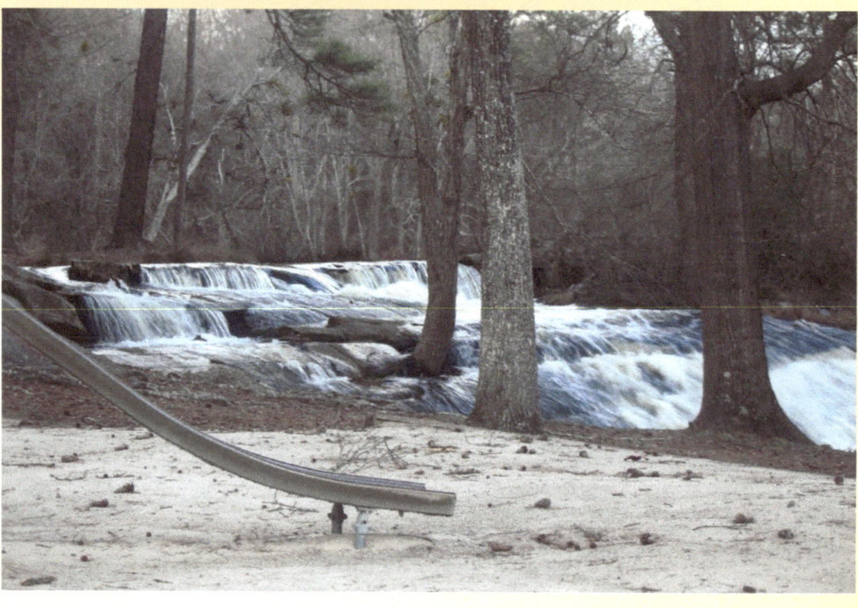
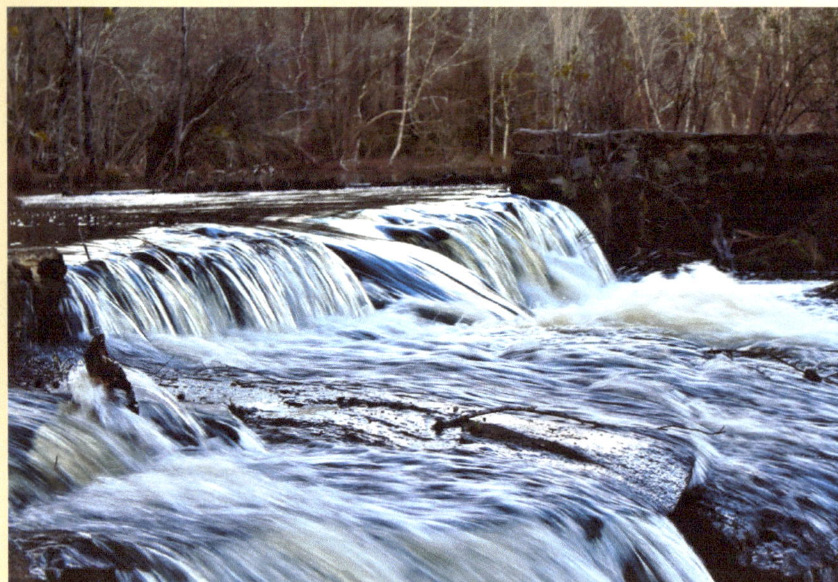
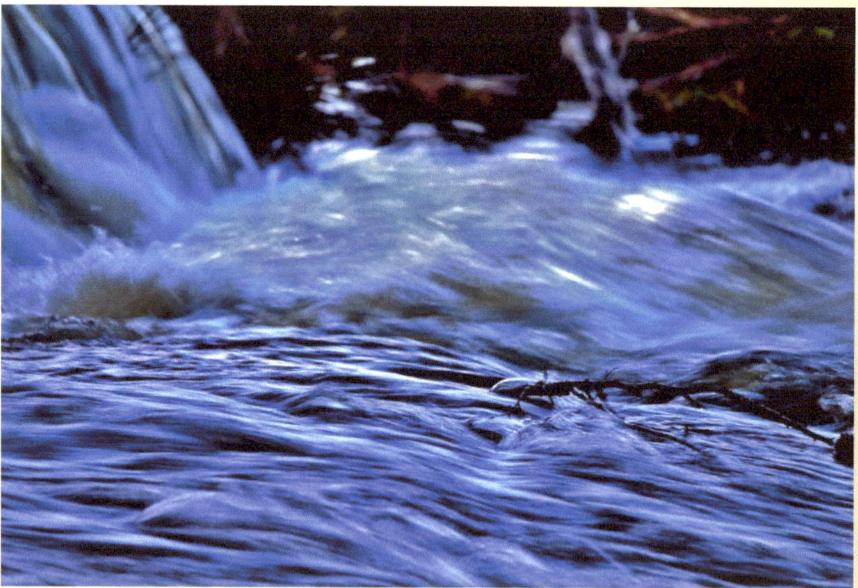

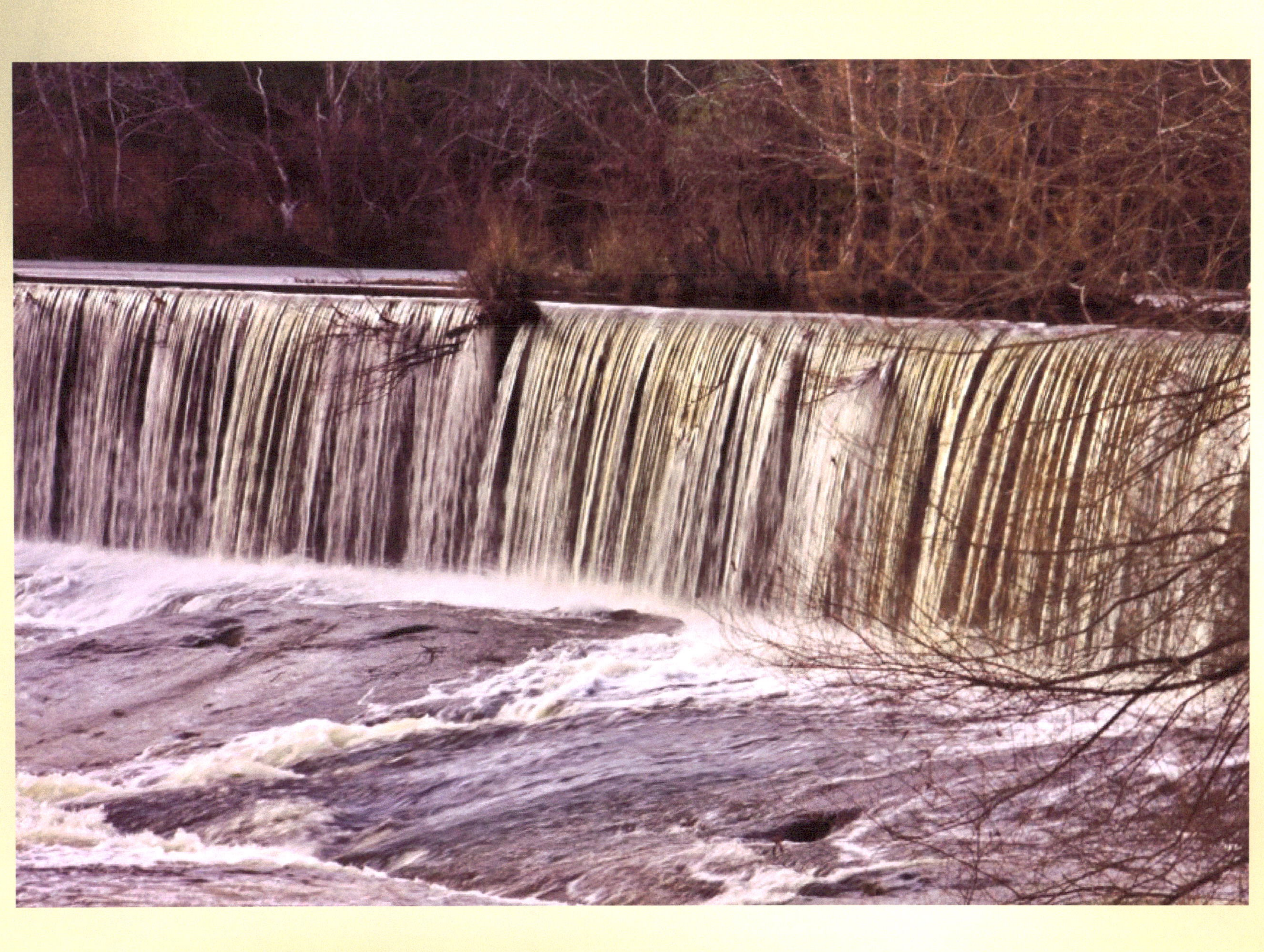

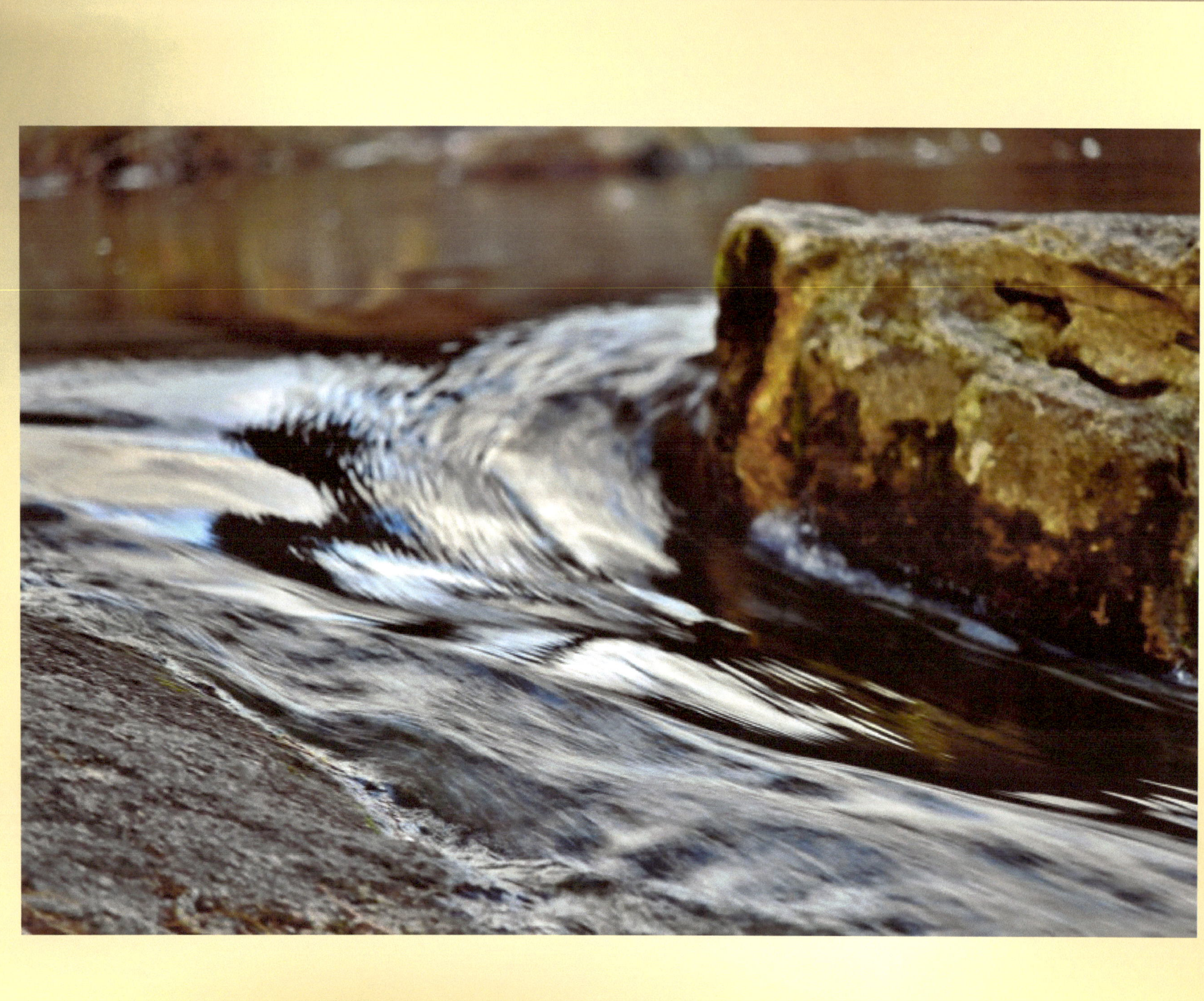

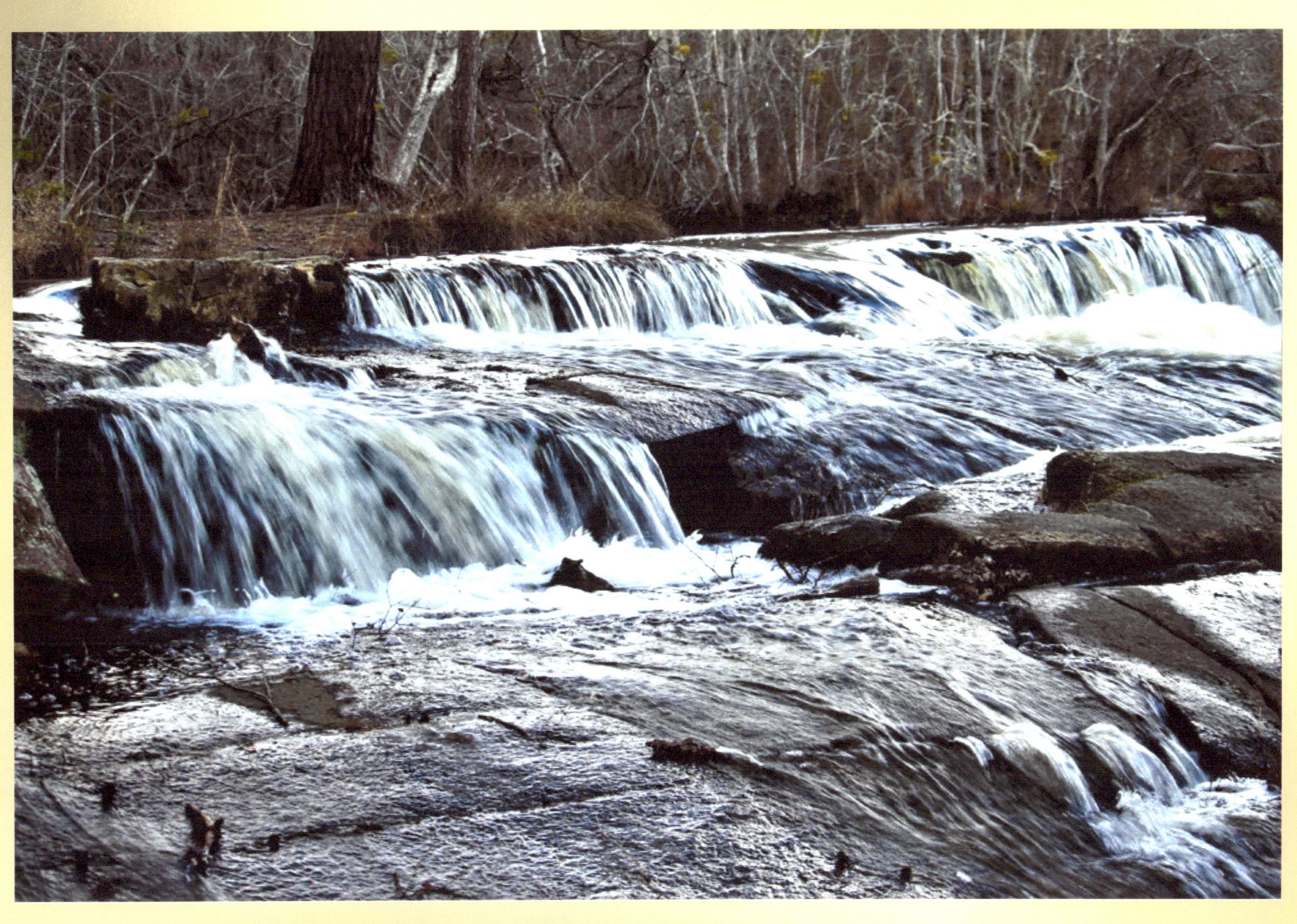

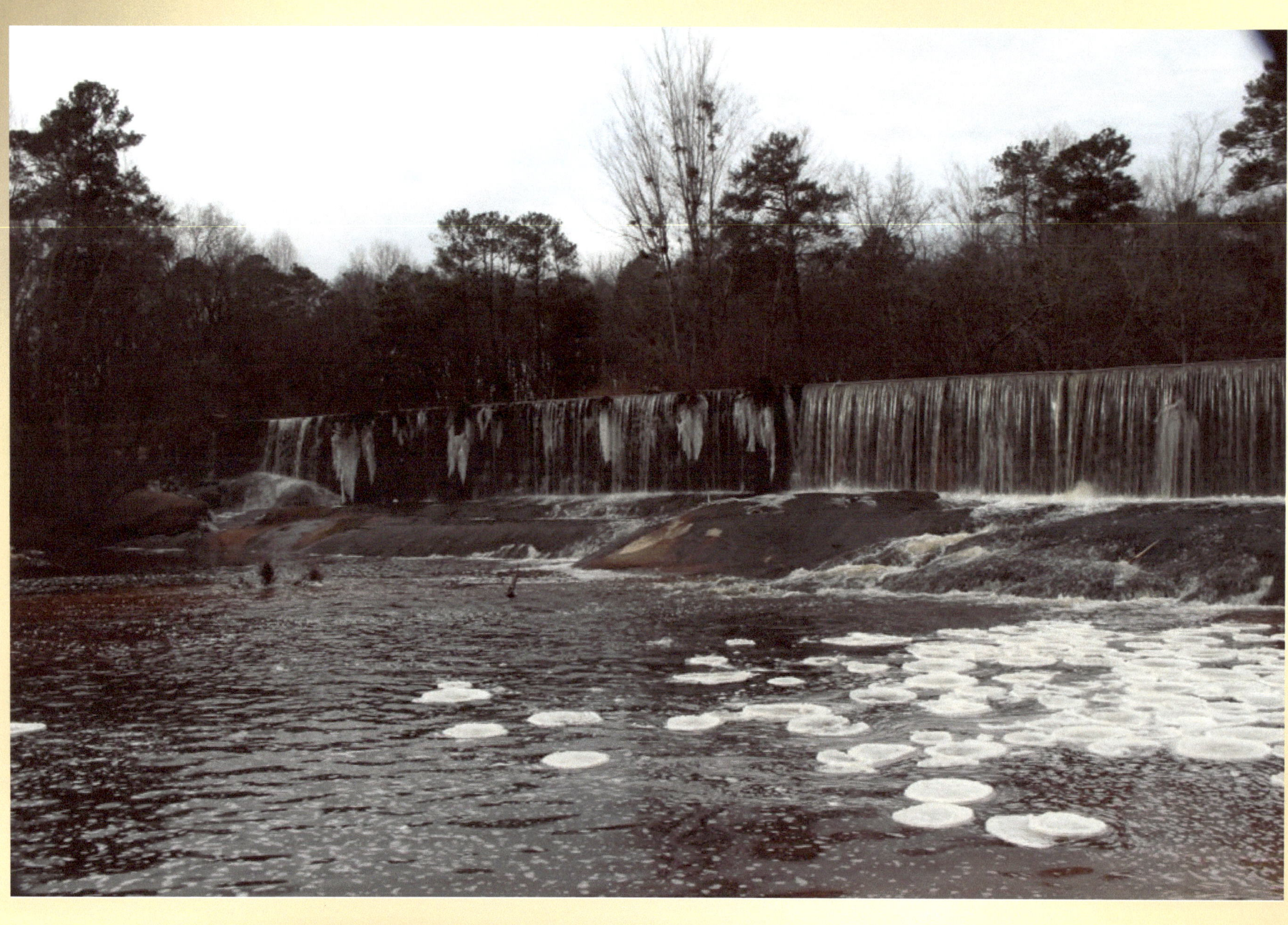

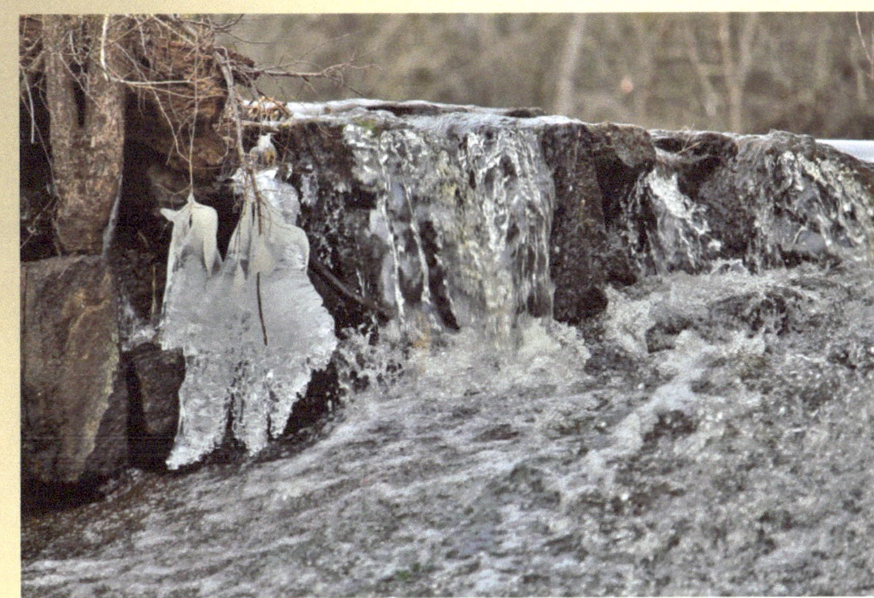

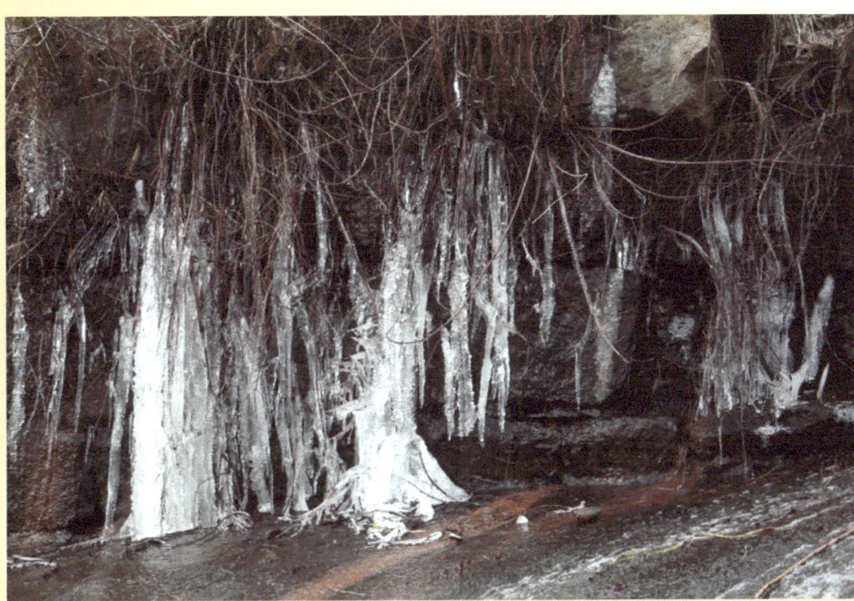

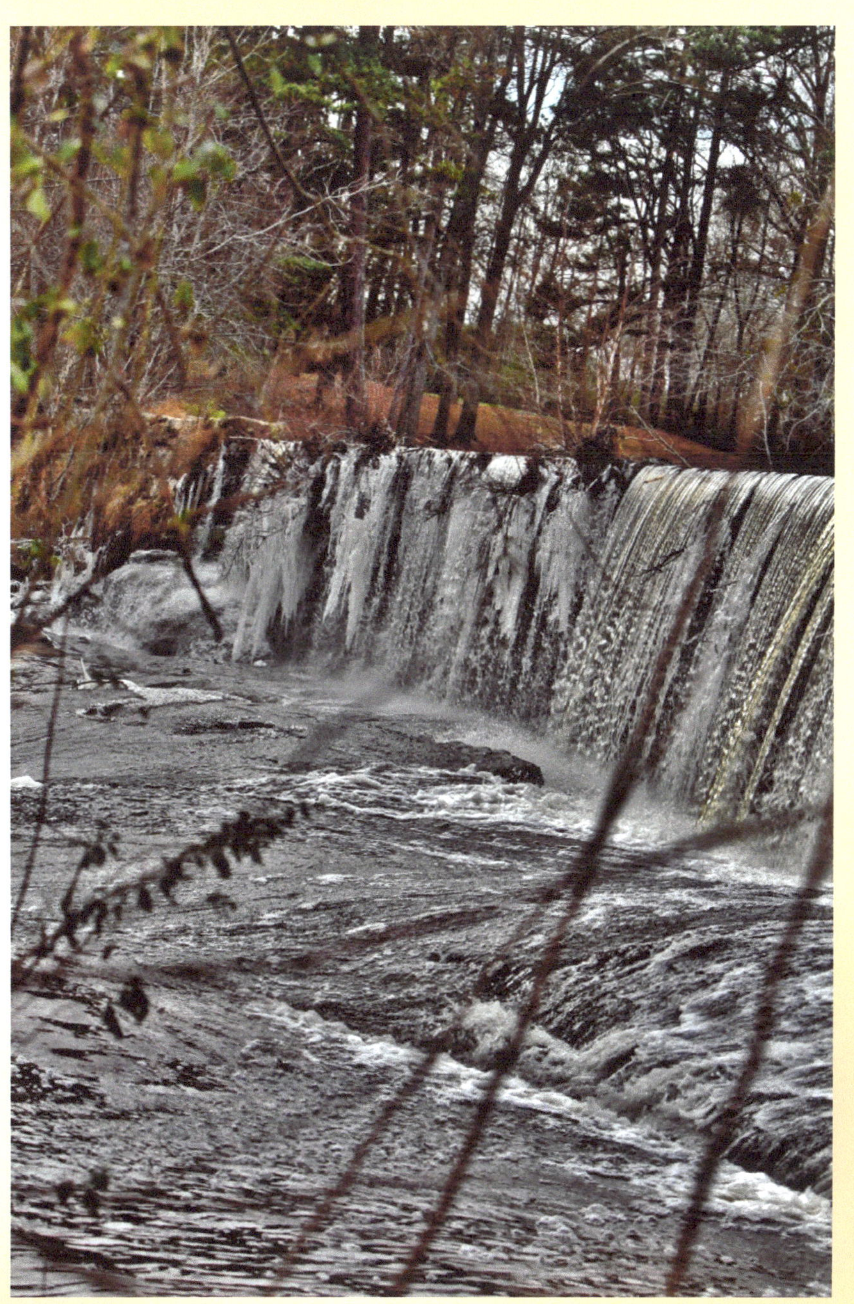

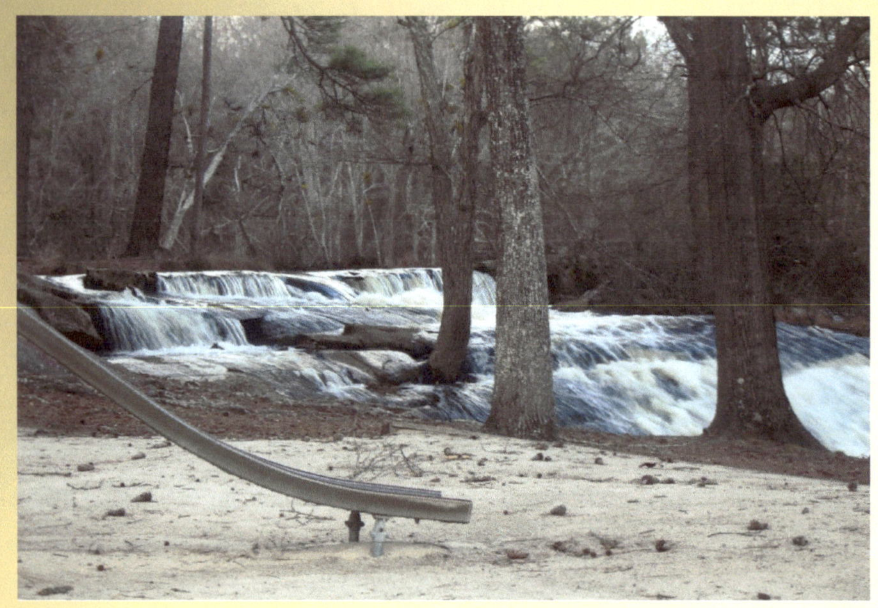
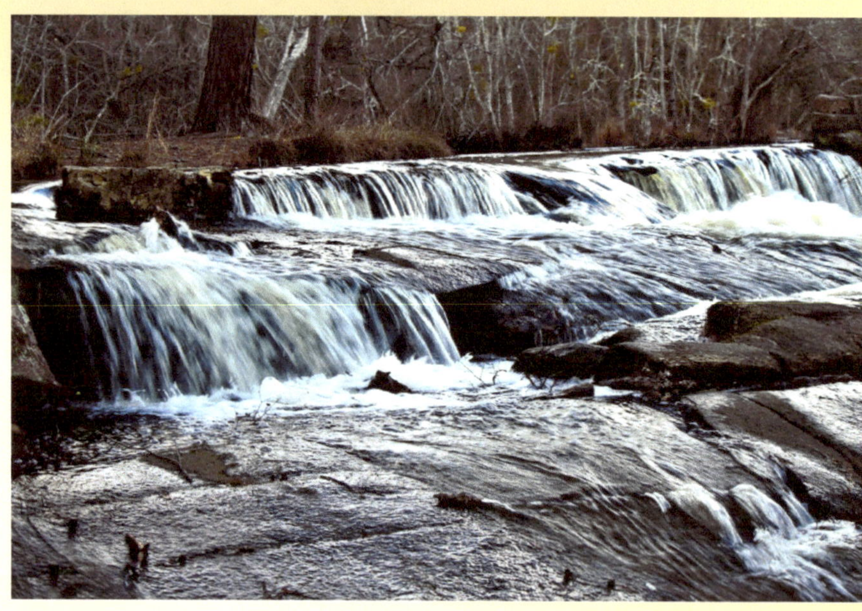
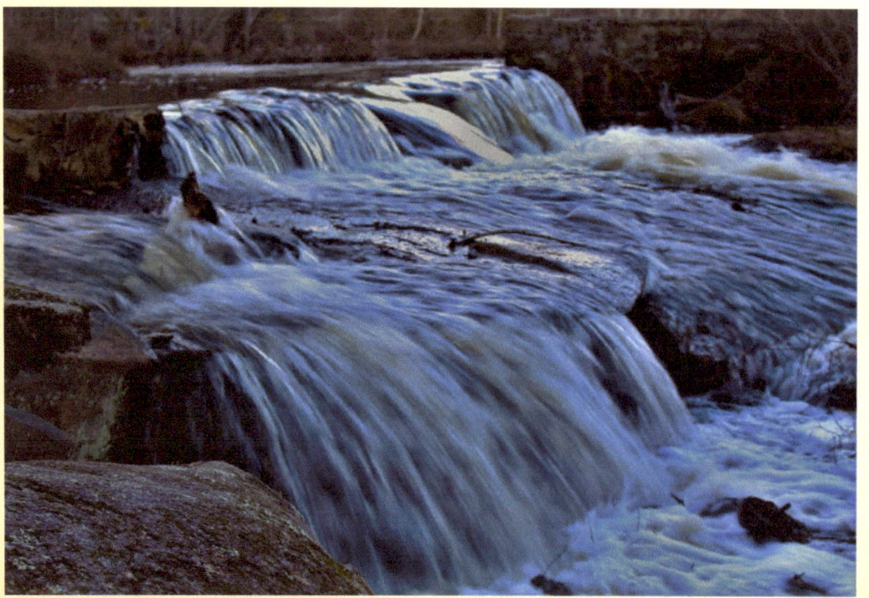

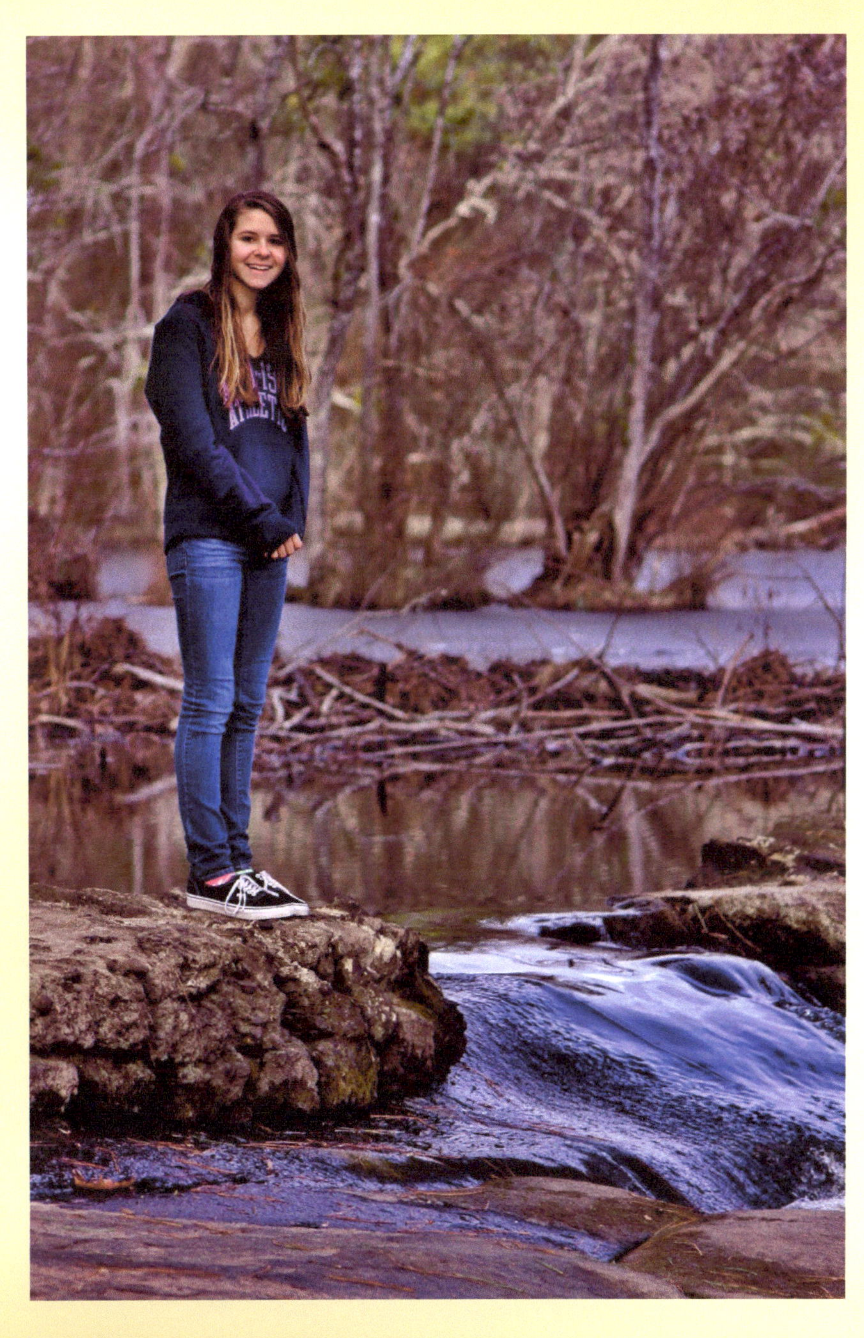

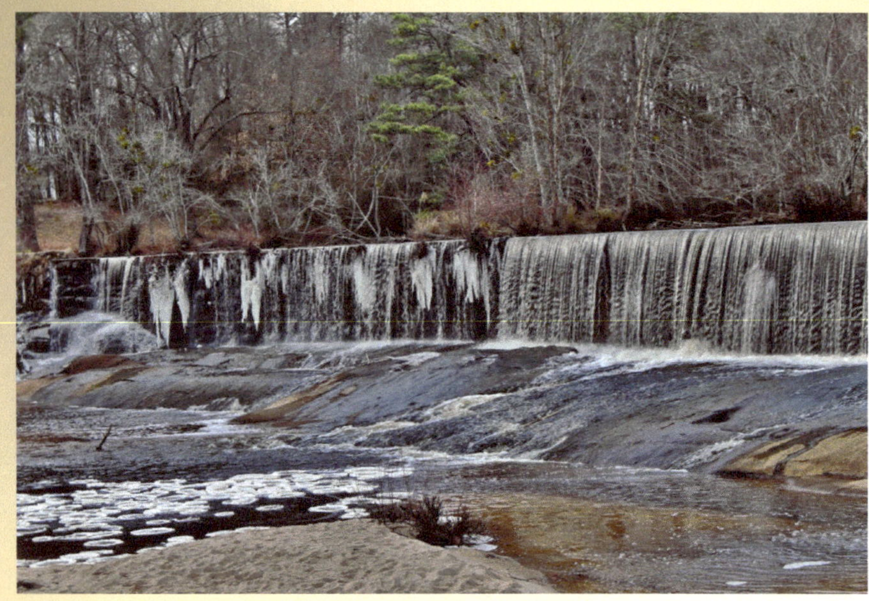

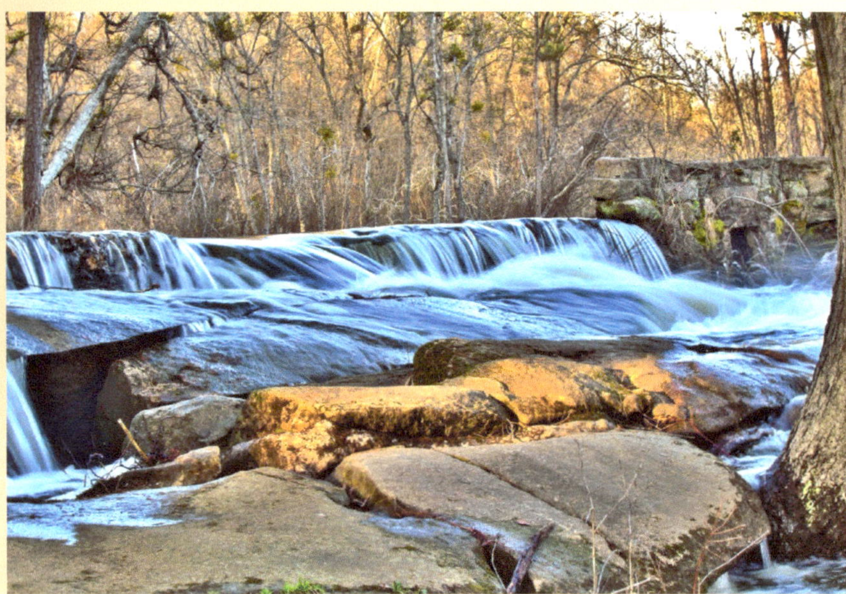

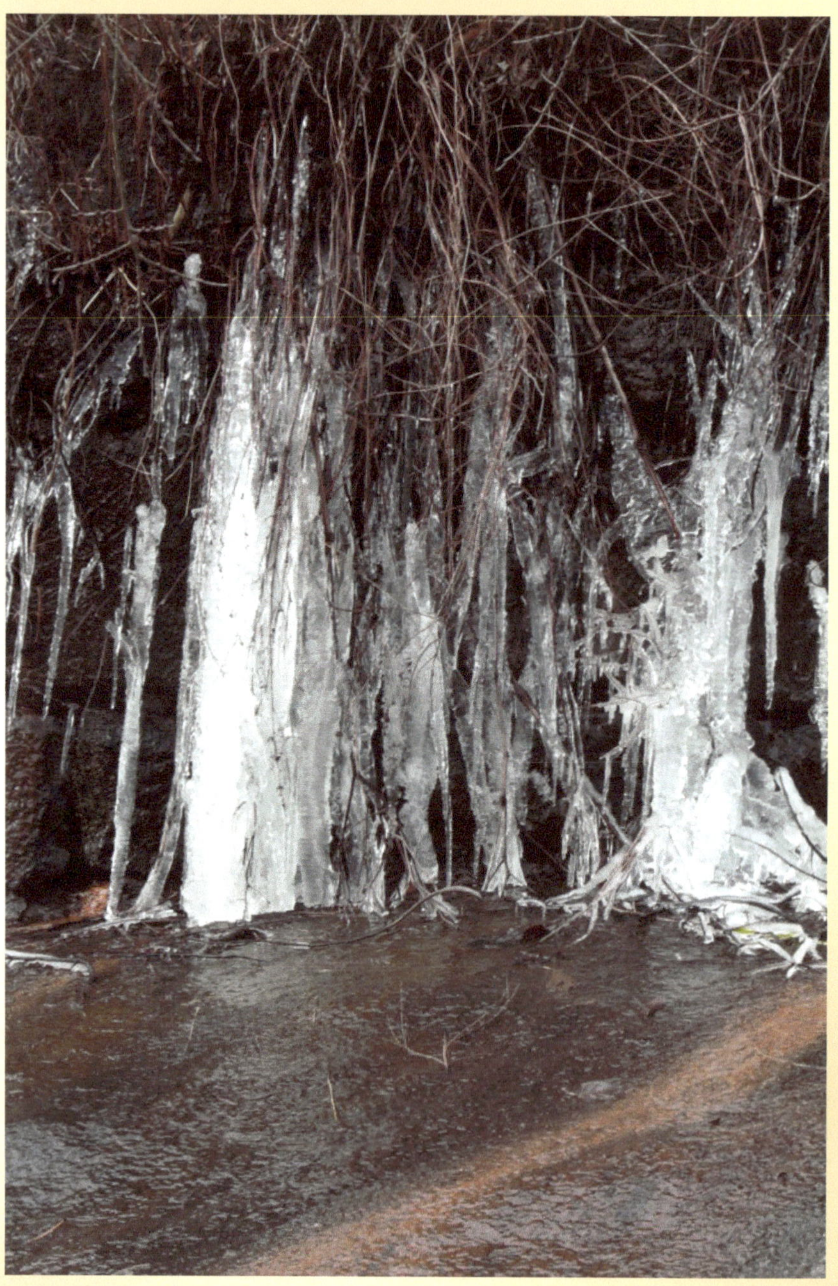

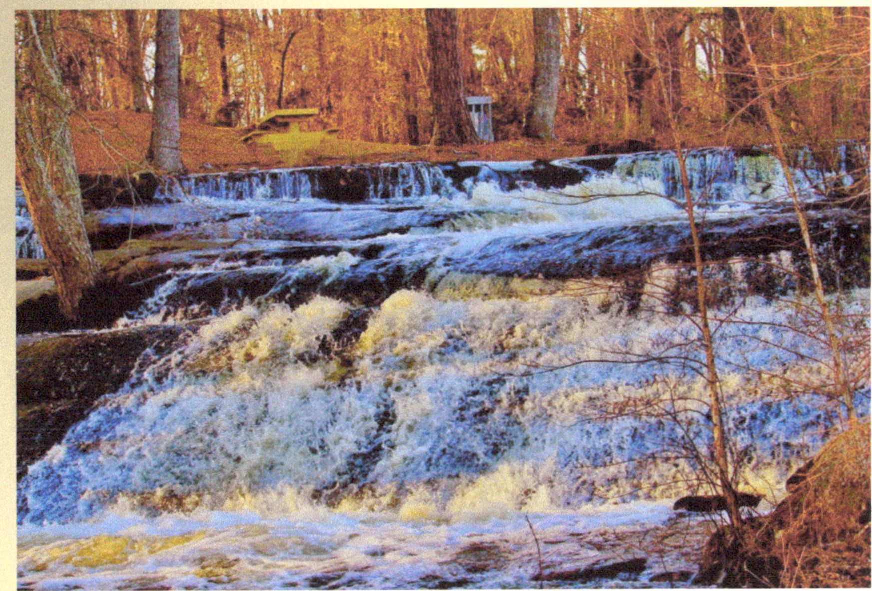

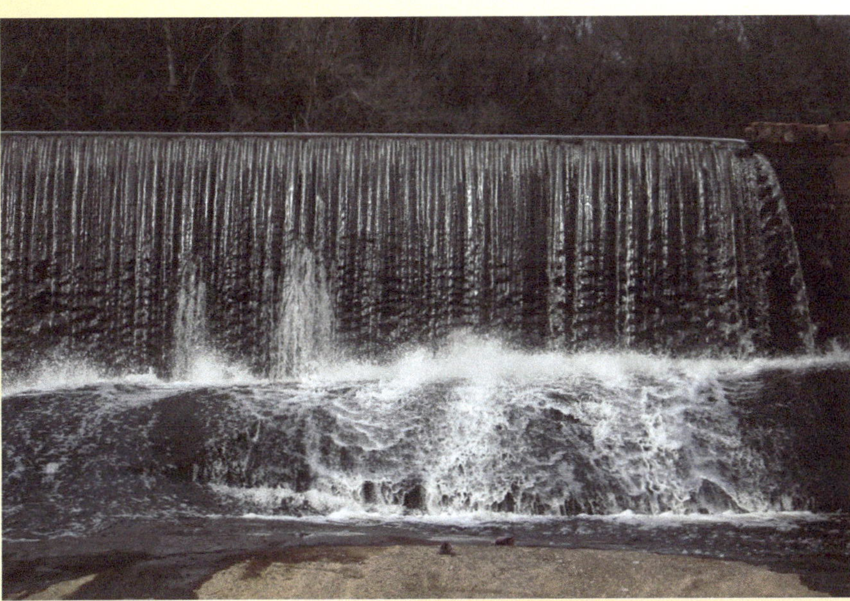

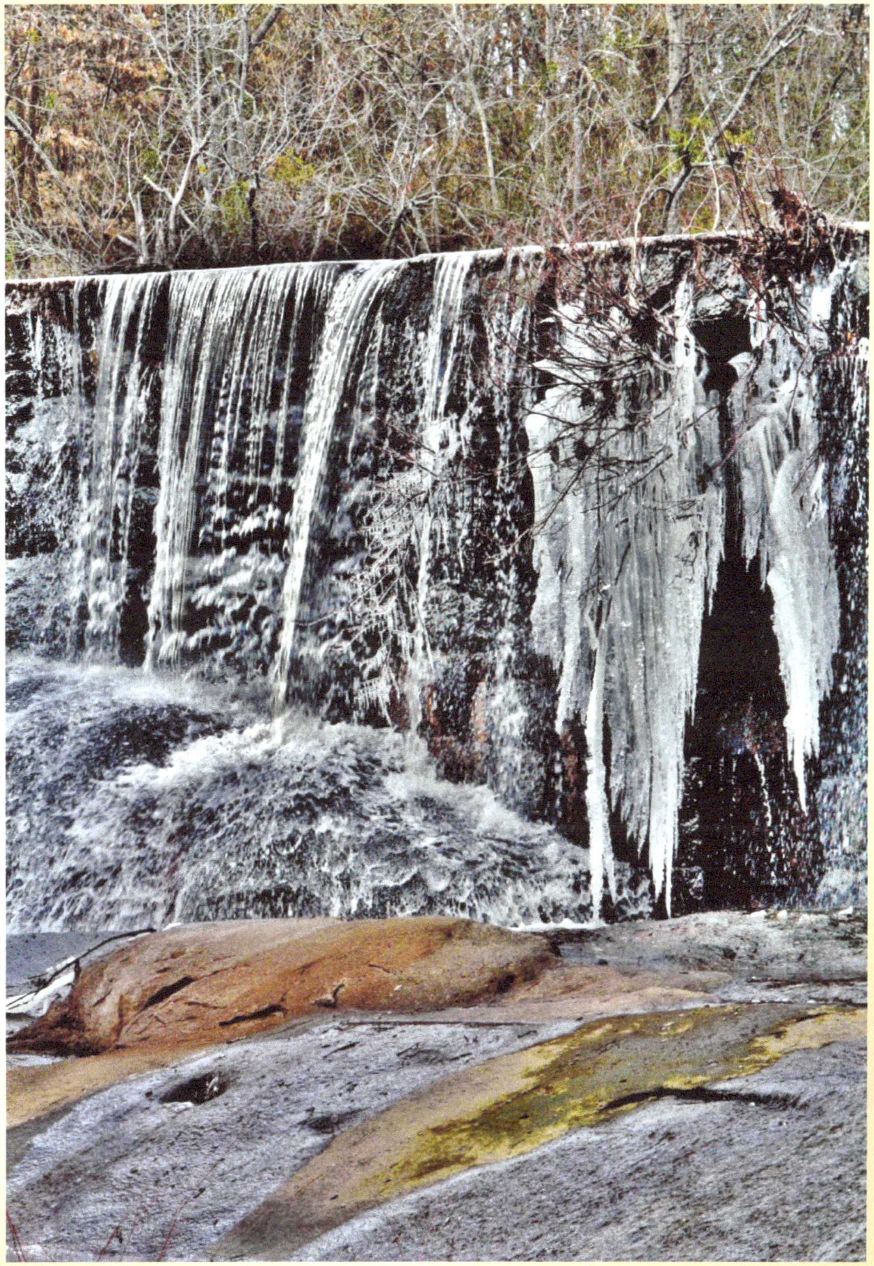

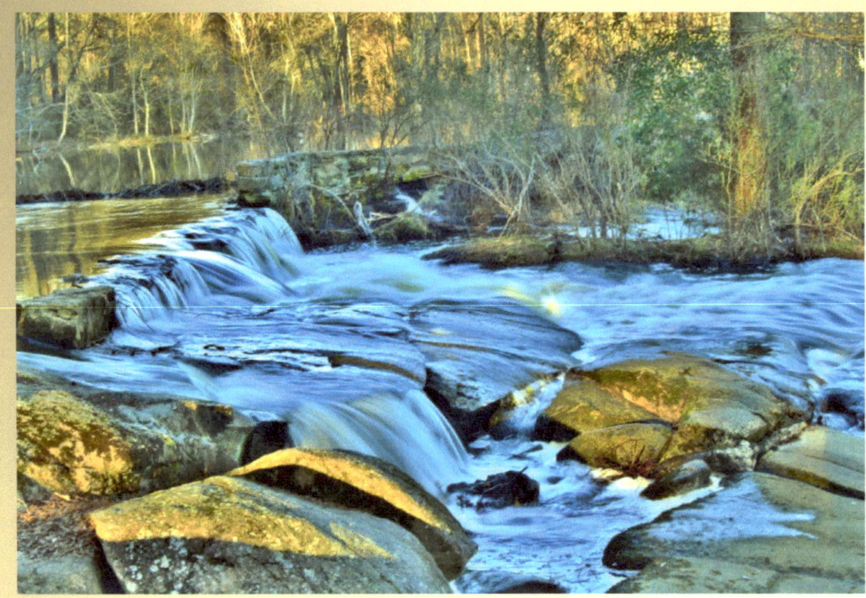

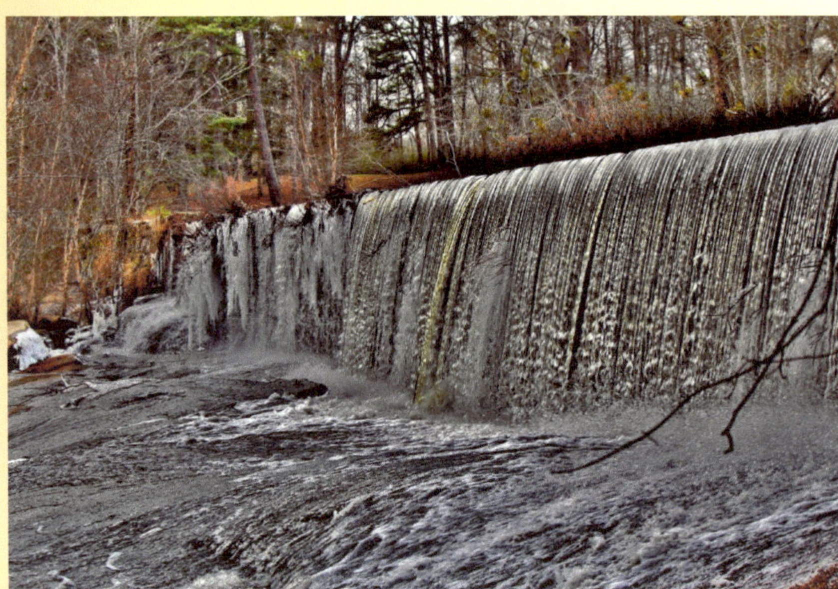

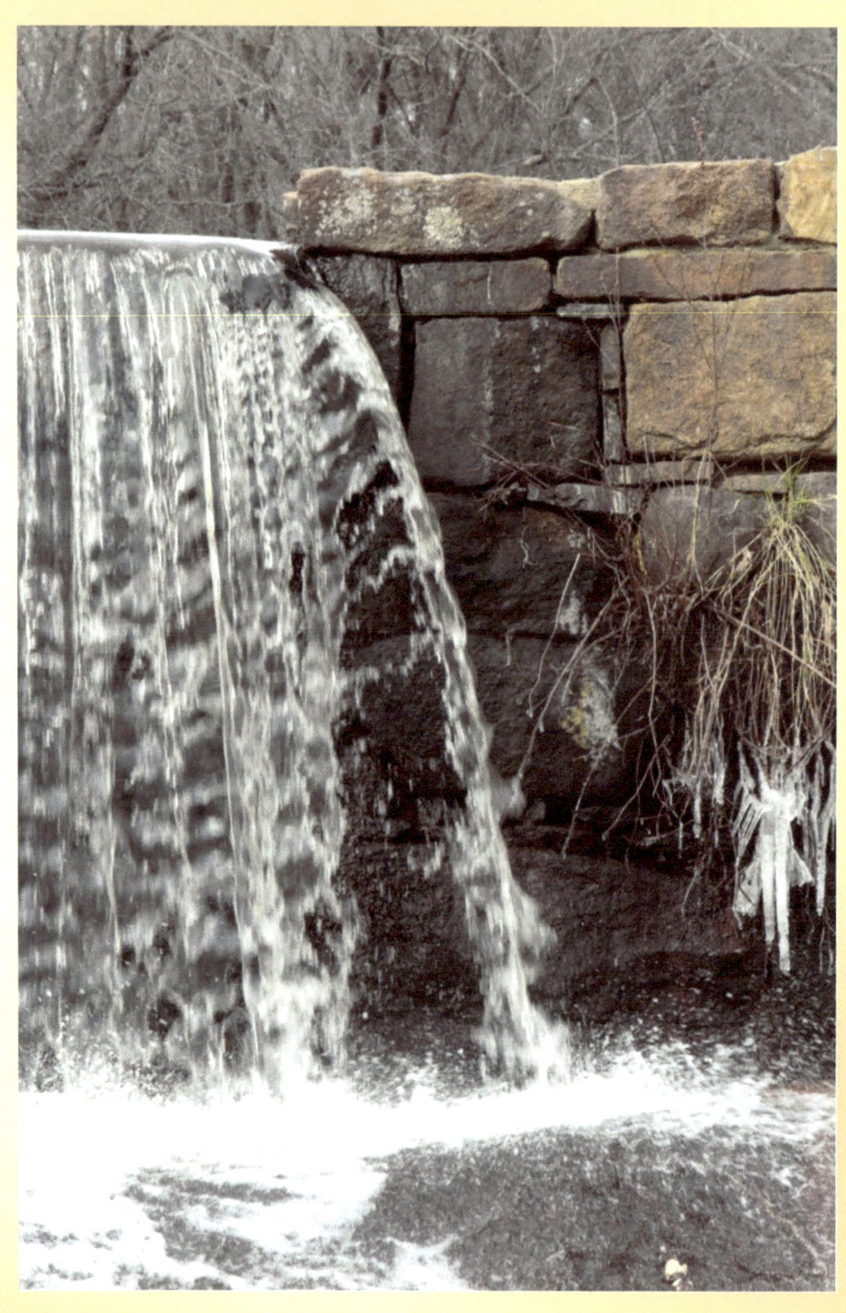

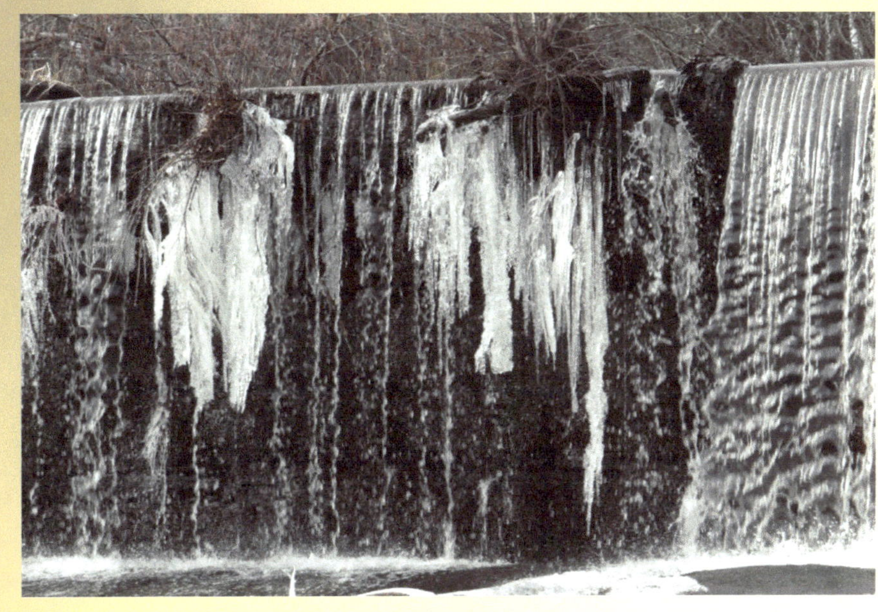

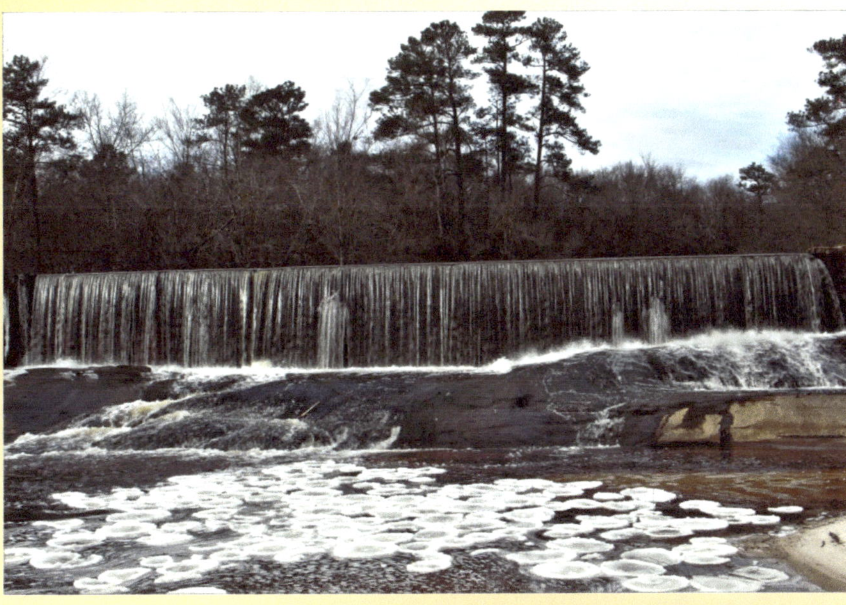

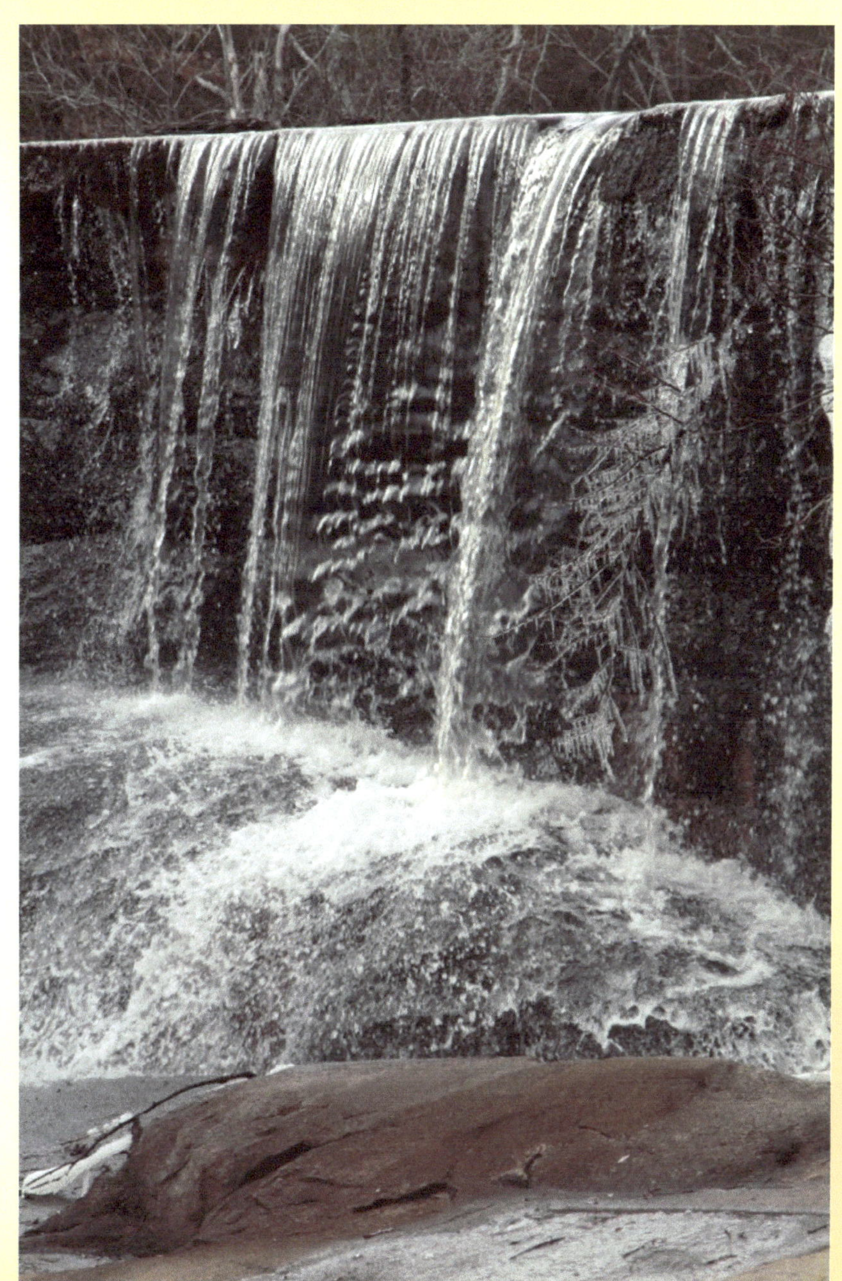

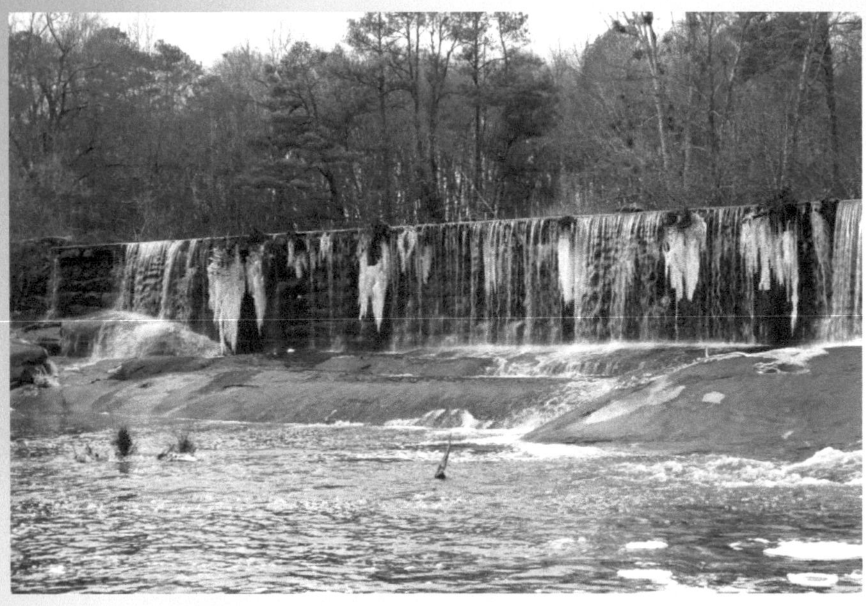
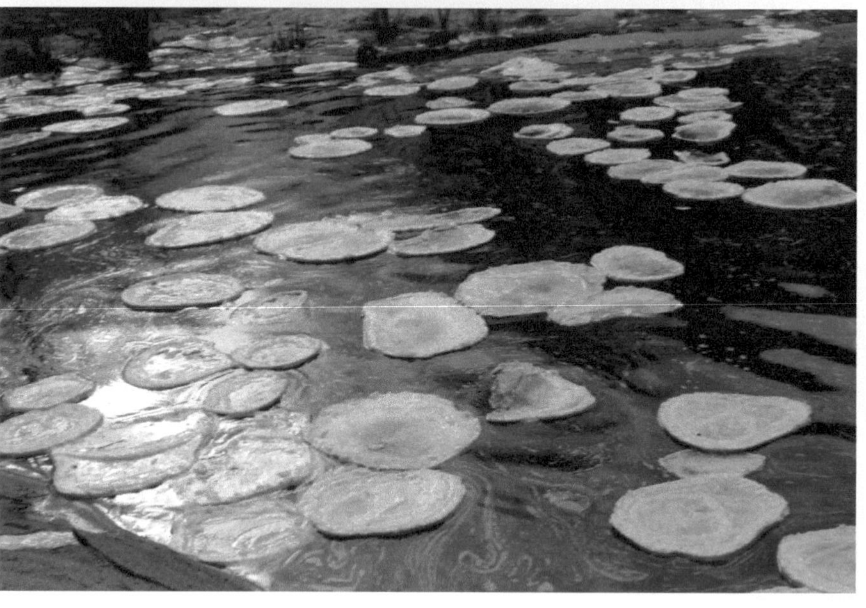
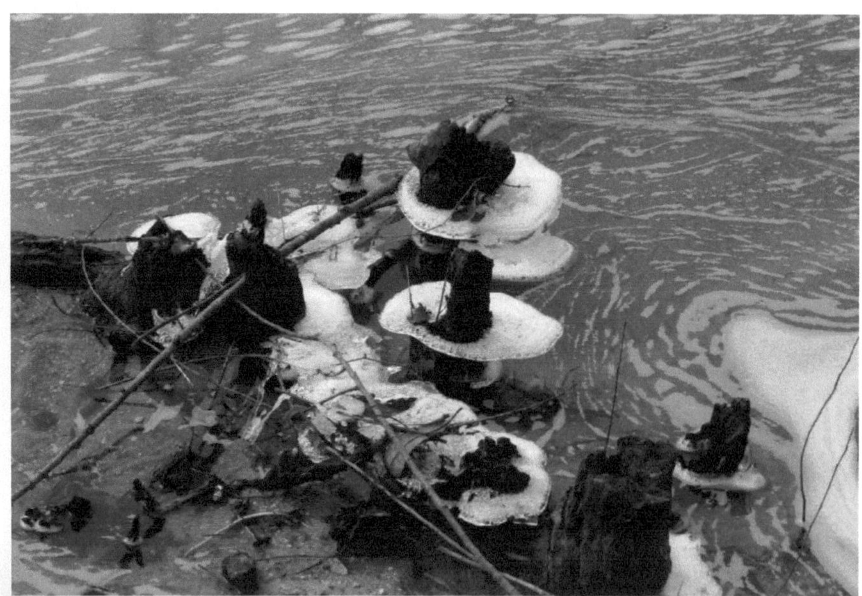

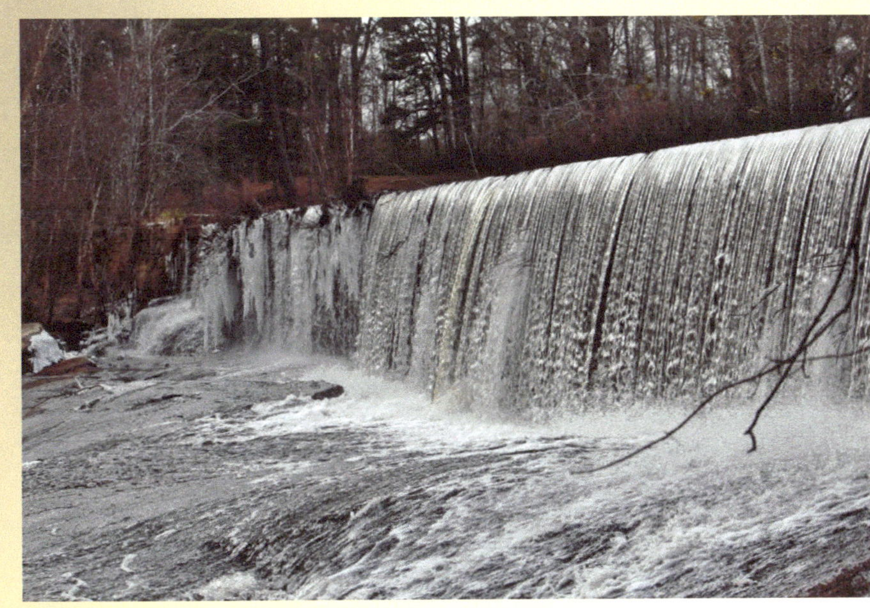
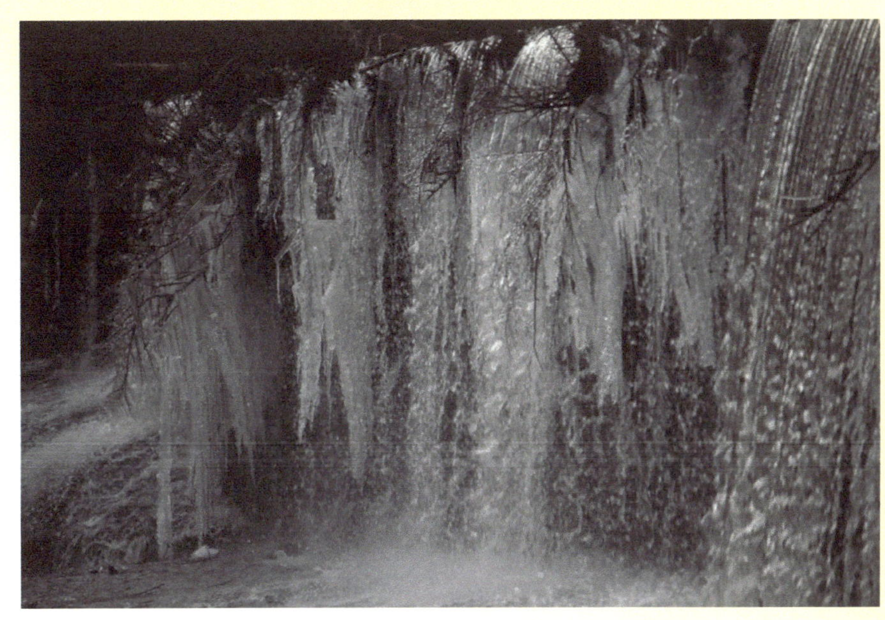
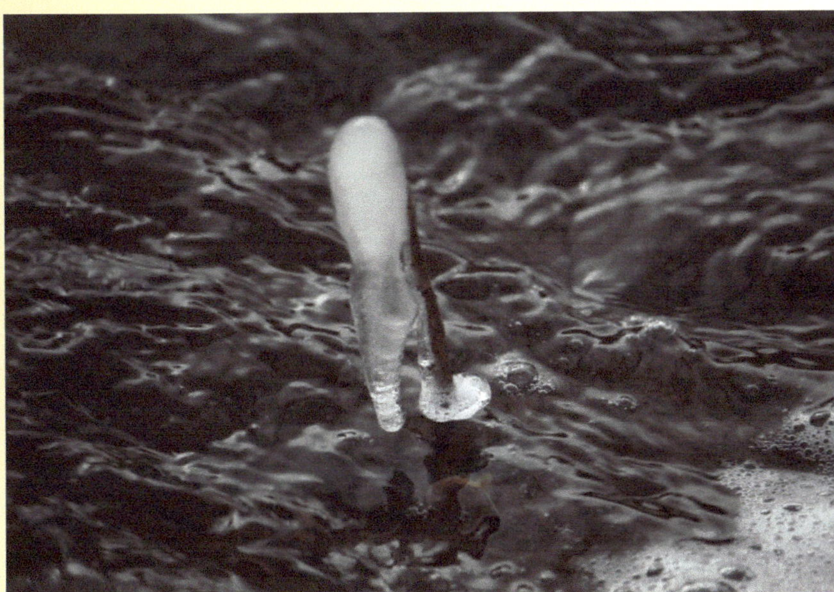
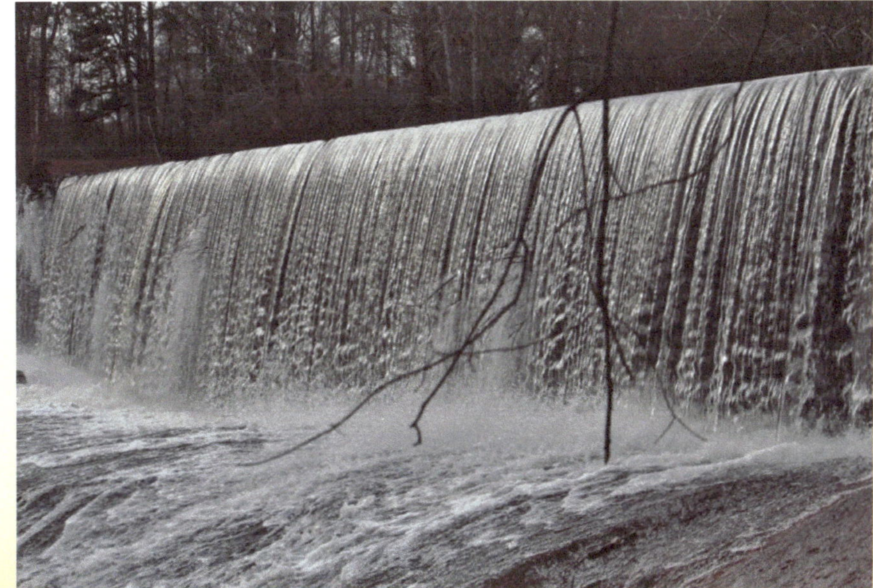

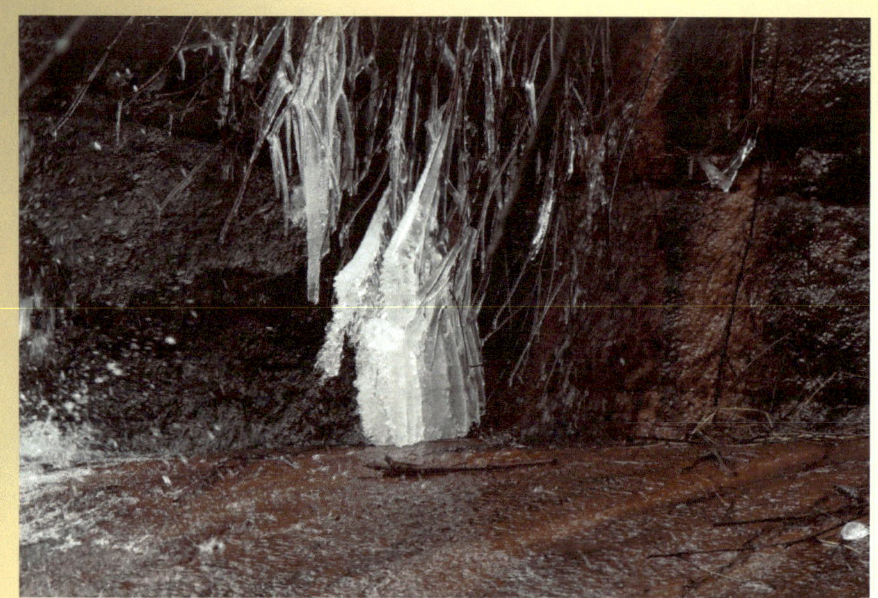

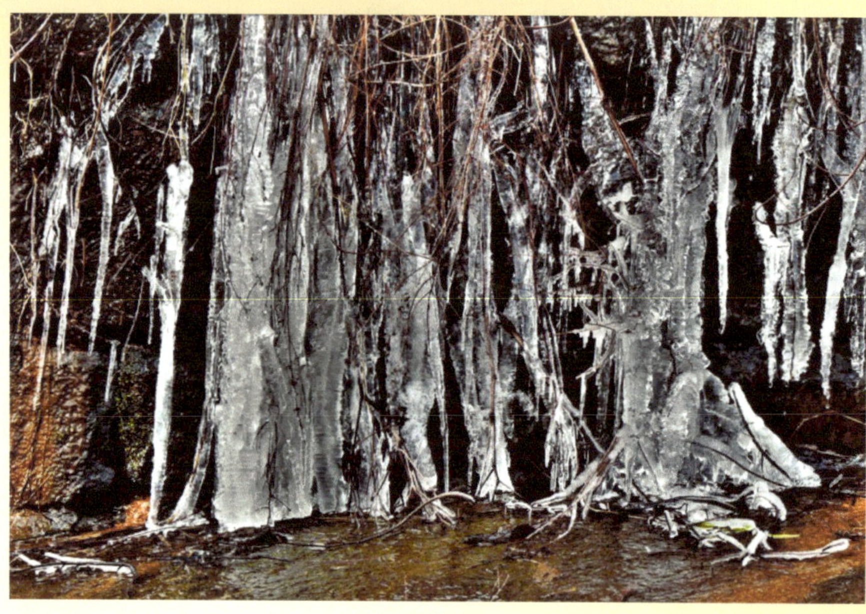

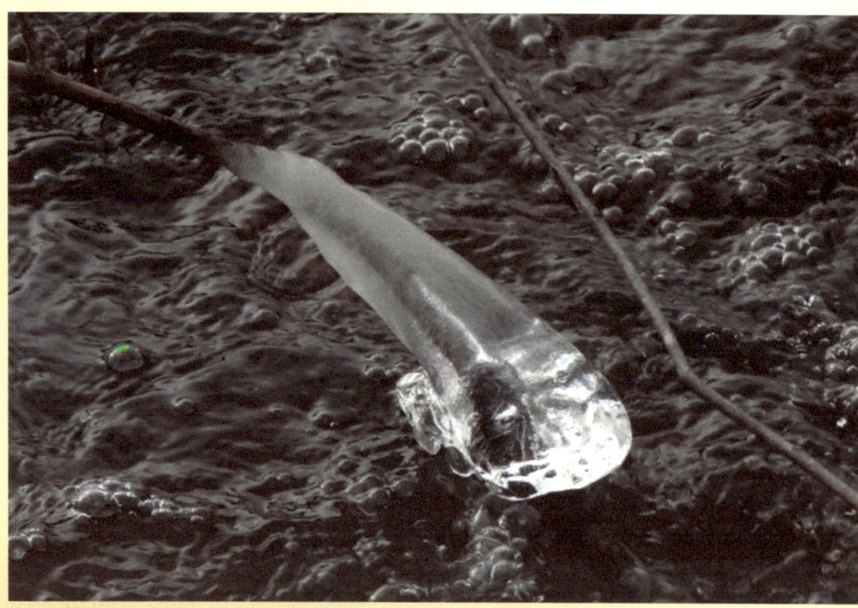

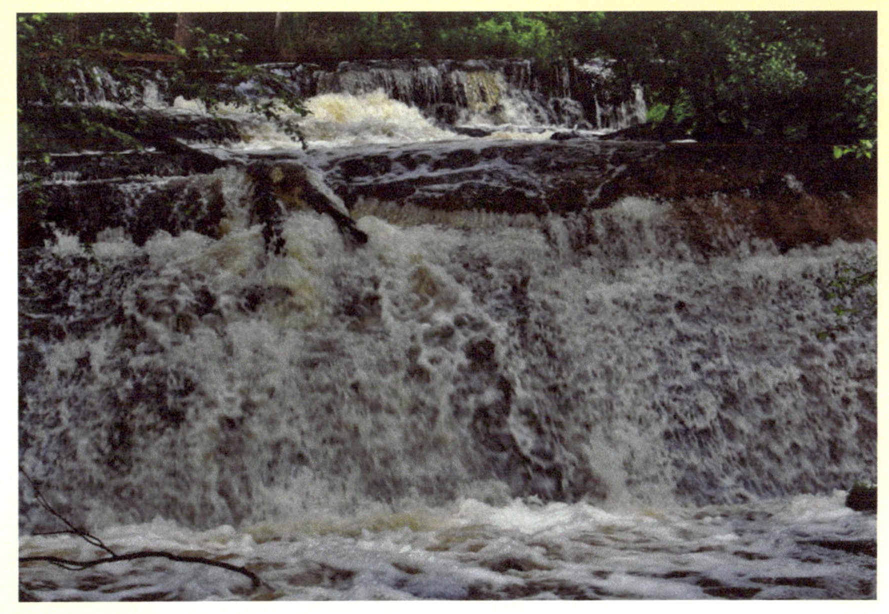

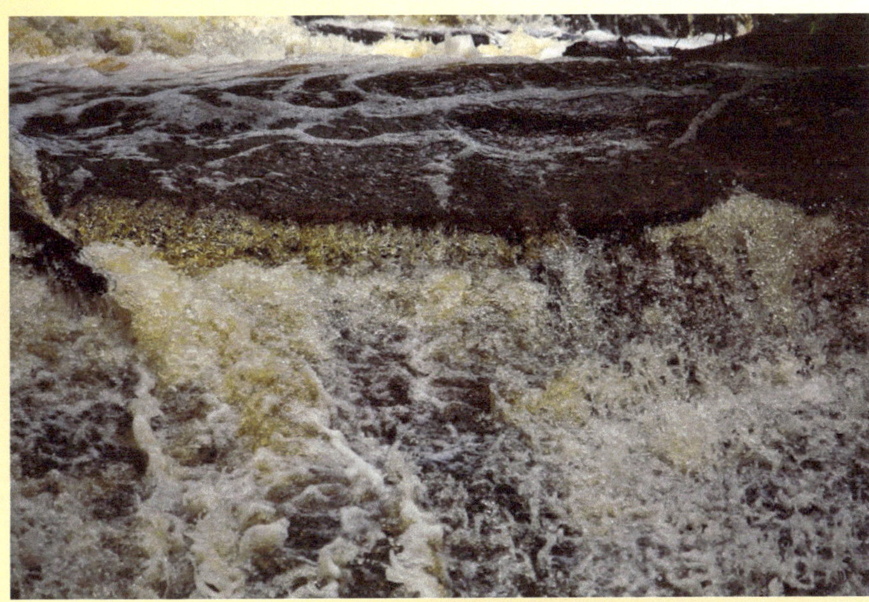

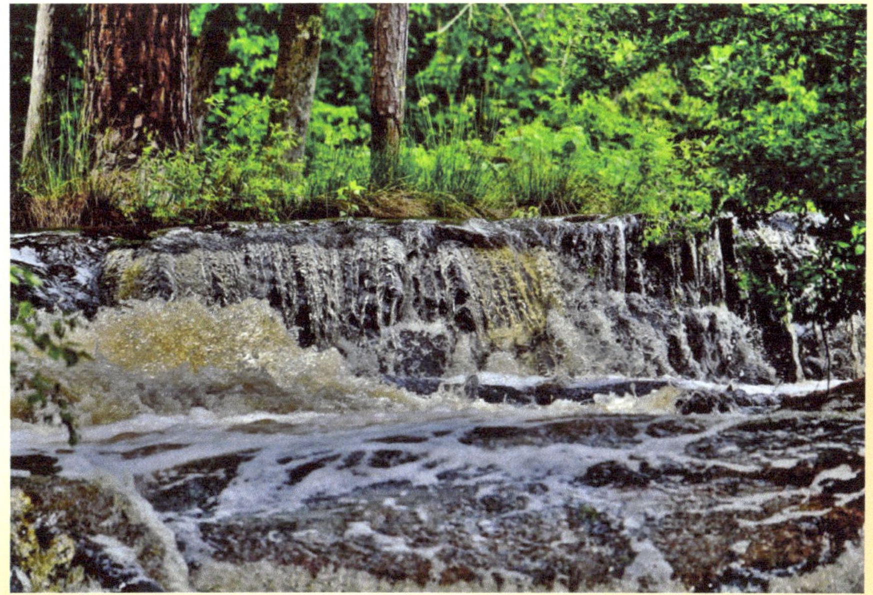

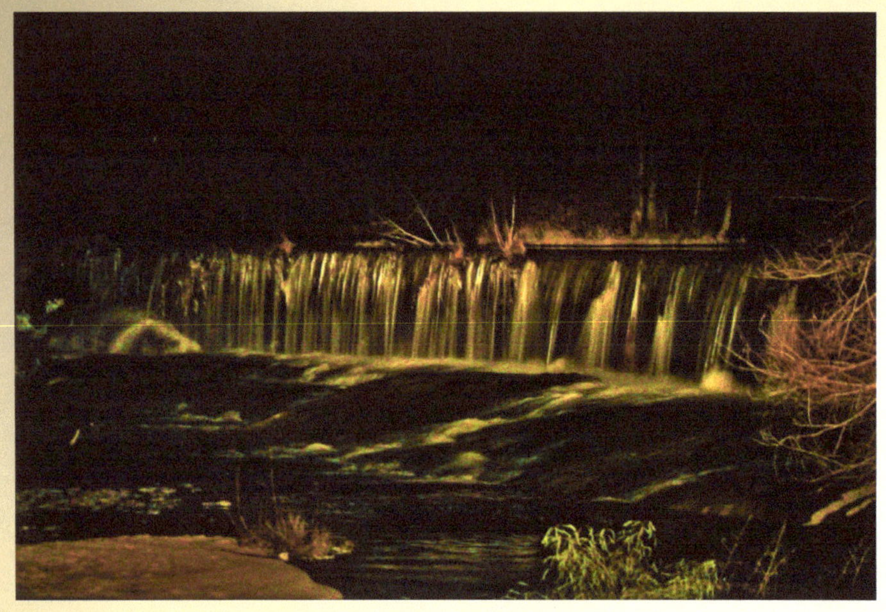

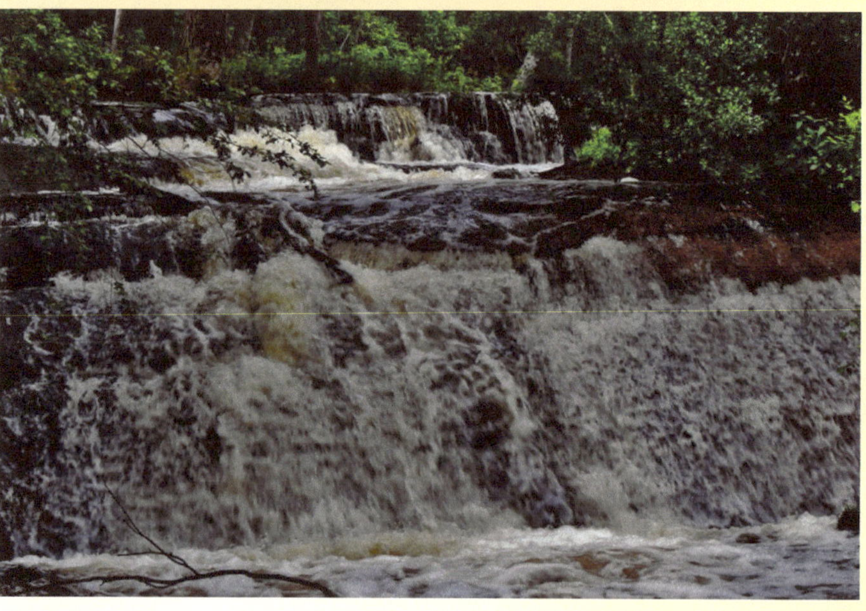

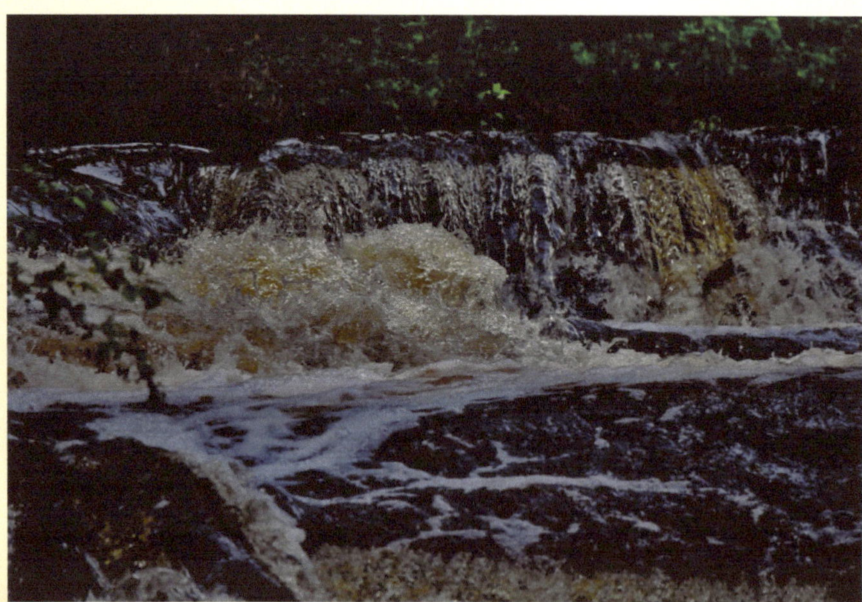

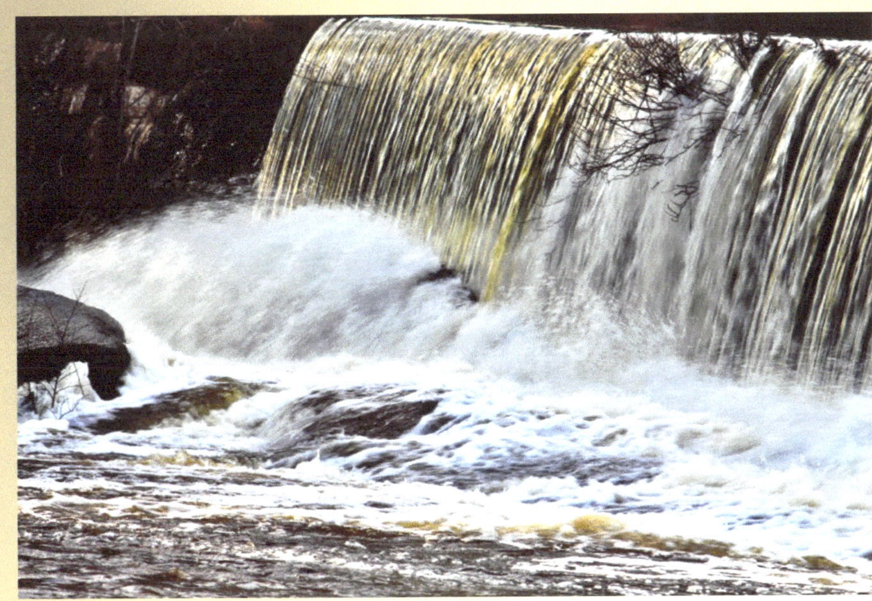
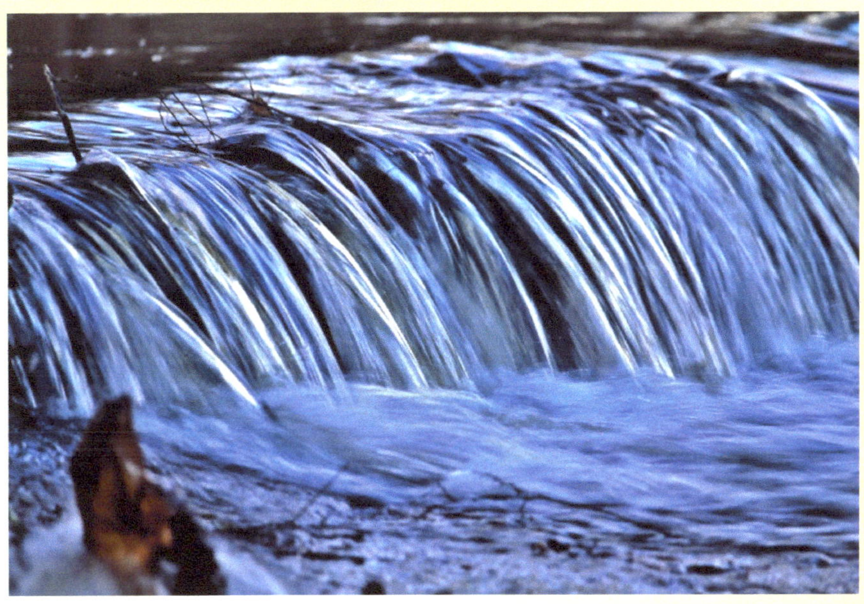
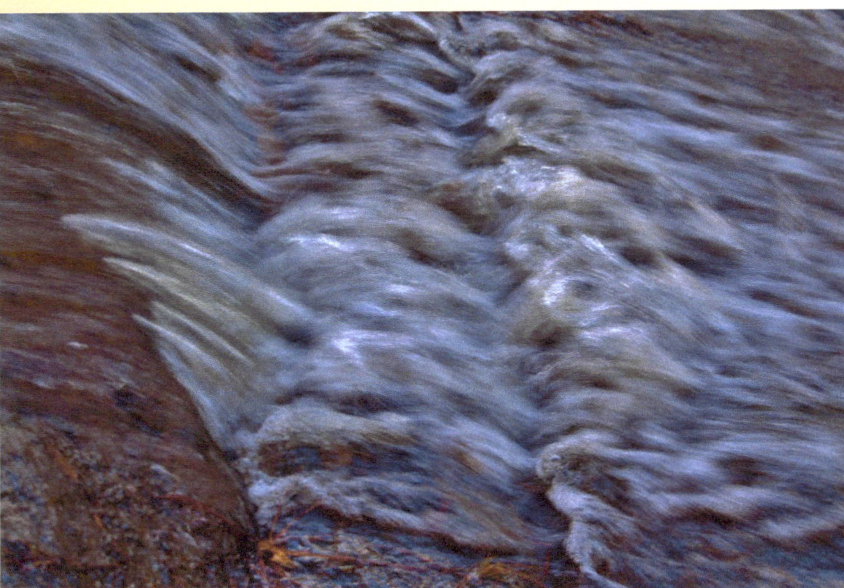
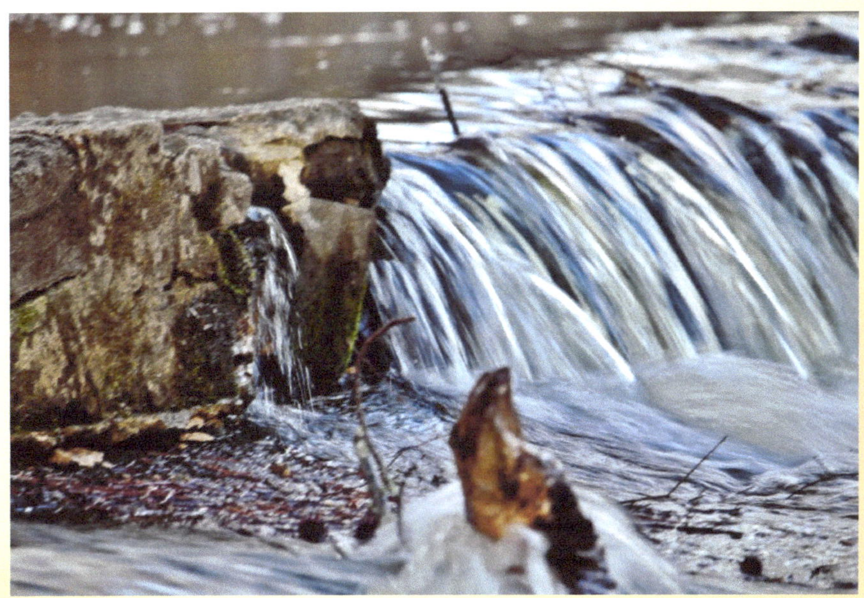

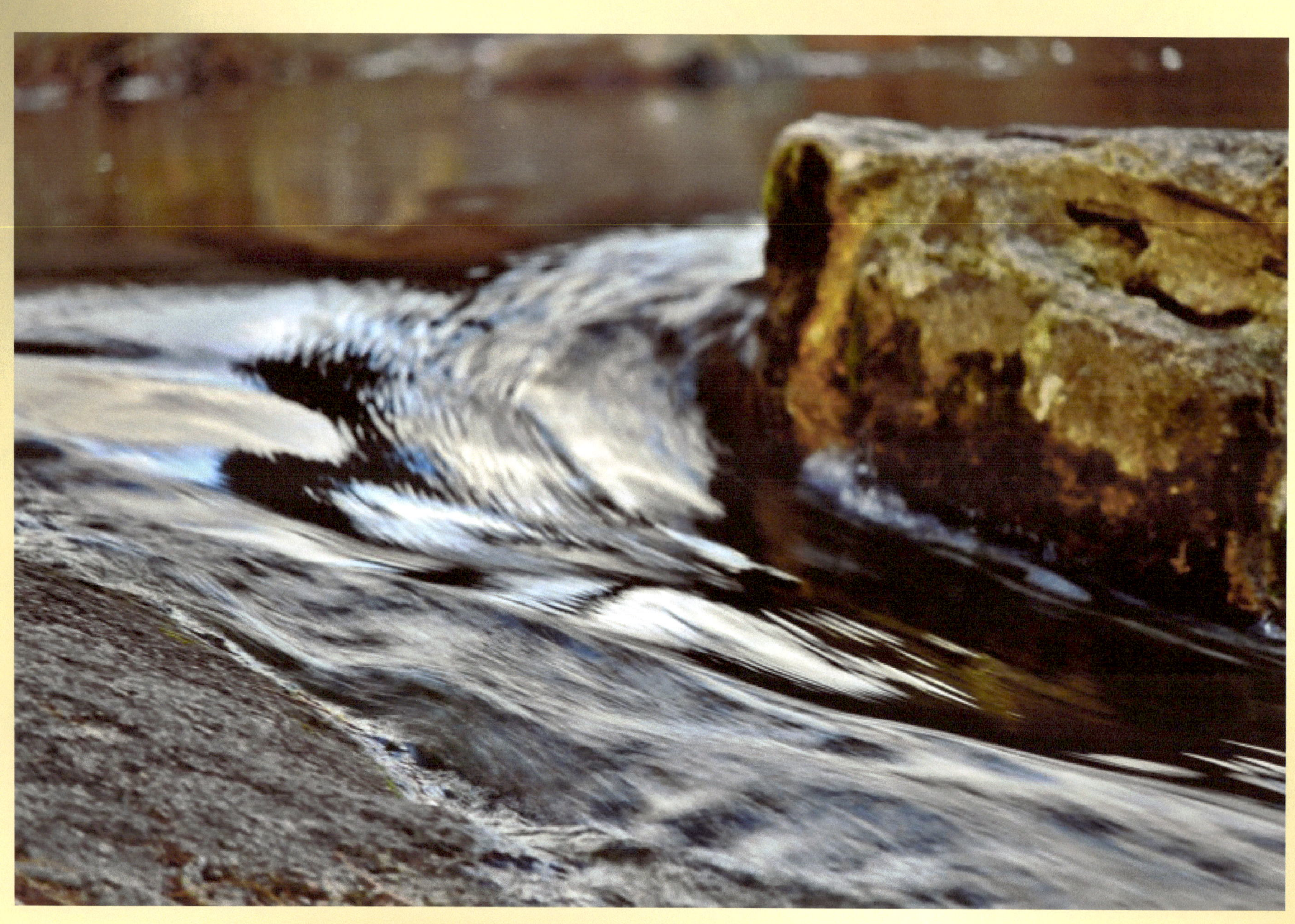

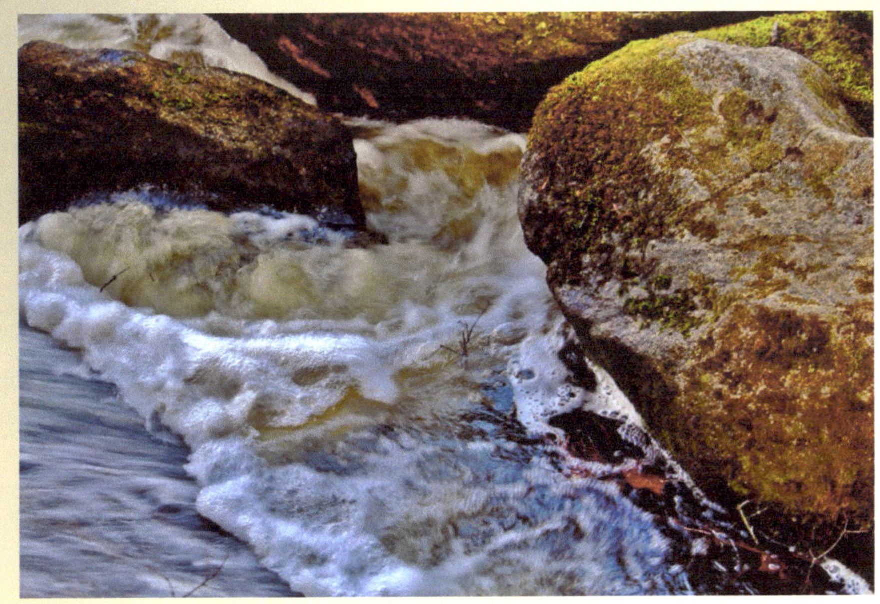

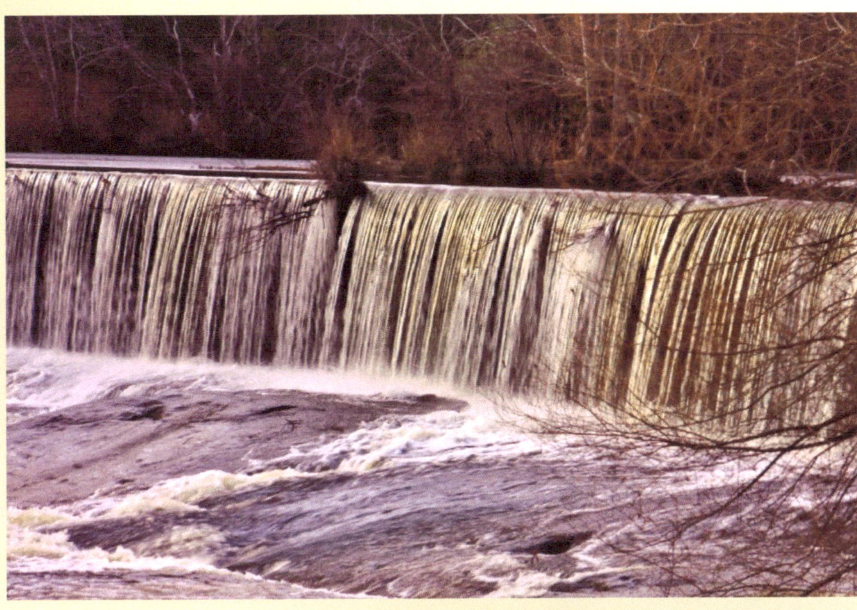

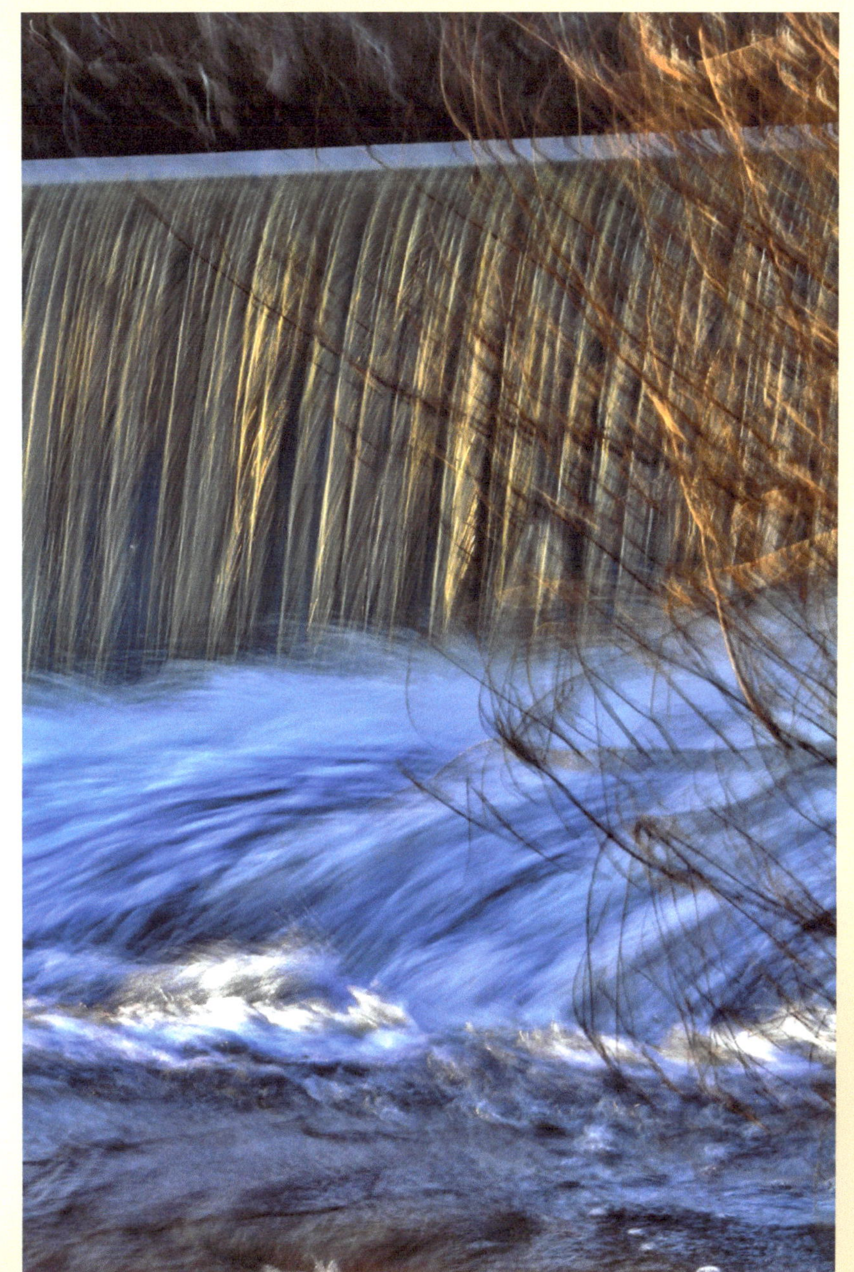

The second section is after Hurricane Matthew. If you will notice the difference in the trees surrounding the Dam. After Matthew came through a Tornado made a direct hit on the Park and Dam and traveled several miles leaving quite a lot of damage. It also damaged the bridge crossing Little River. I was able to get close to the parking lot with my equipment since they had the roads blocked. While using my telephoto lens, I was fortunate to get a lot of shots while the water was running at top speed and making its own trails between the broken rocks and limbs. Also the water was making a spectacular design around the boulders and the remains of the dam itself.

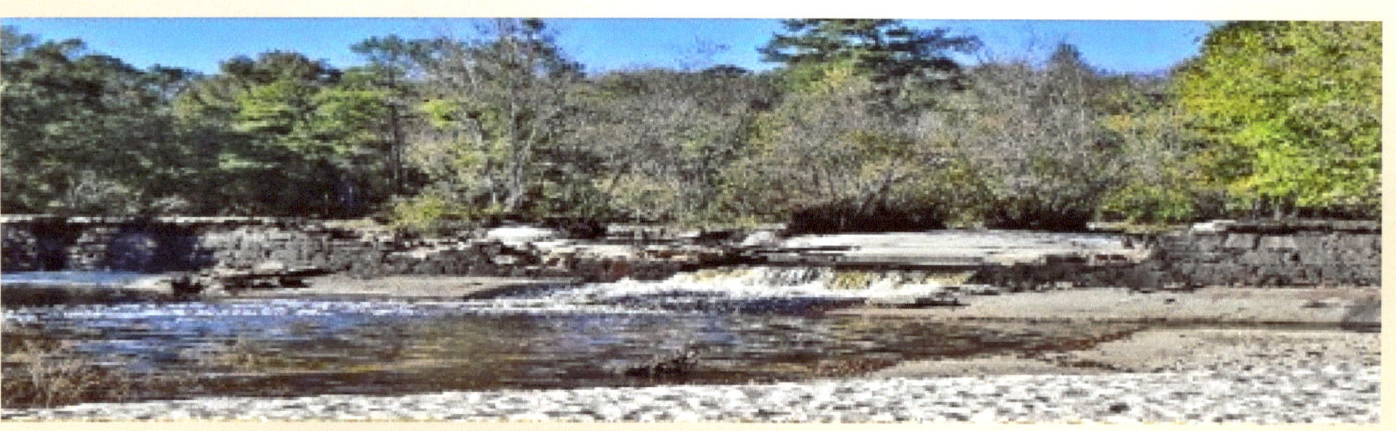

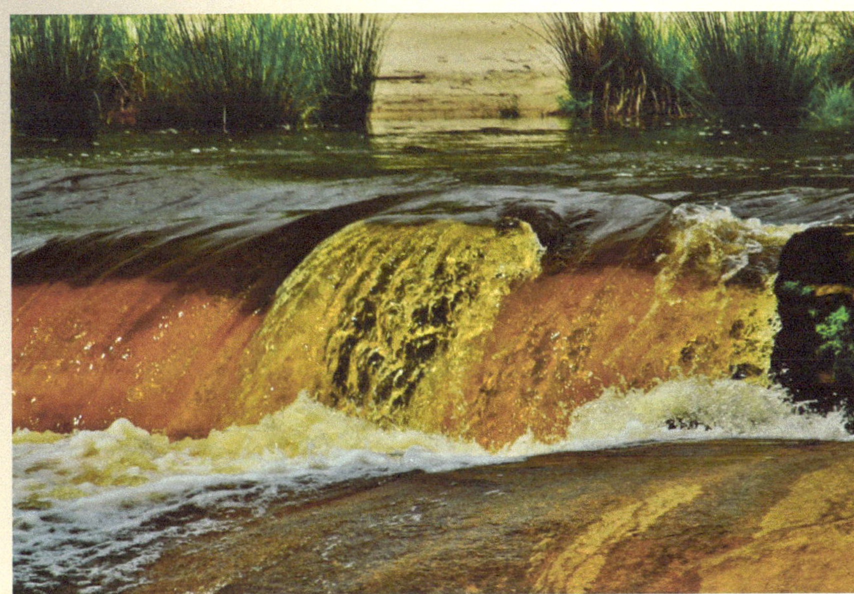
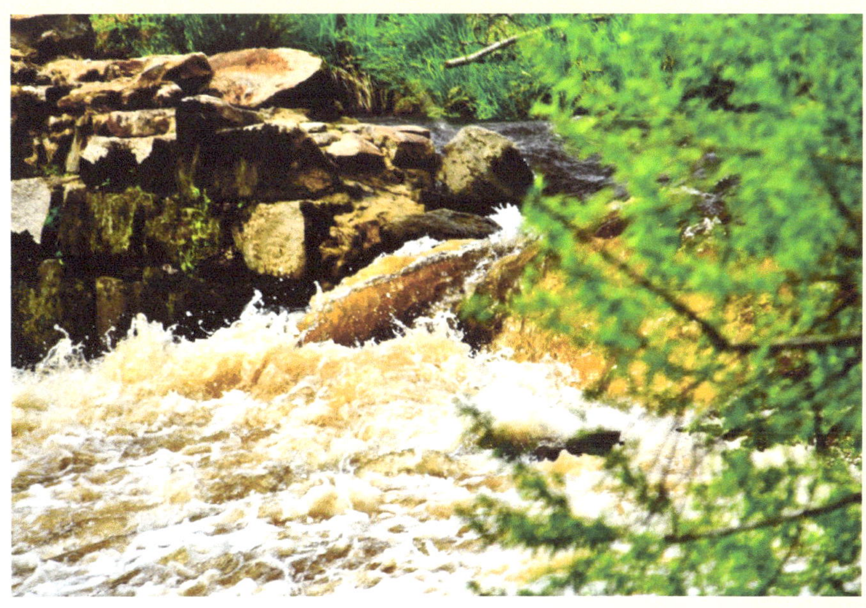
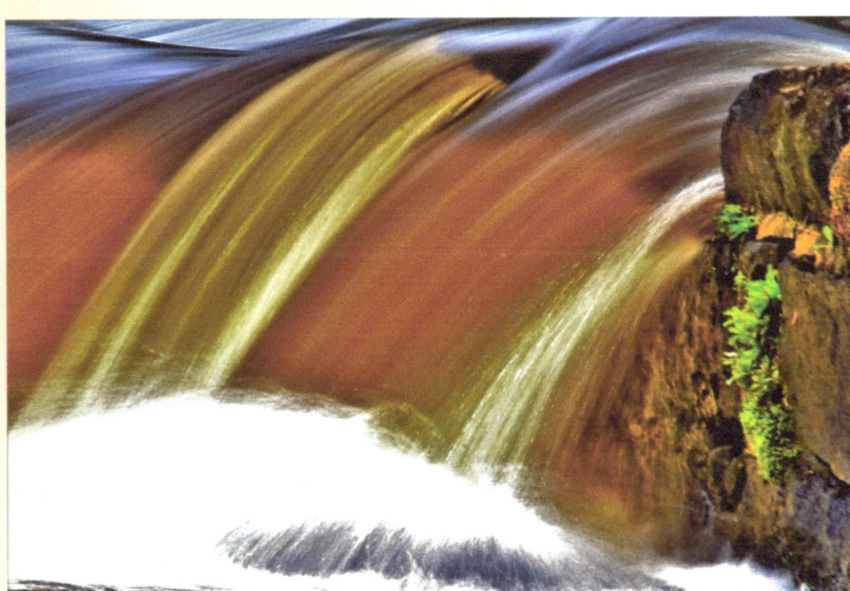
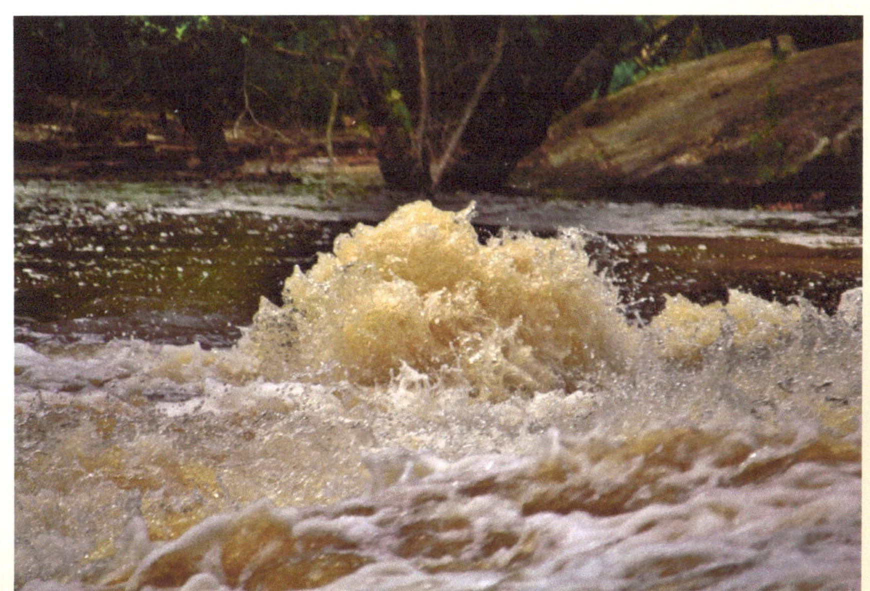

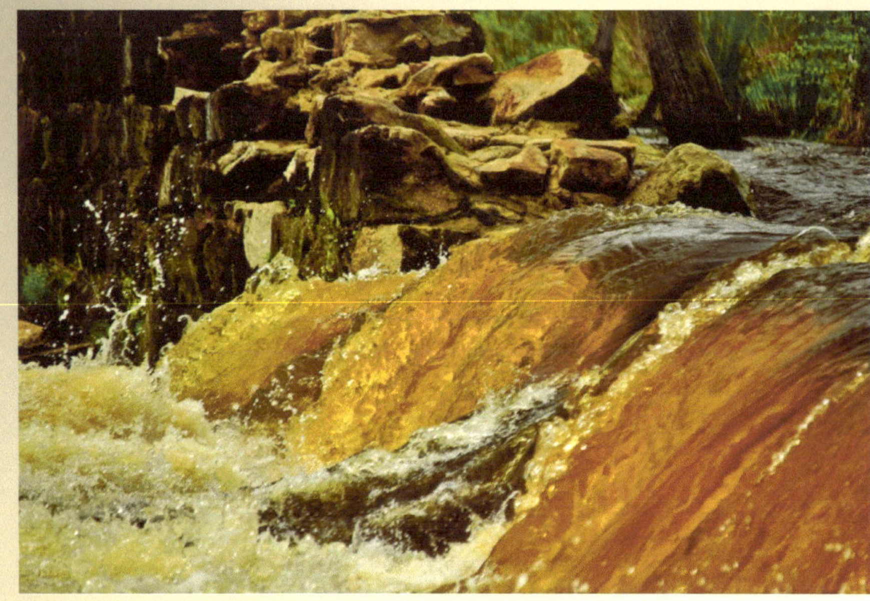
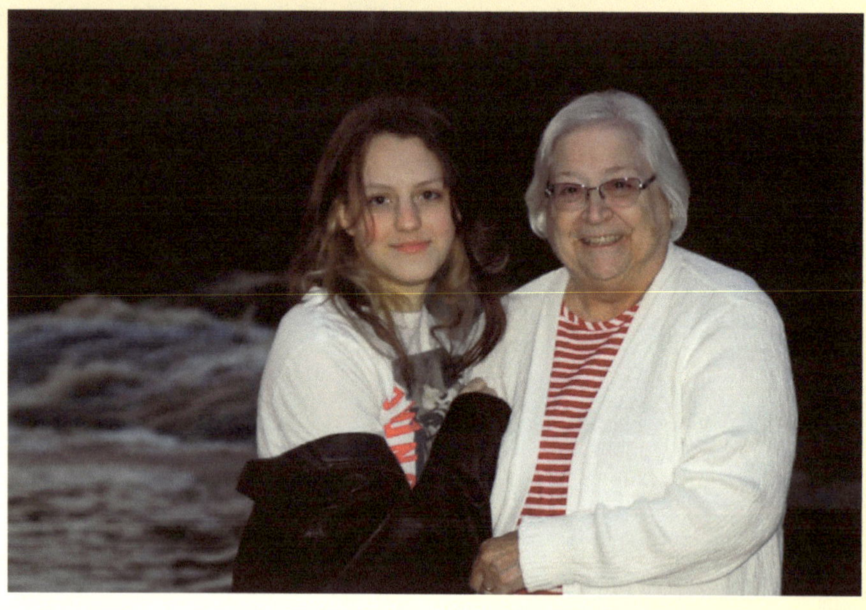
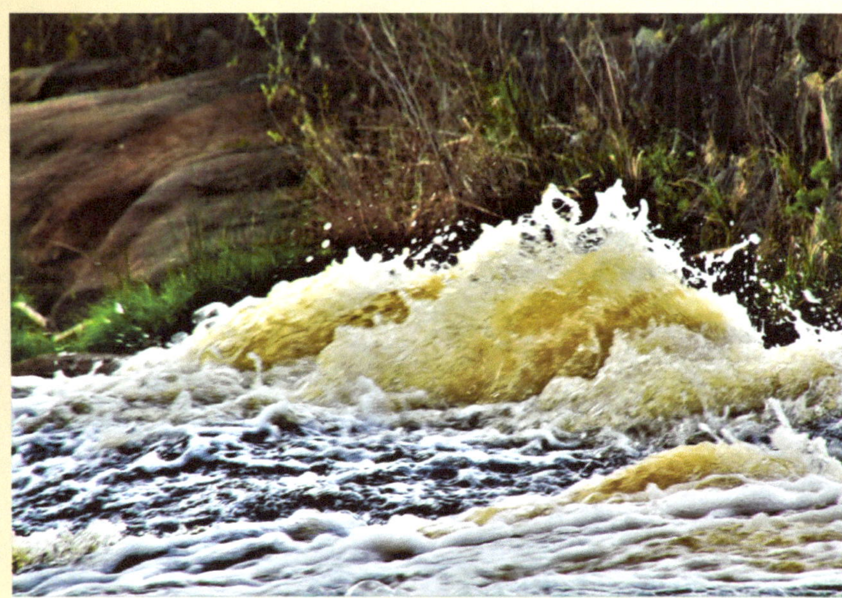
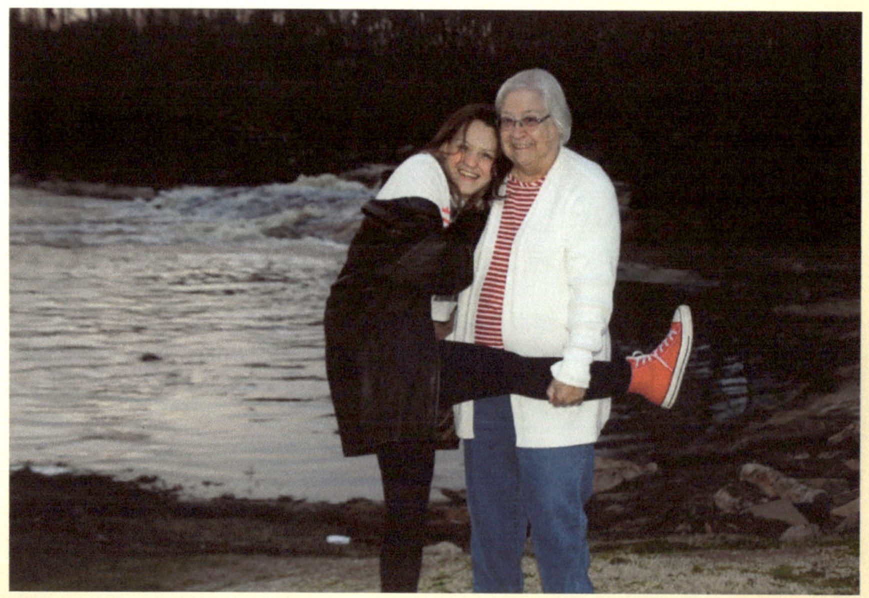

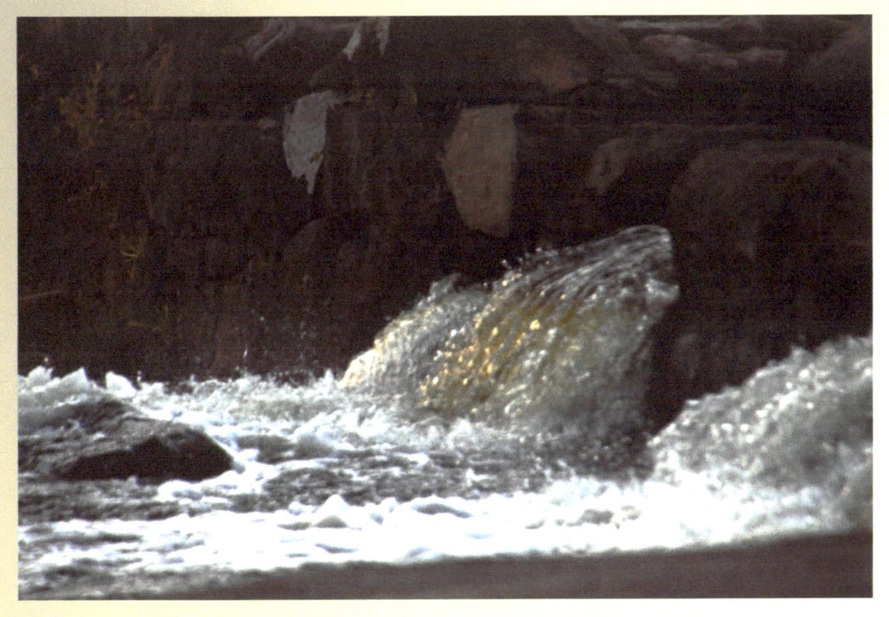
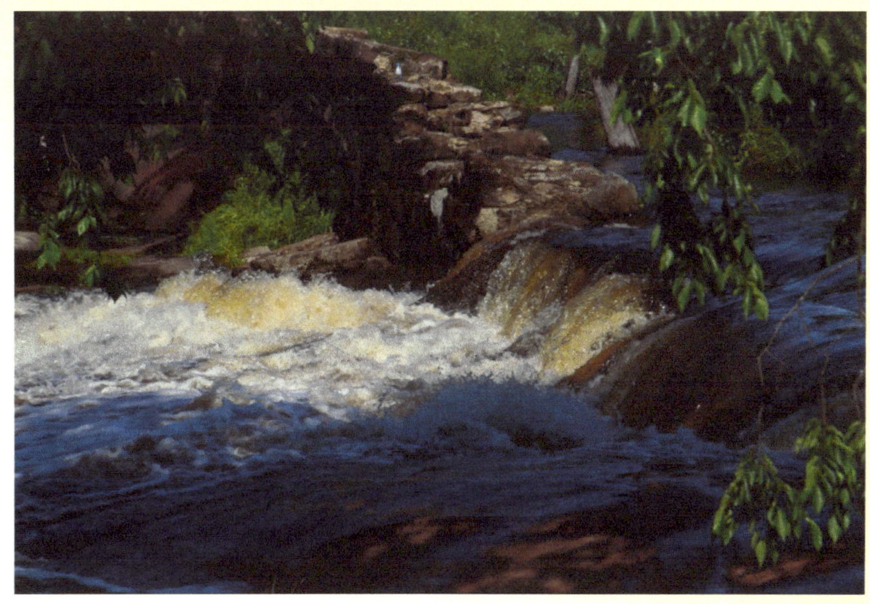
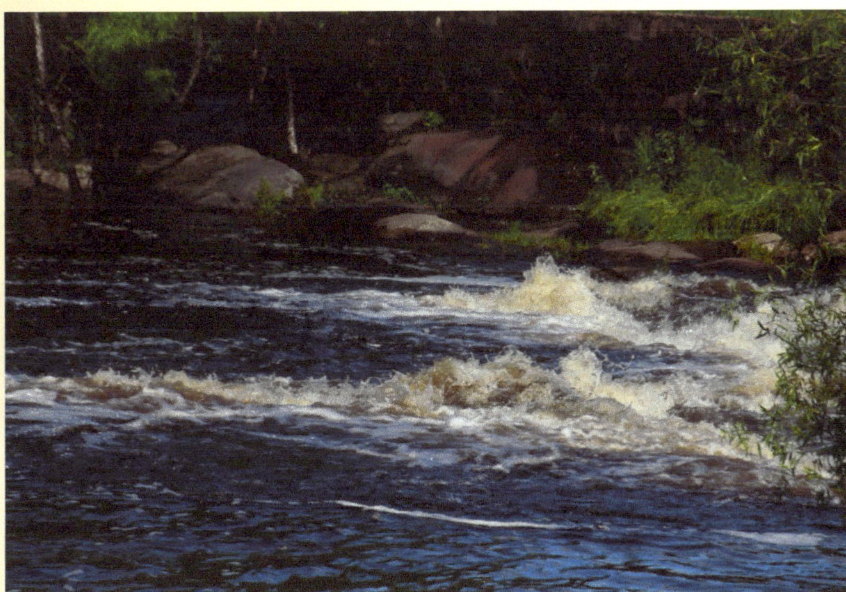
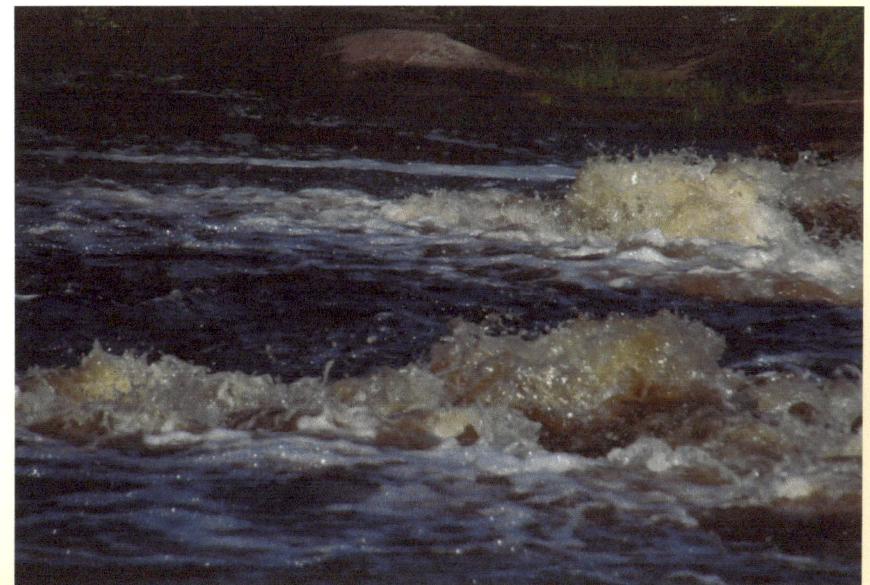

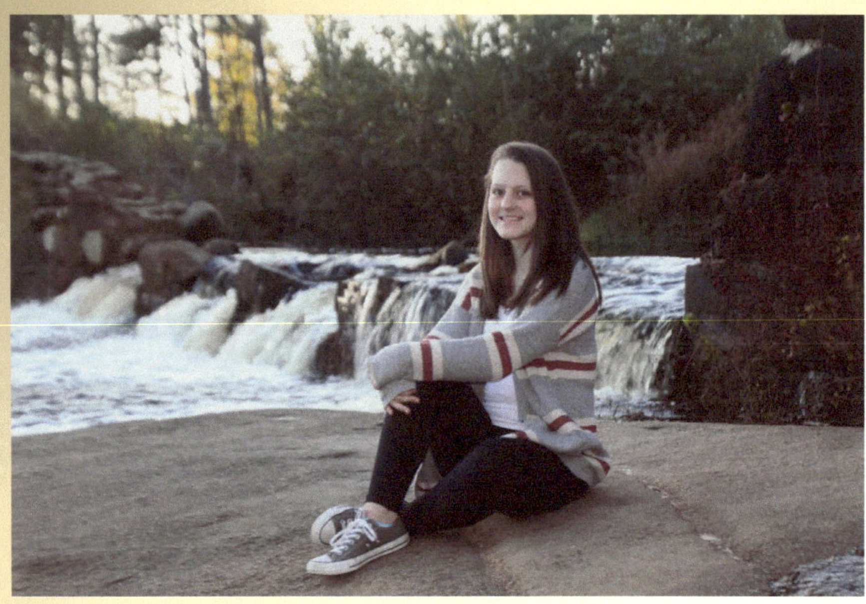
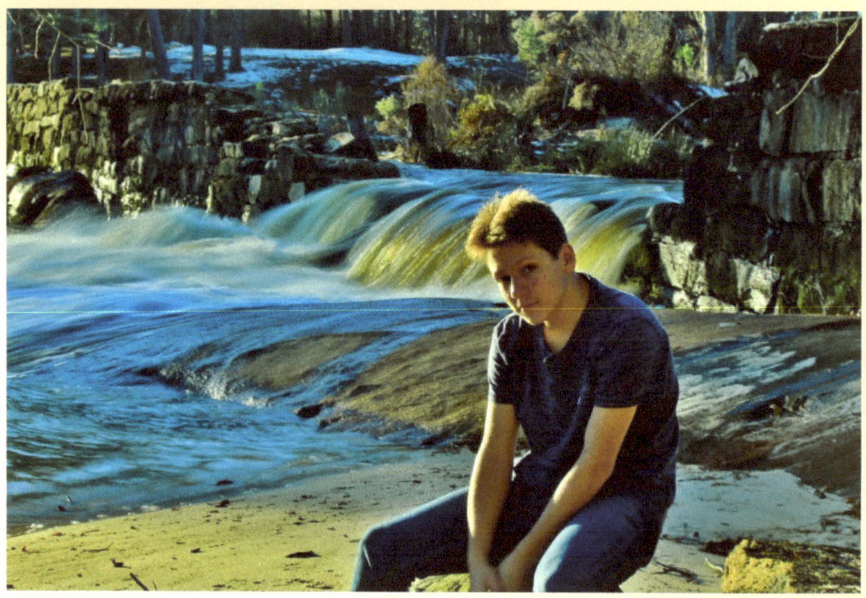
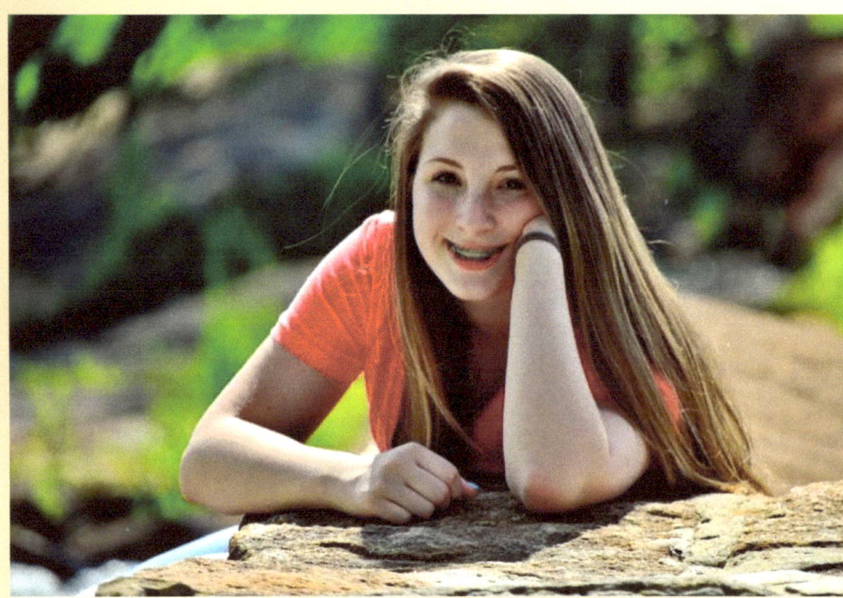
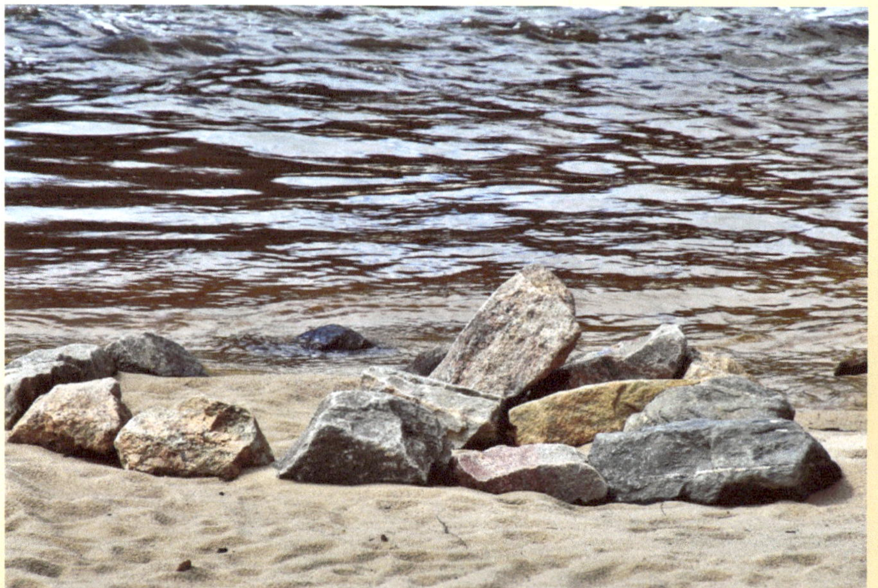

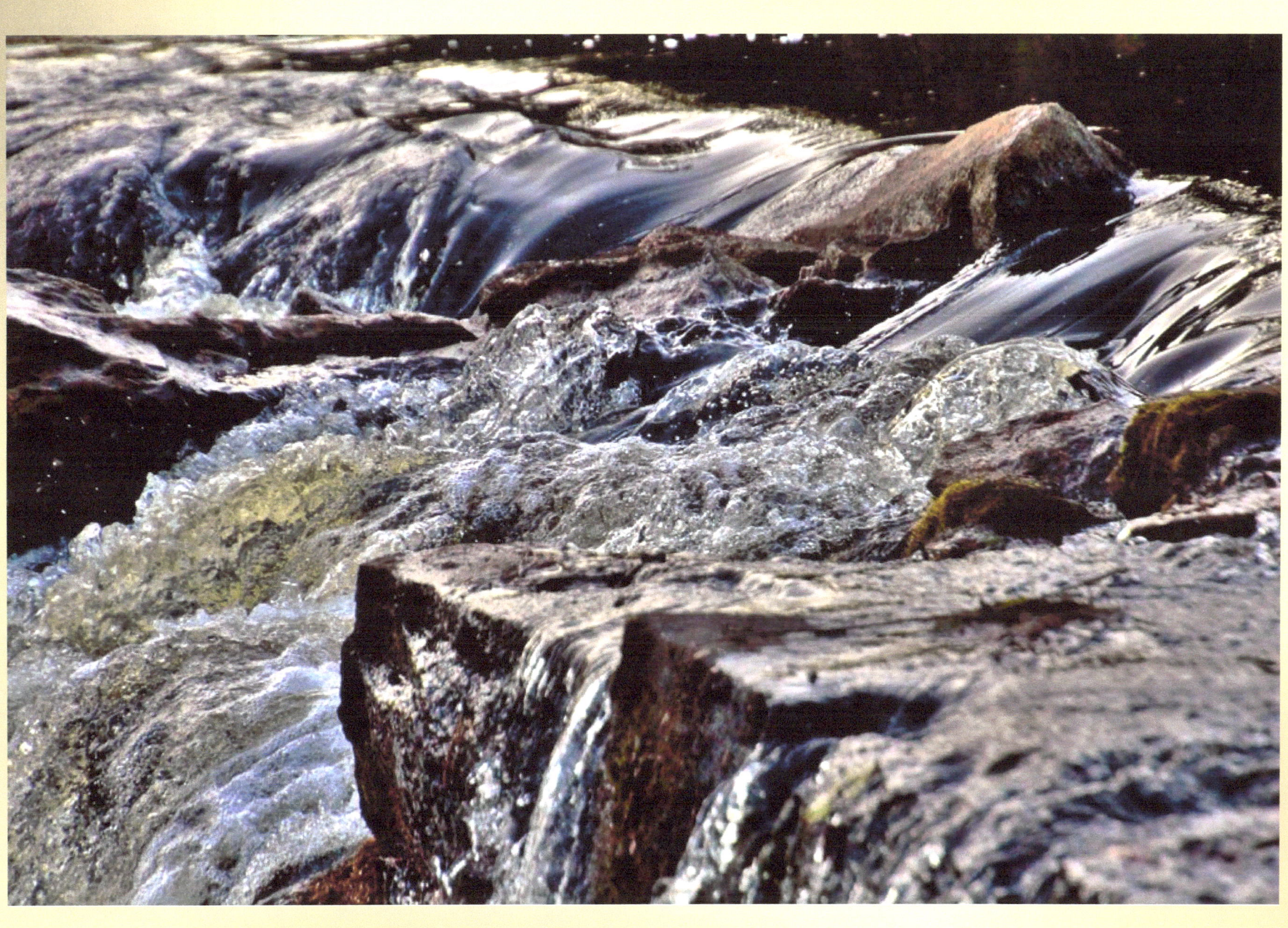

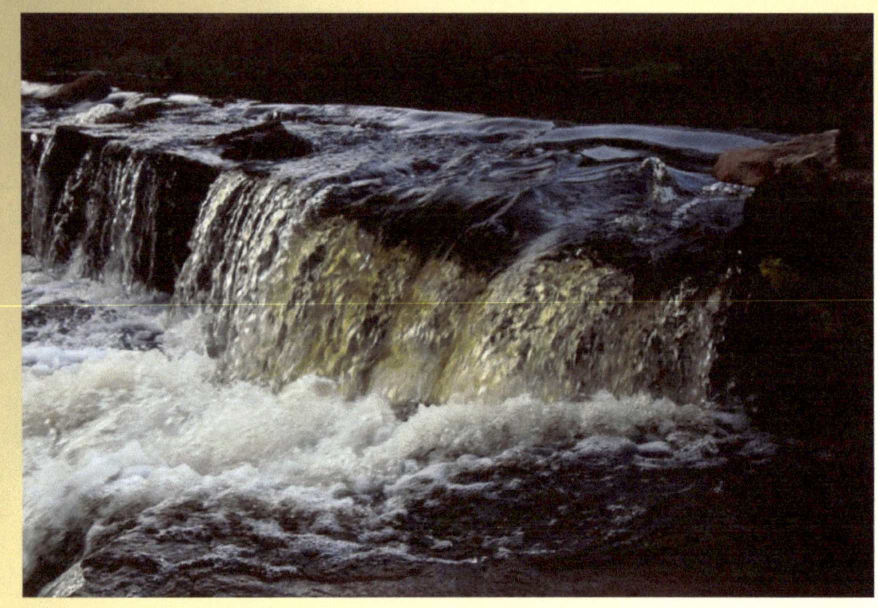
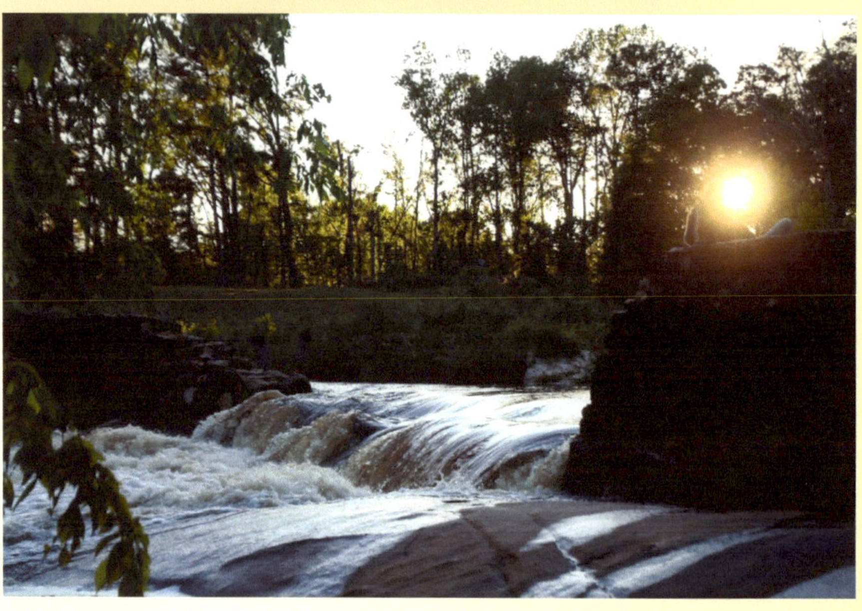
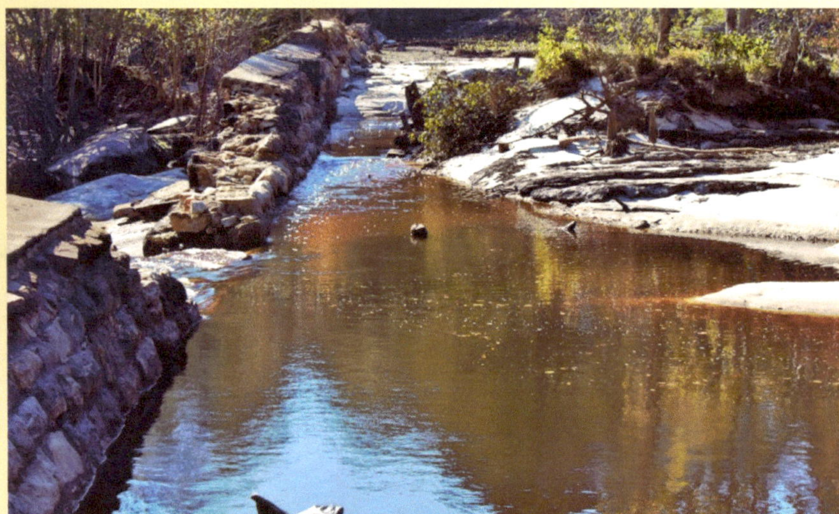
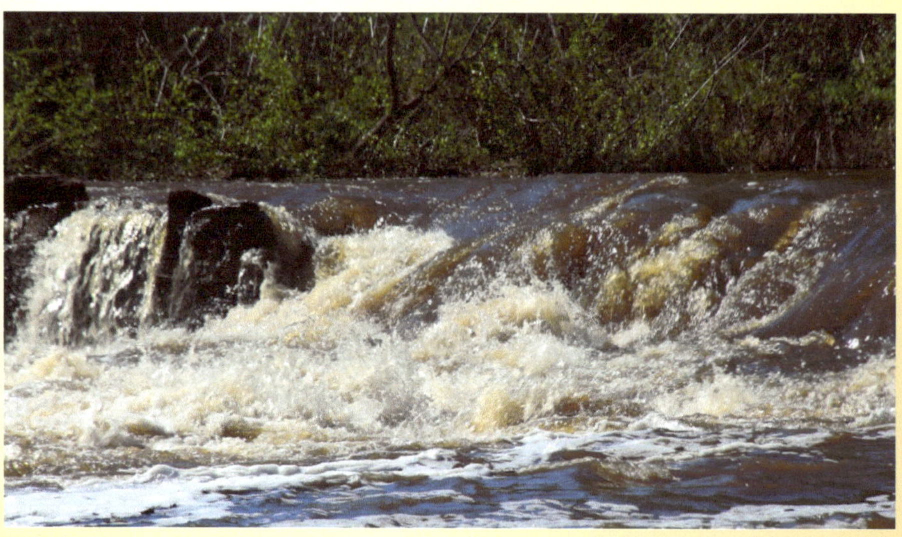

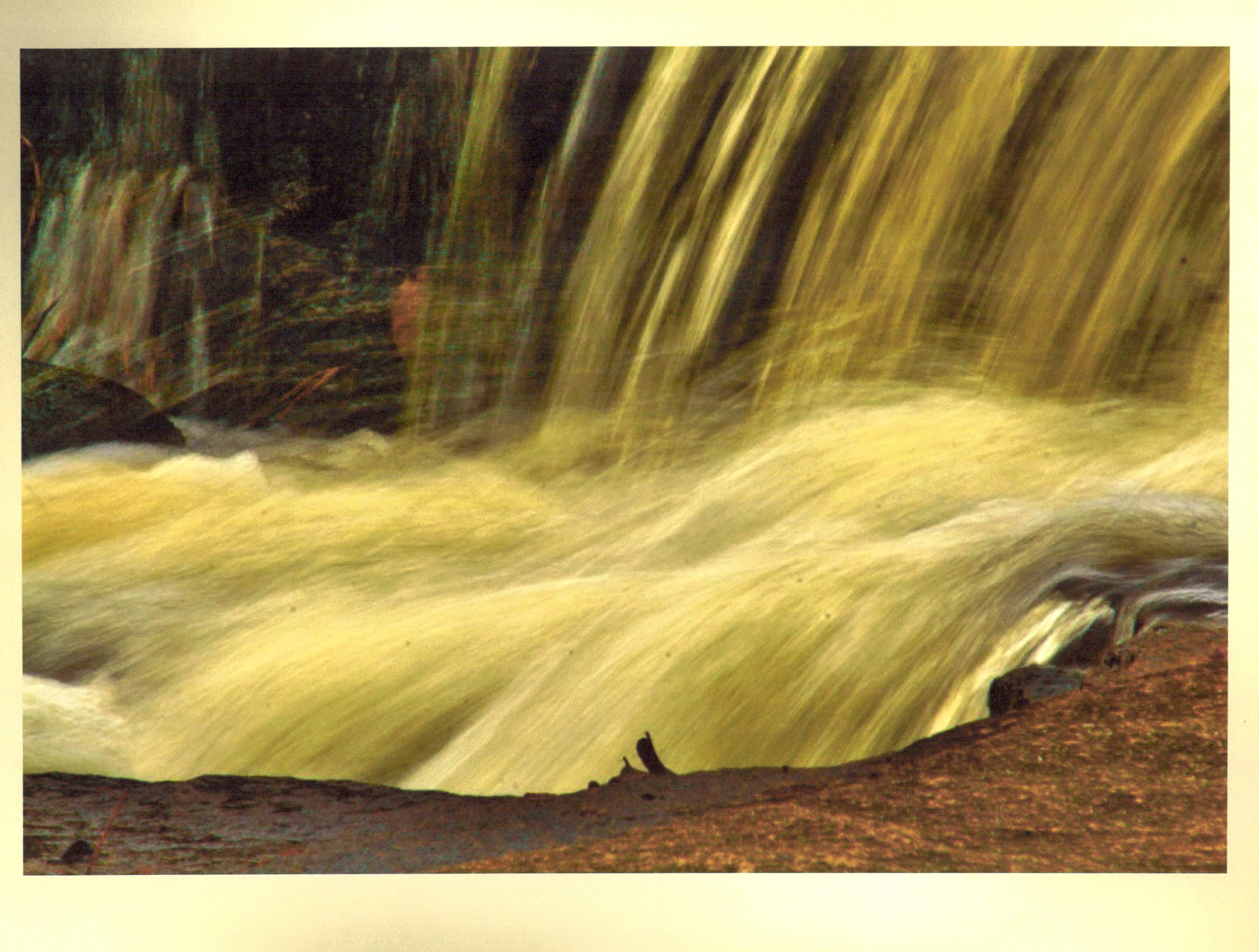

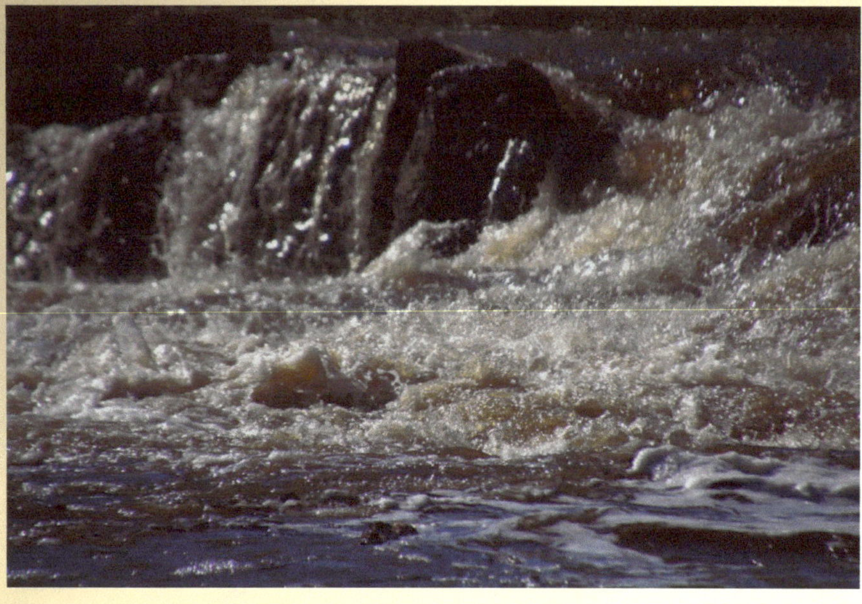

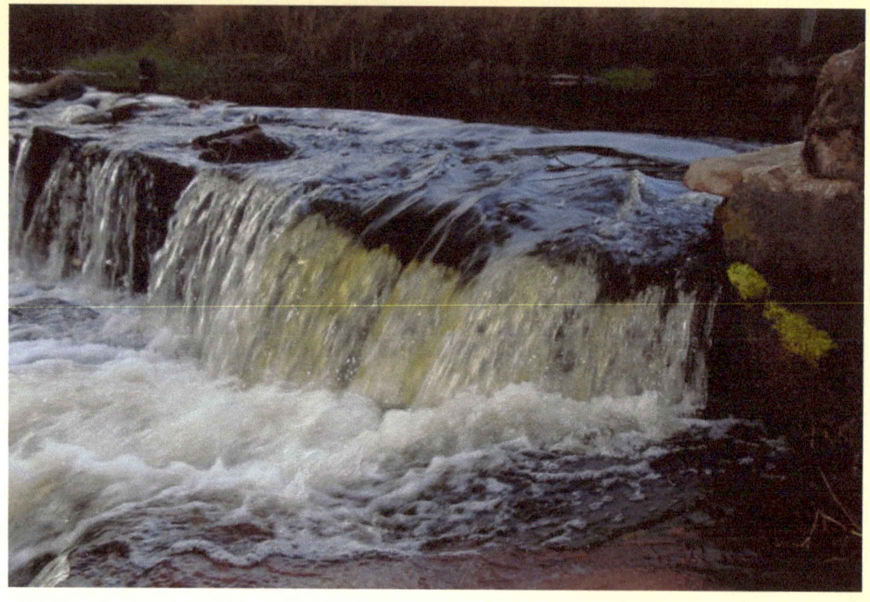

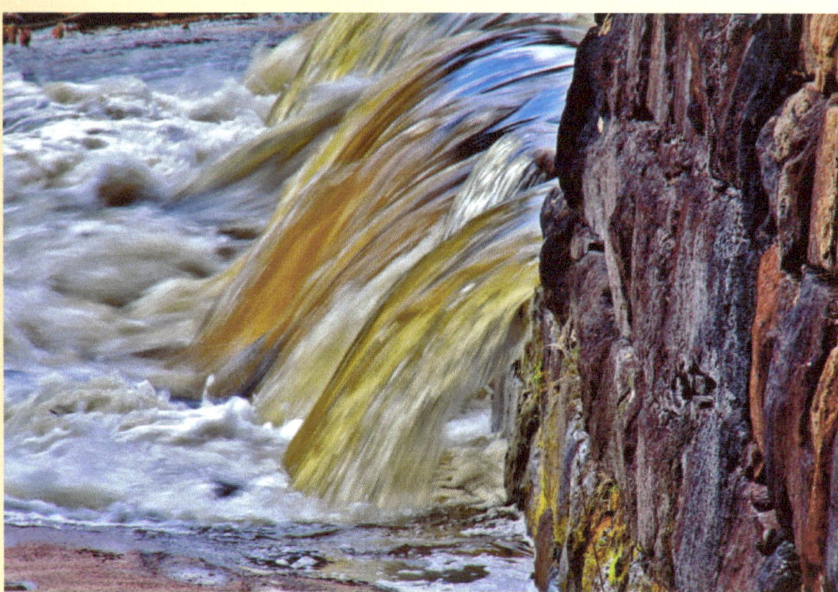

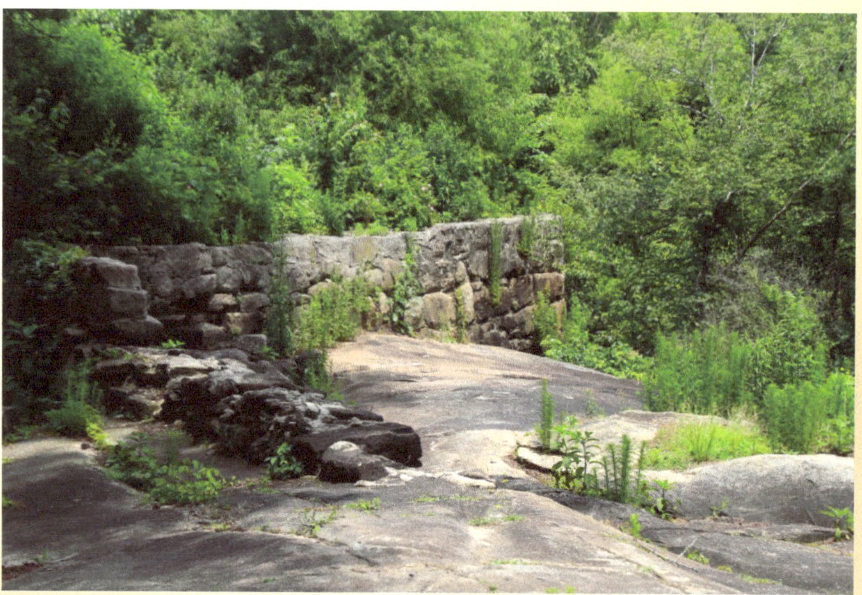

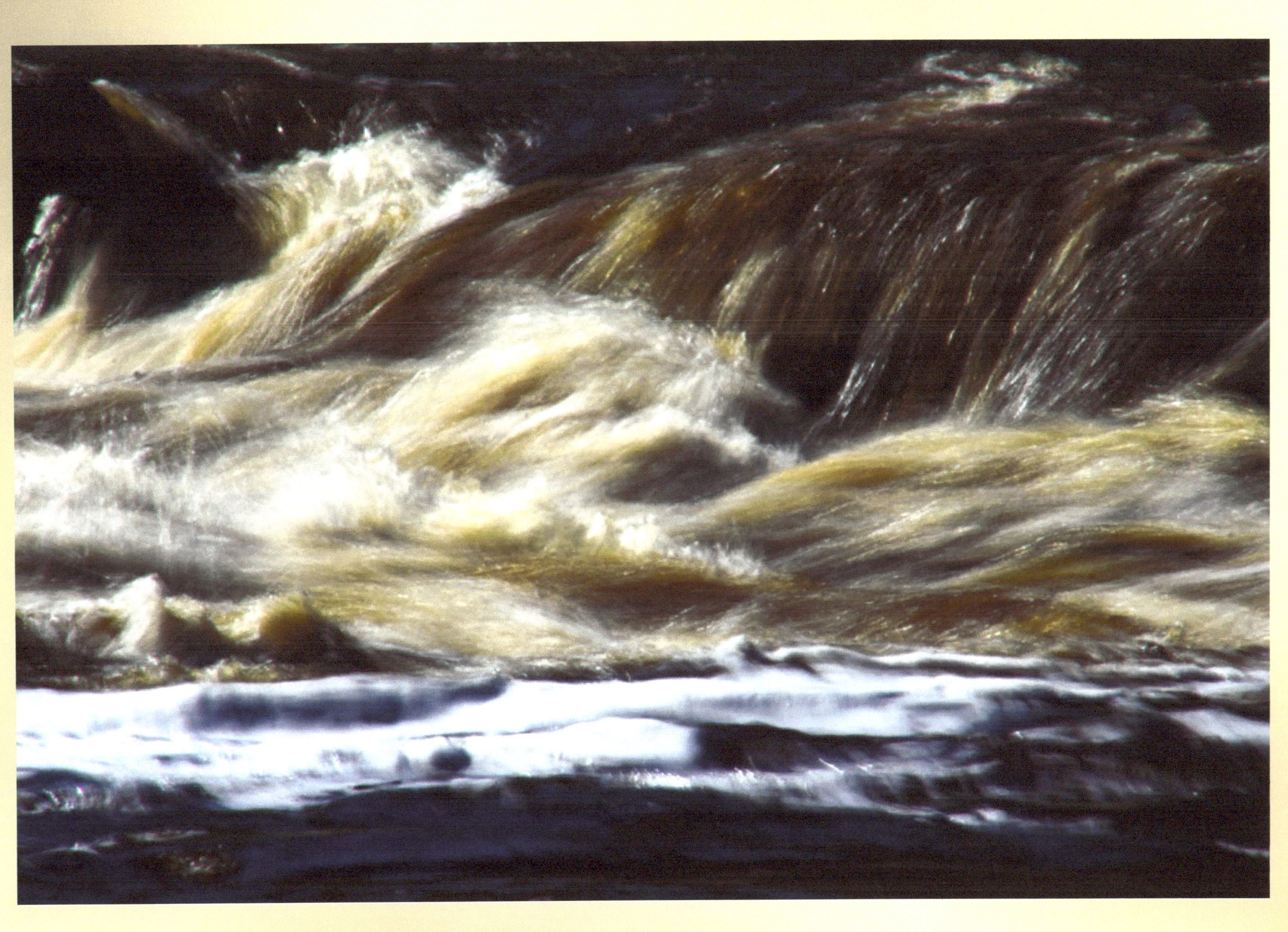

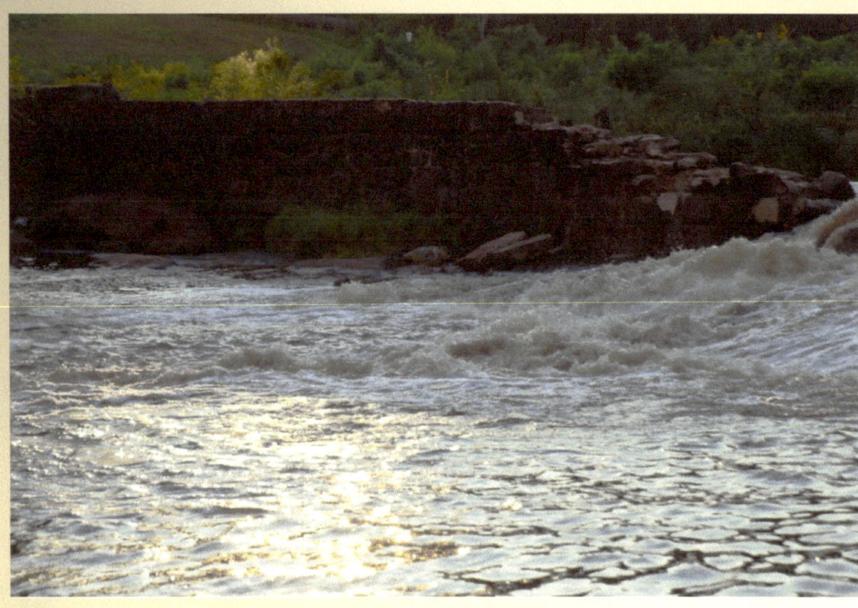
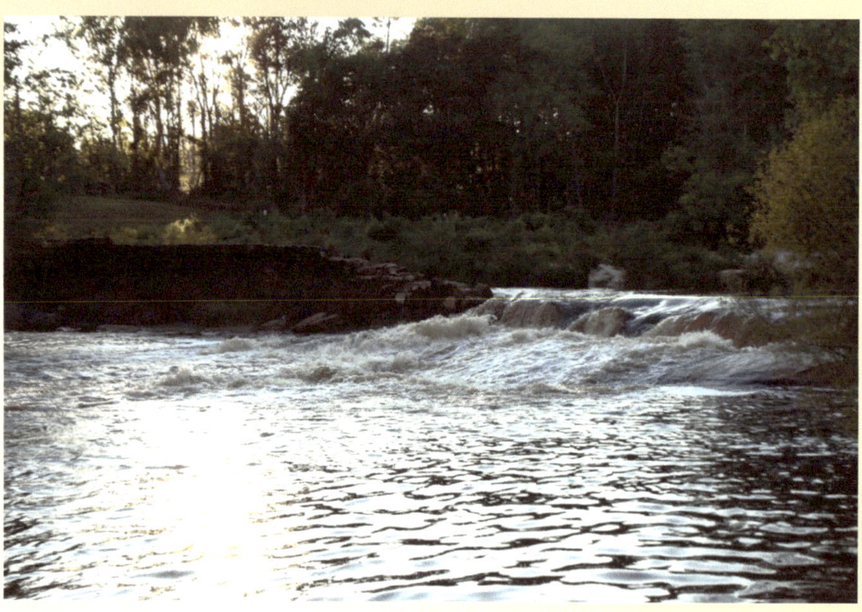
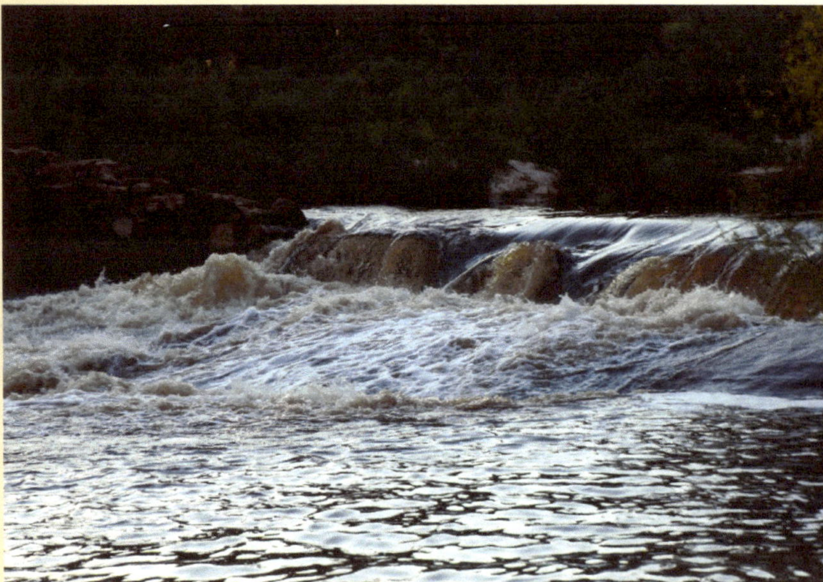
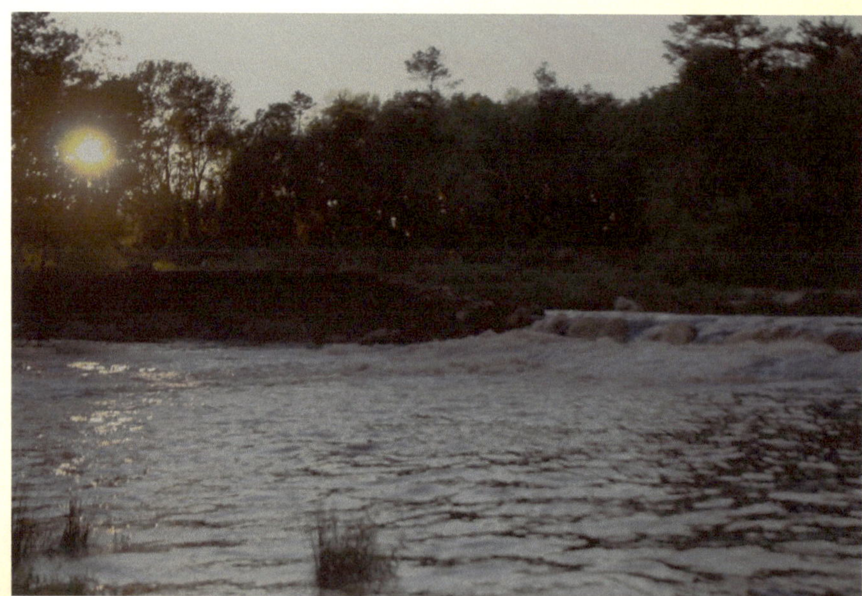

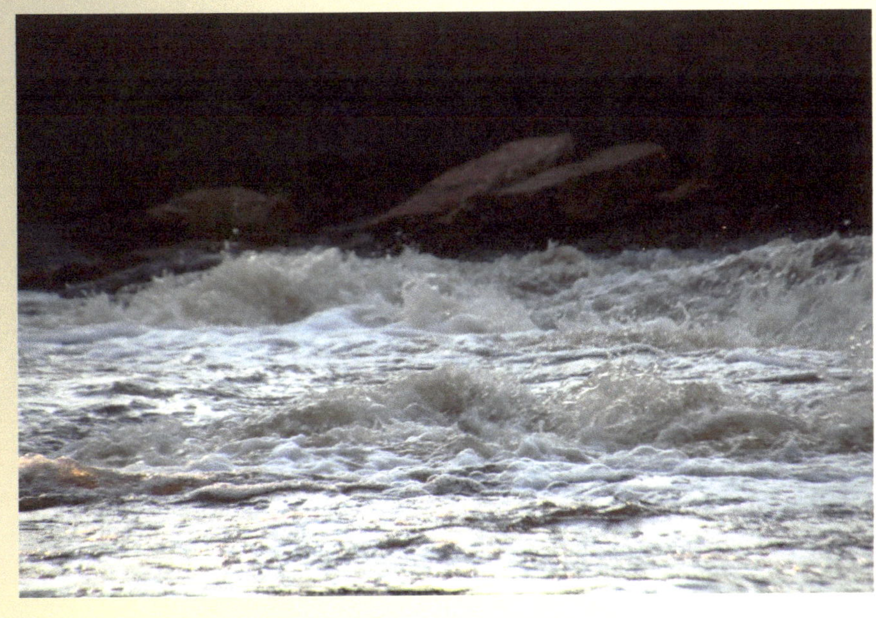
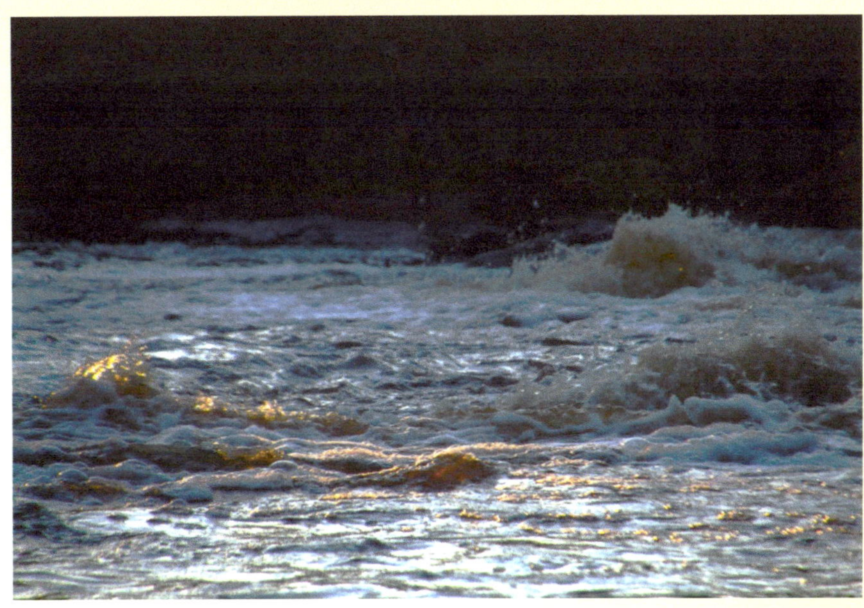
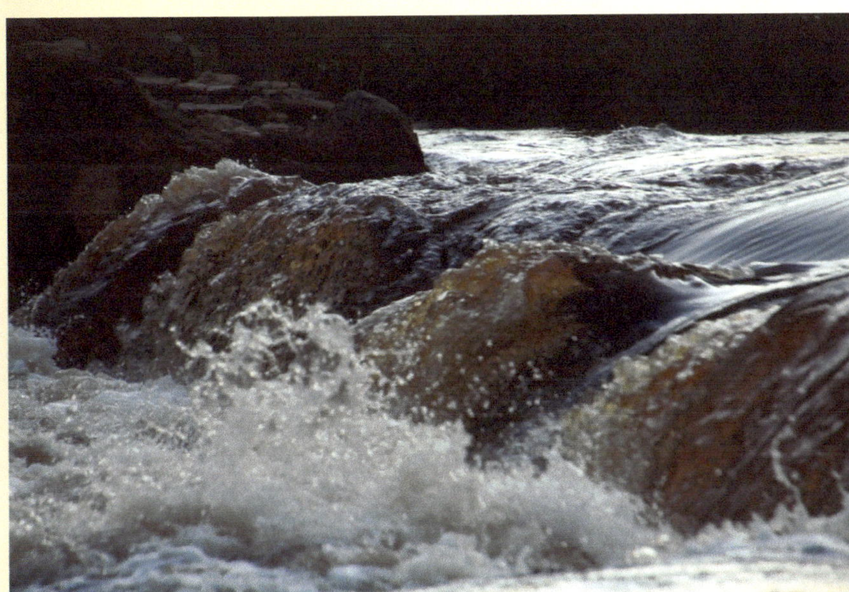
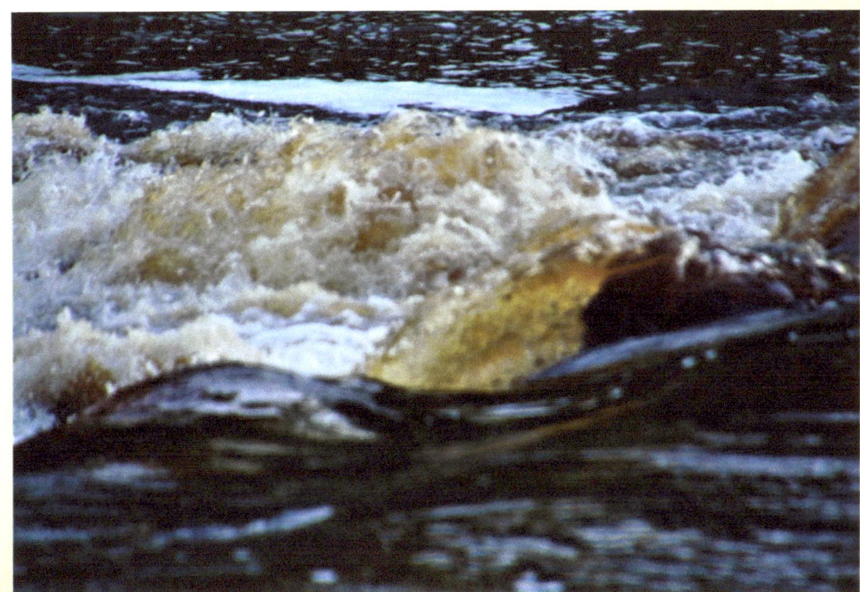

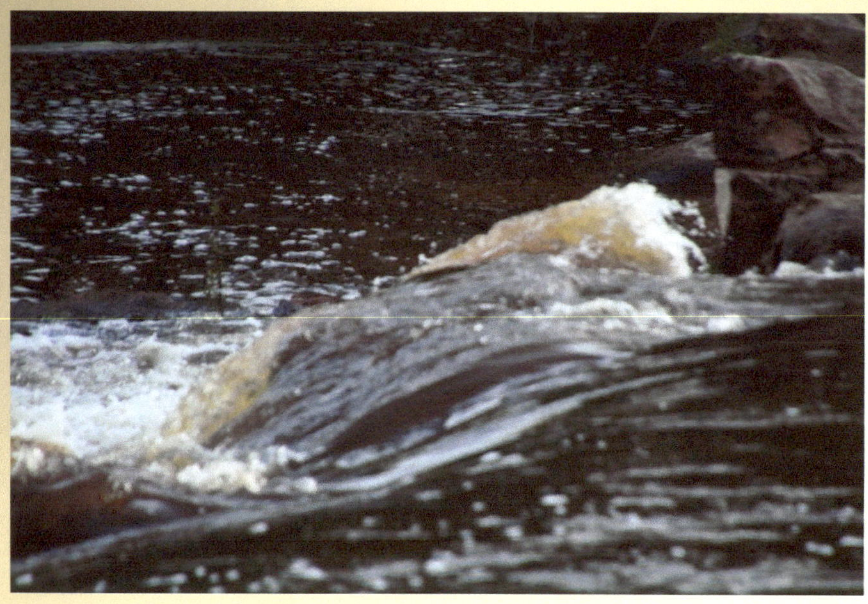
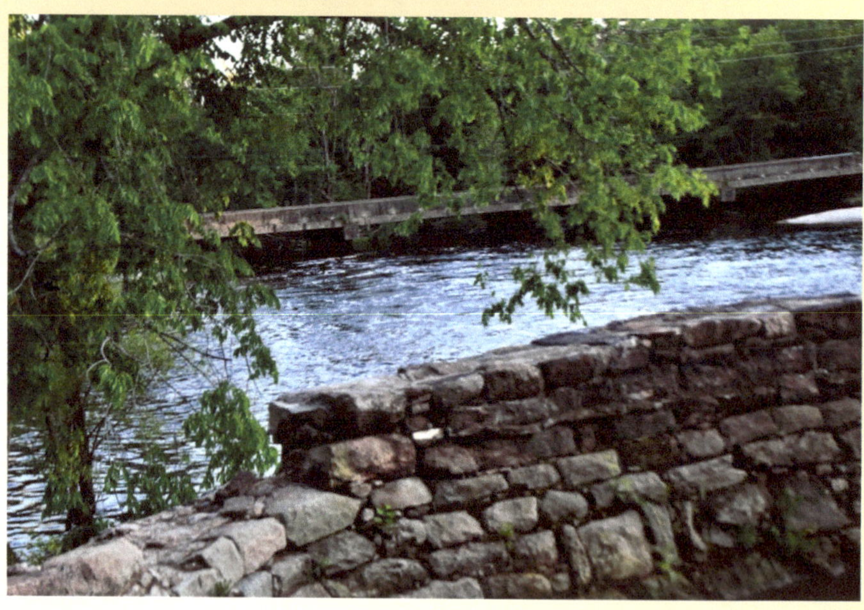
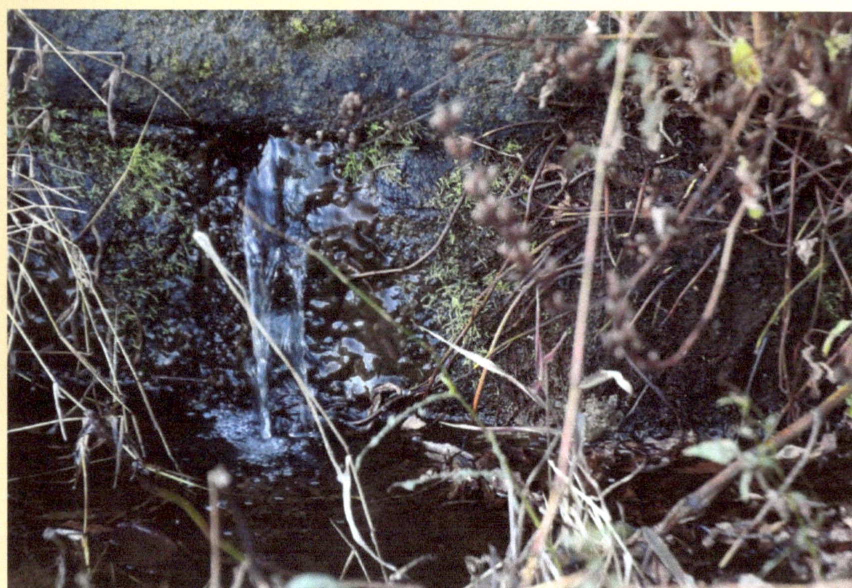
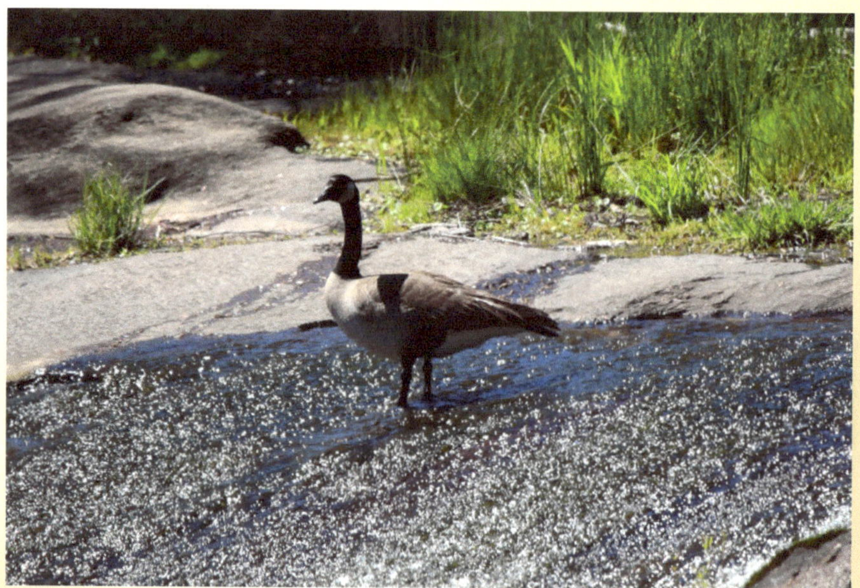

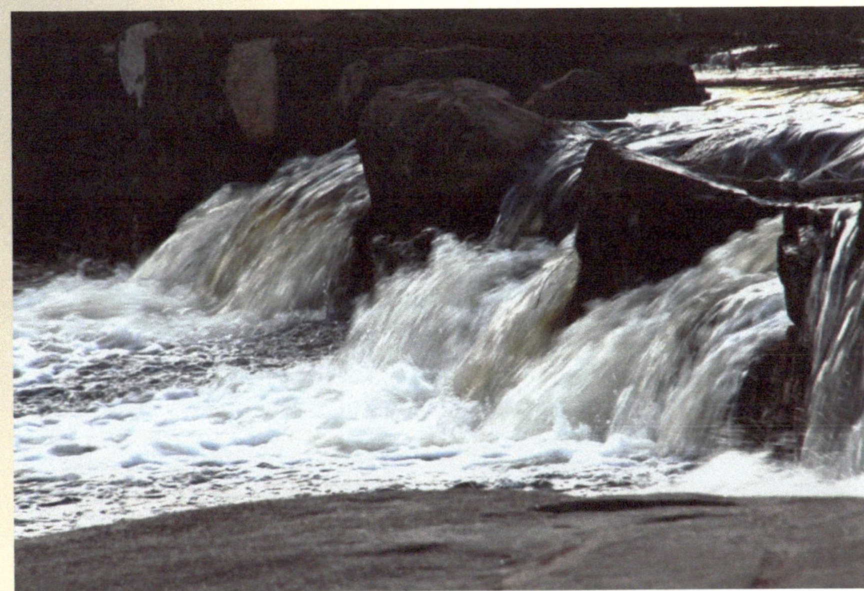
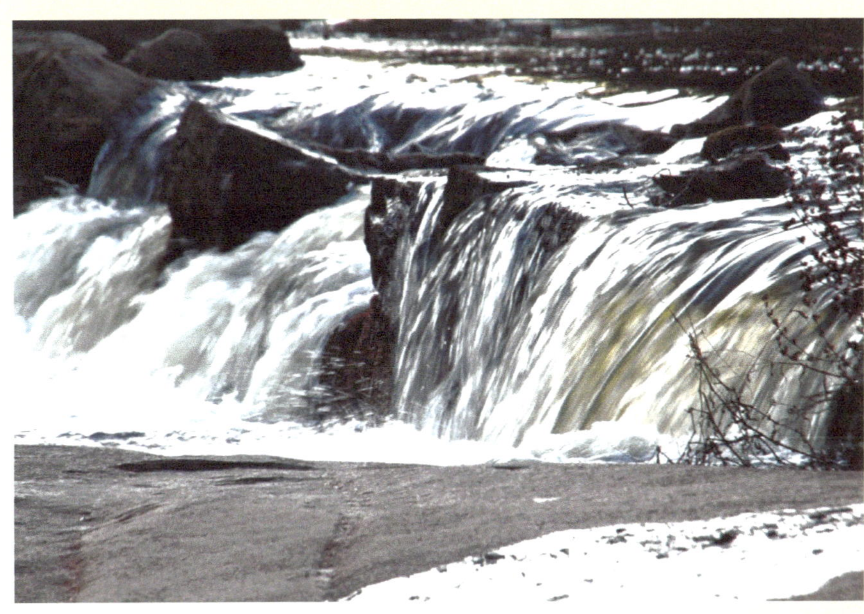
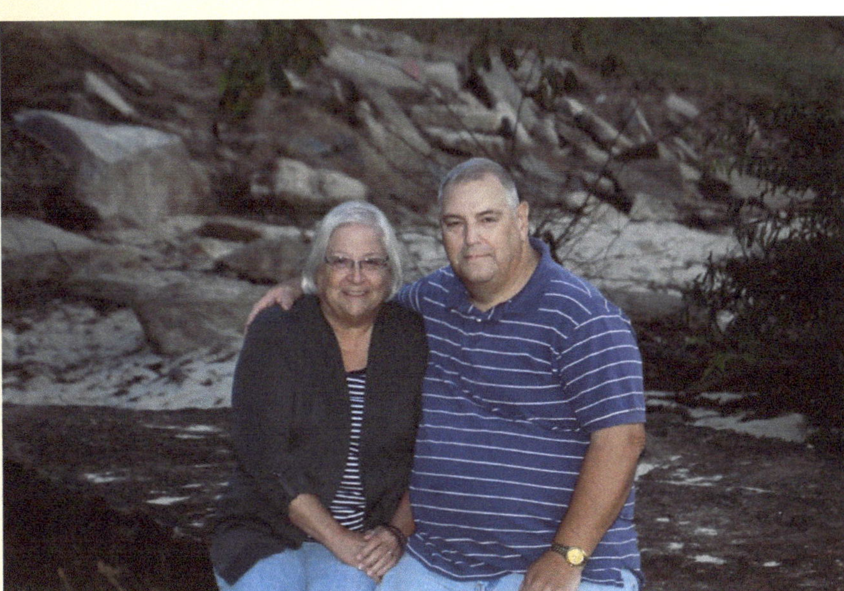
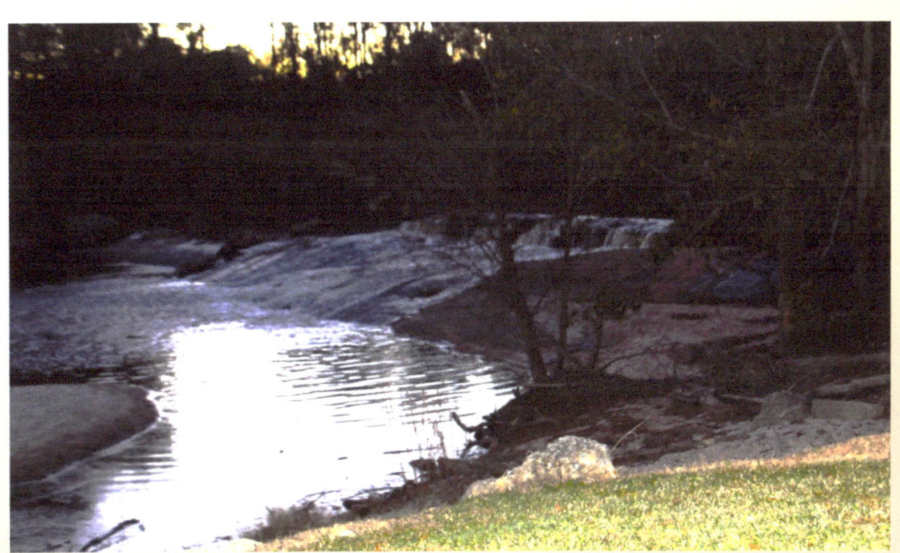

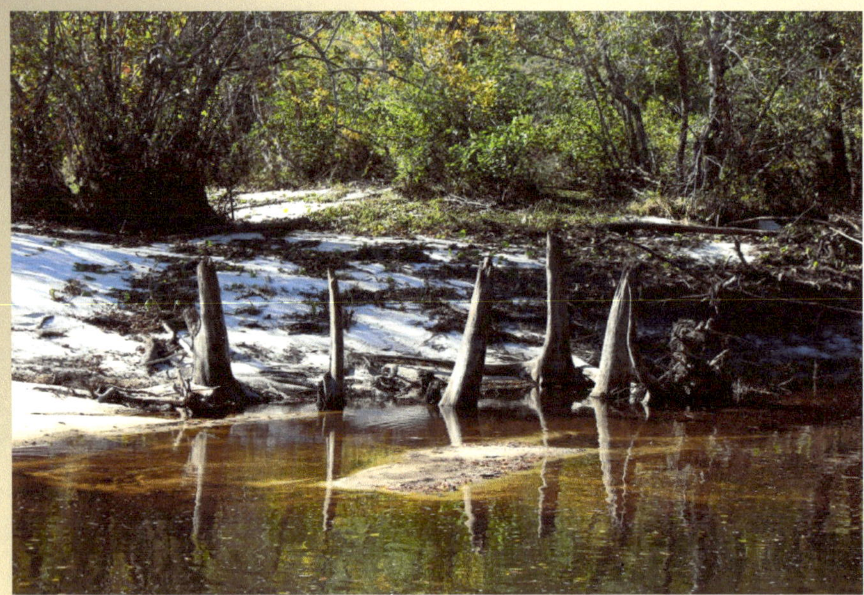
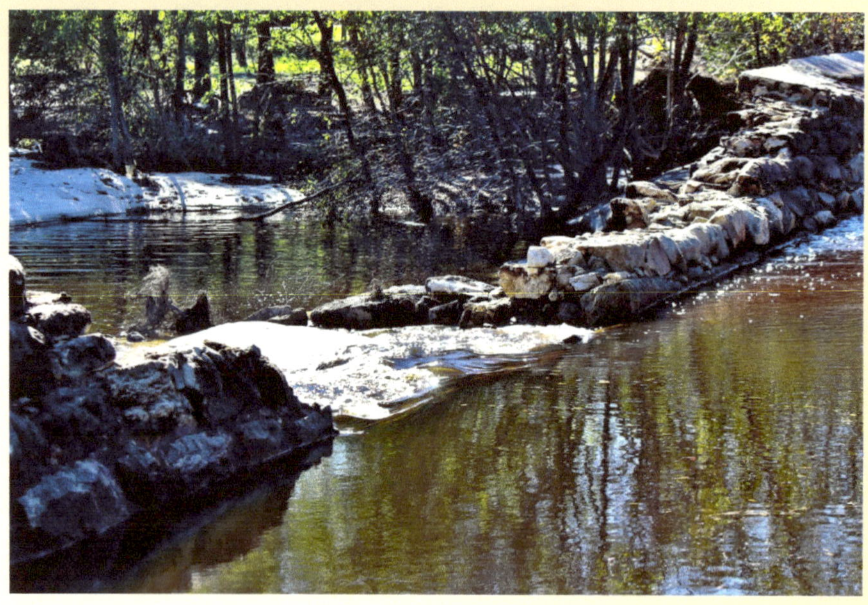
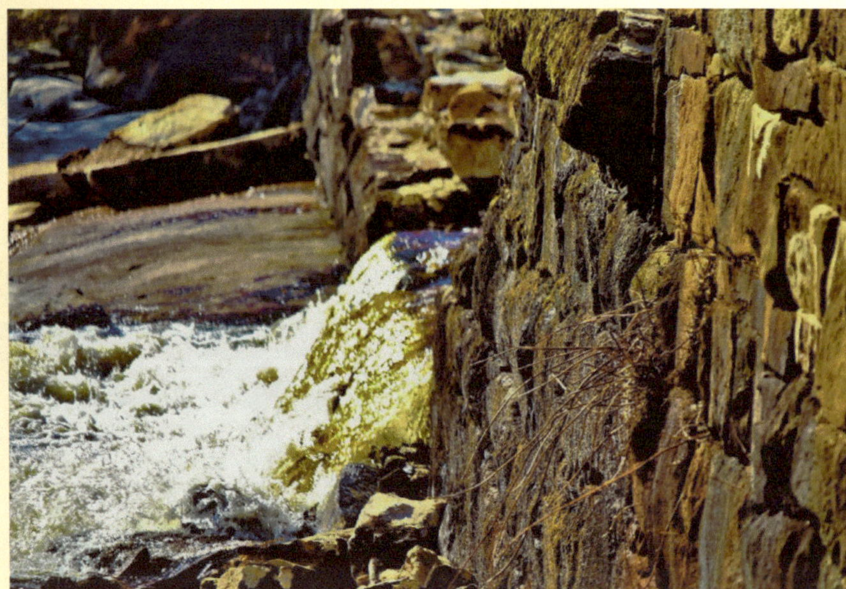
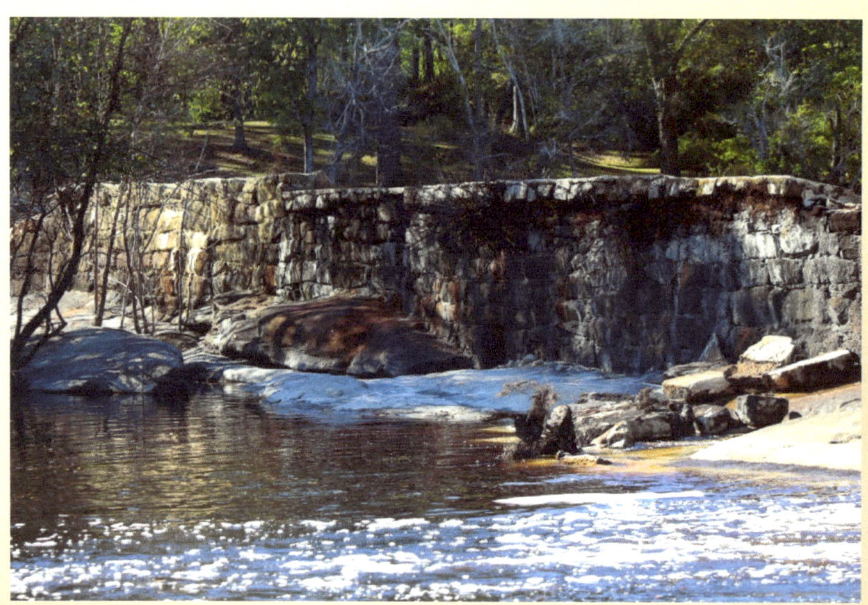

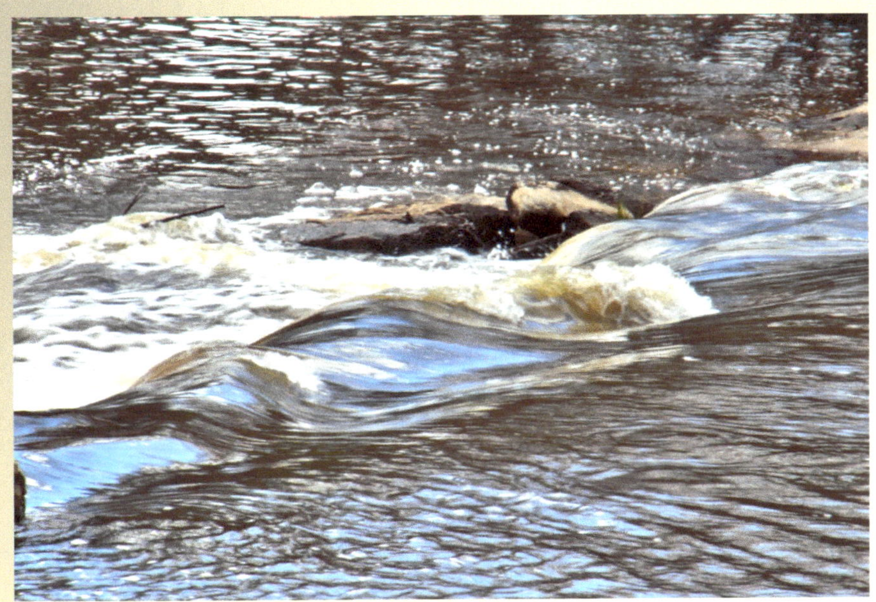
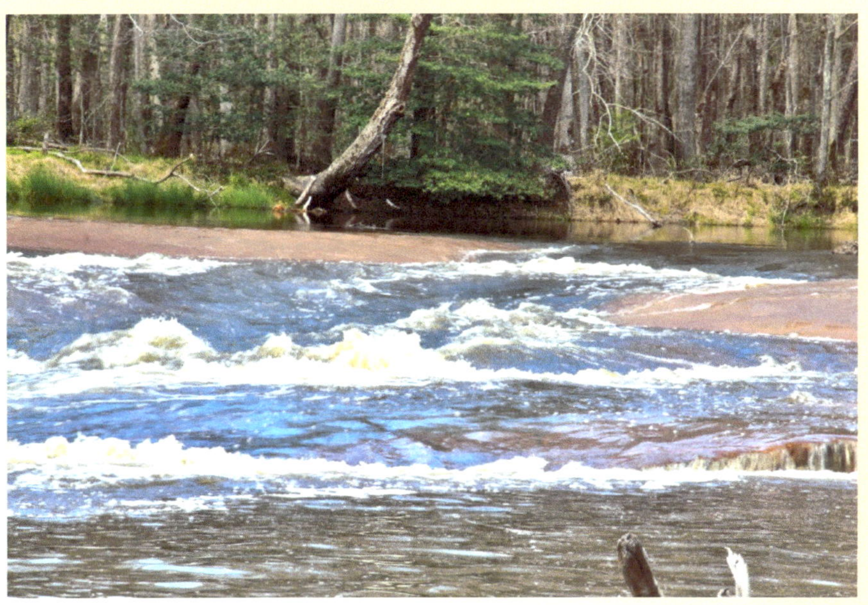
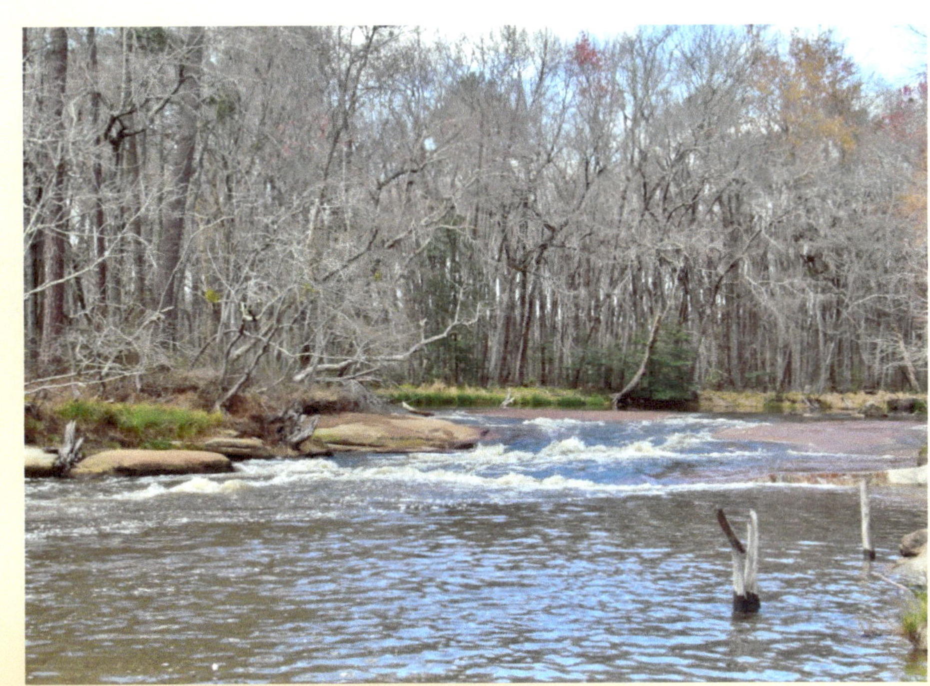

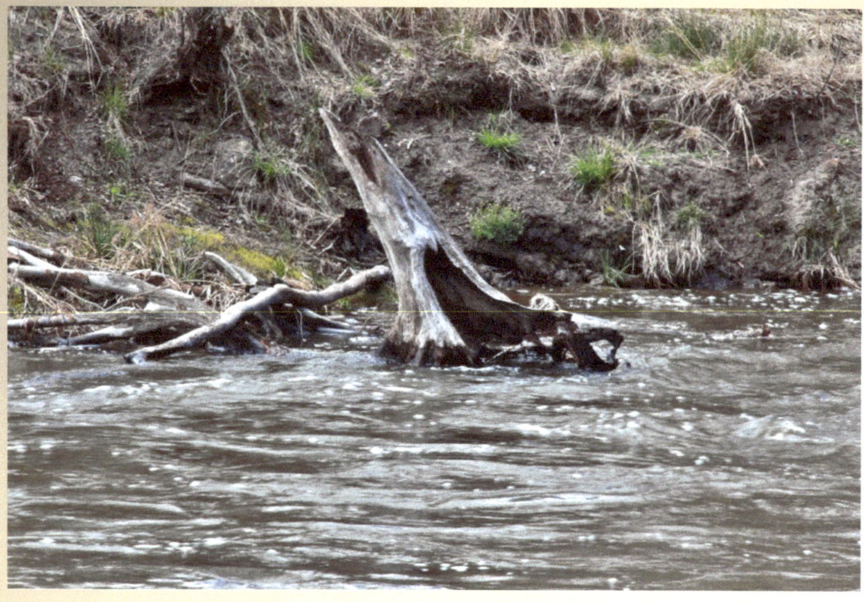
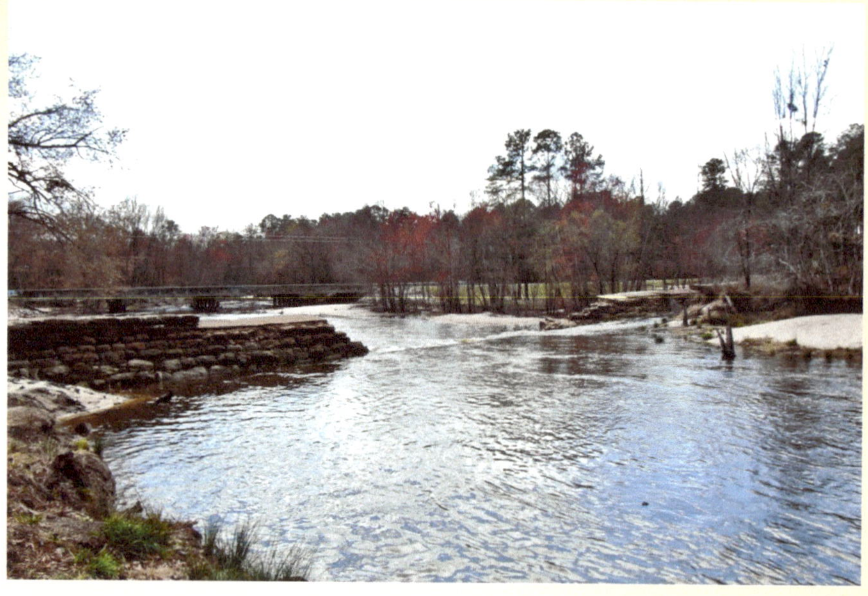
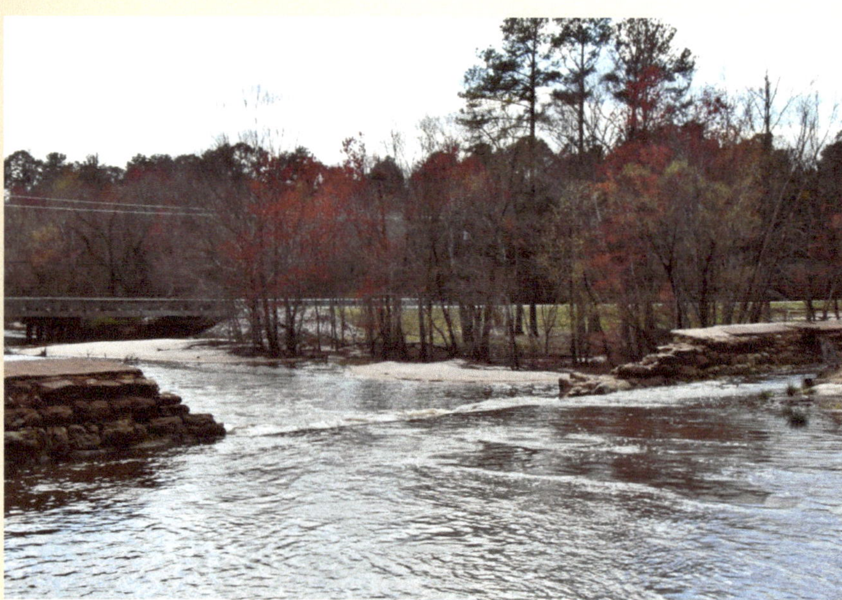
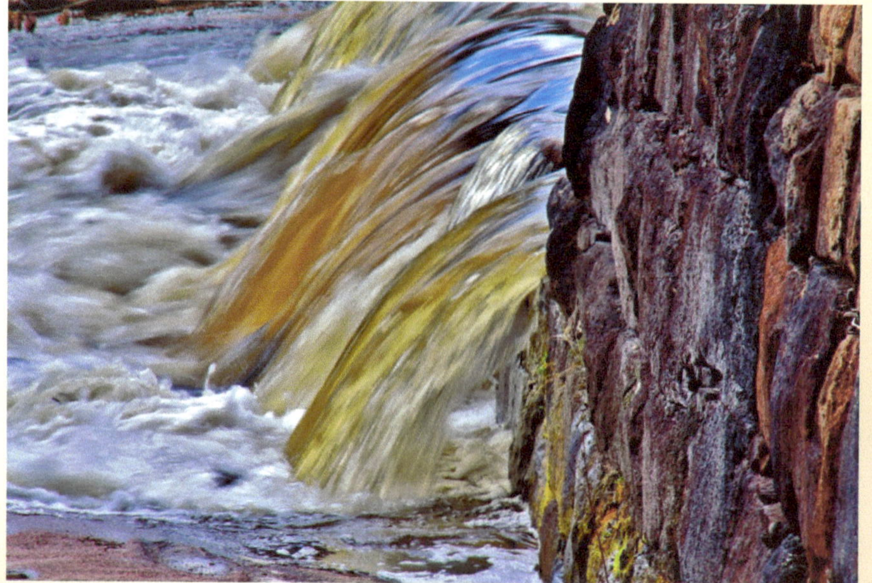

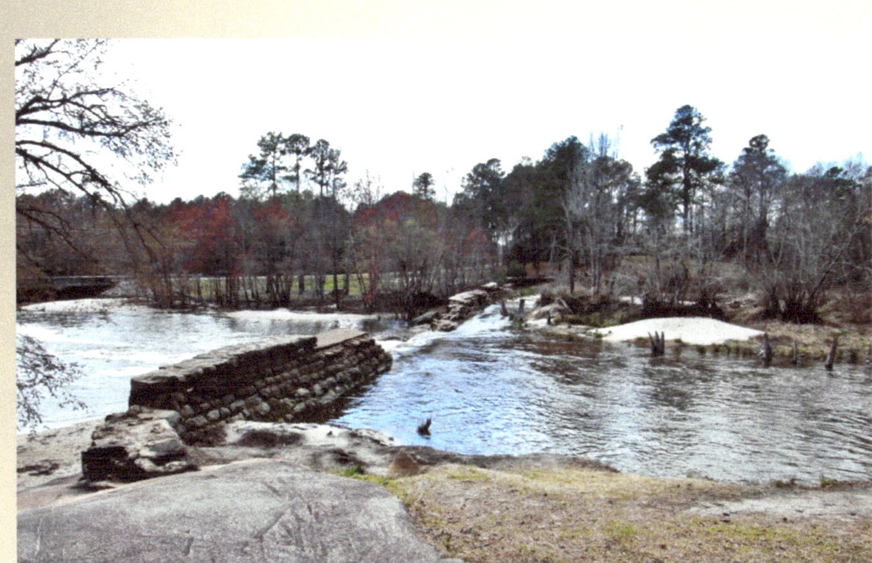

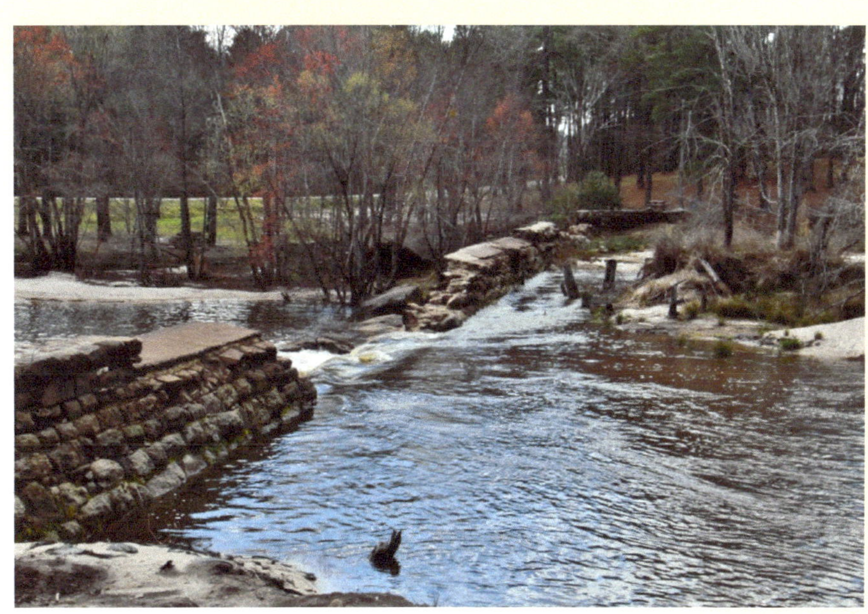

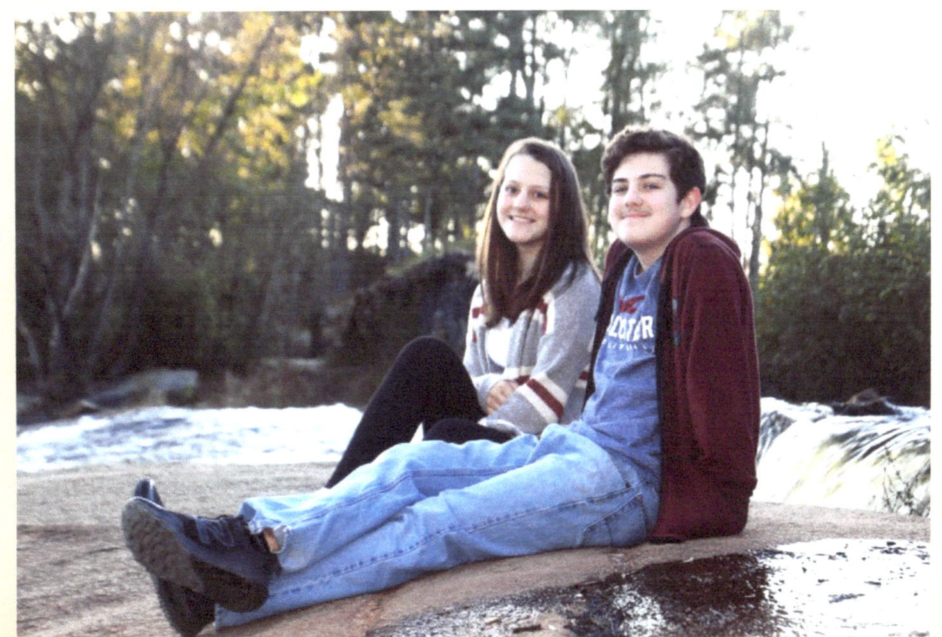

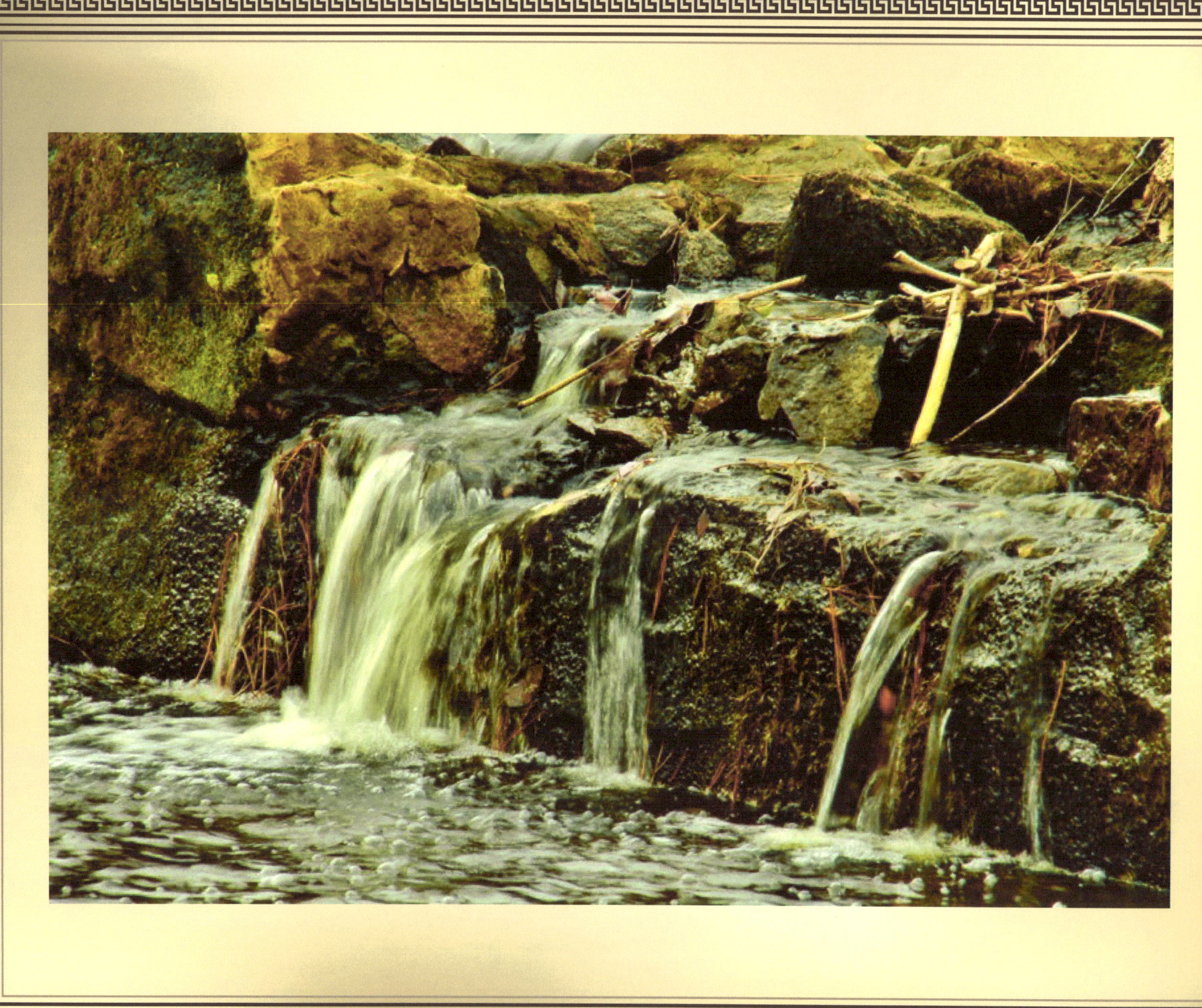

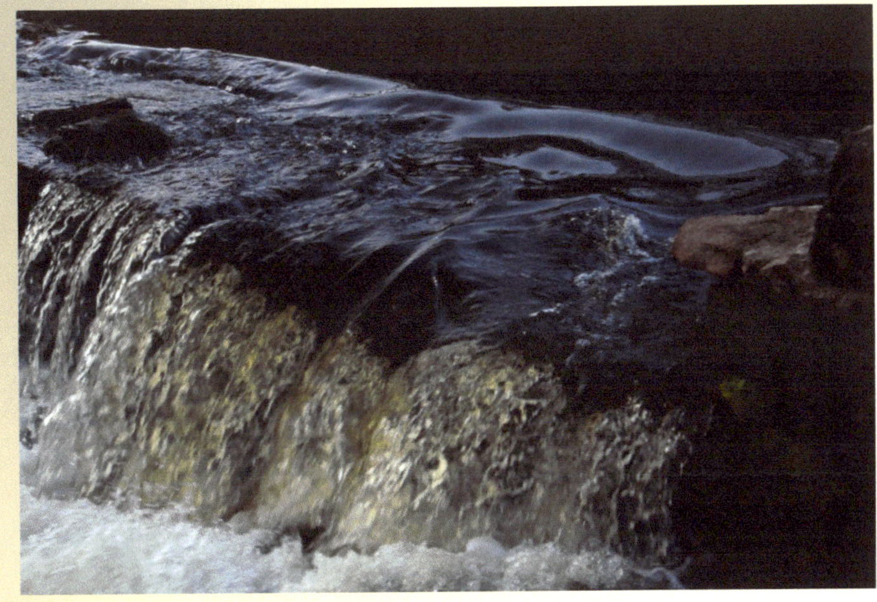
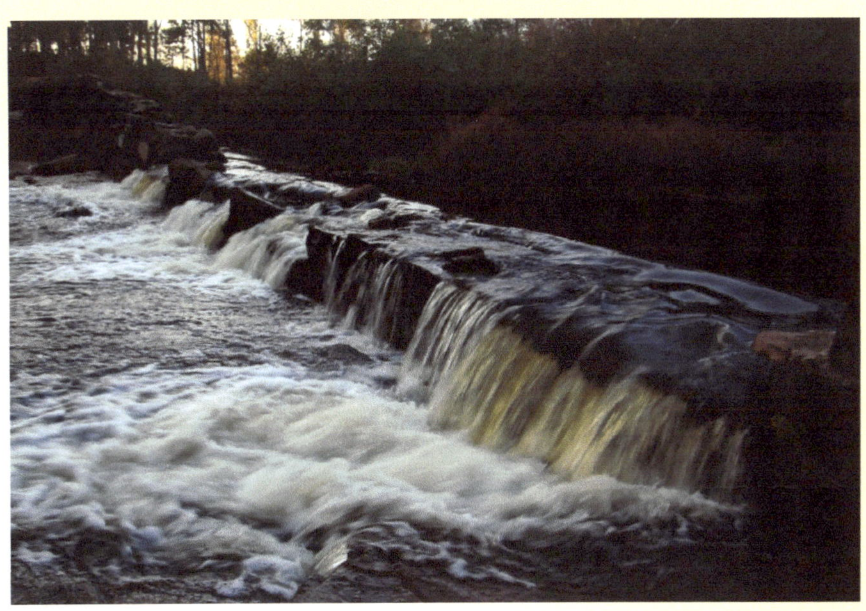
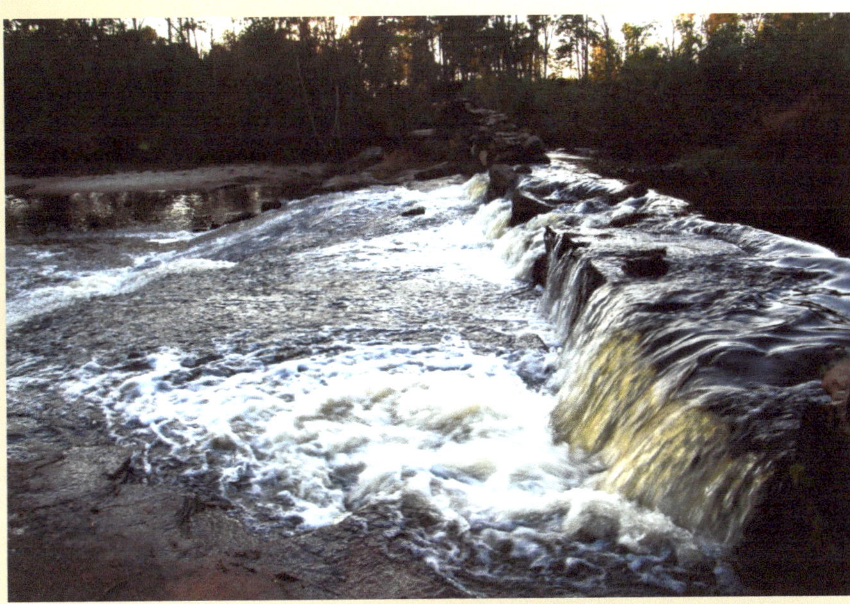
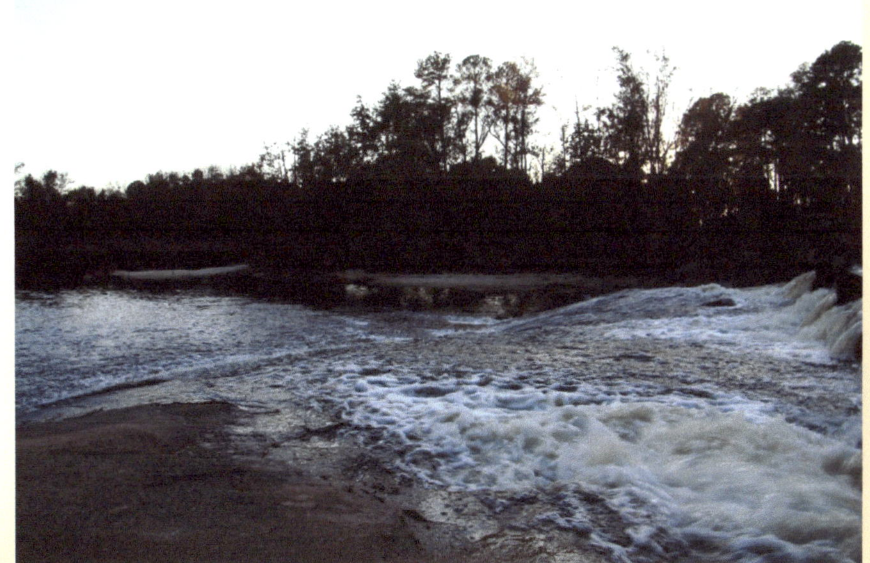

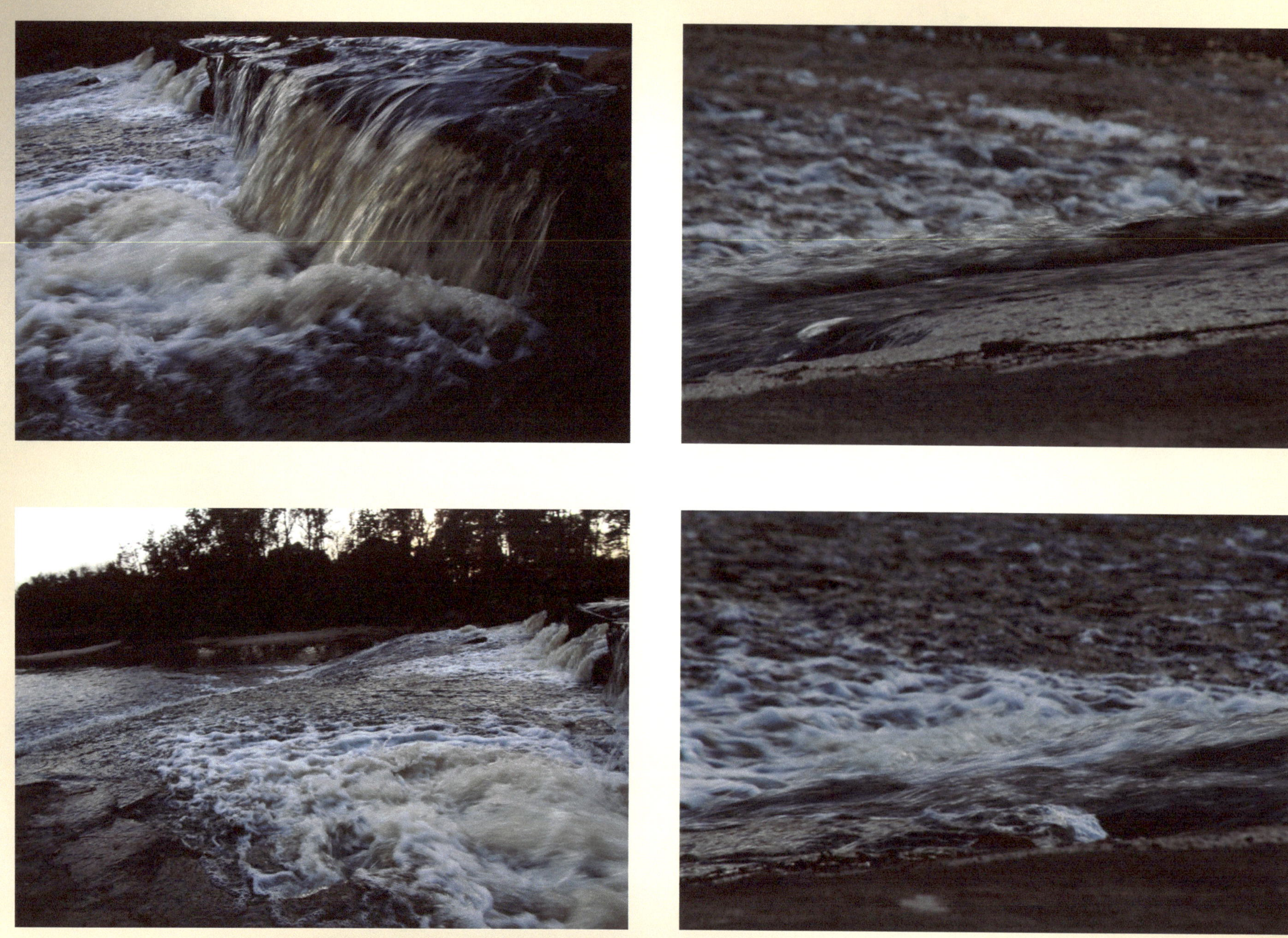

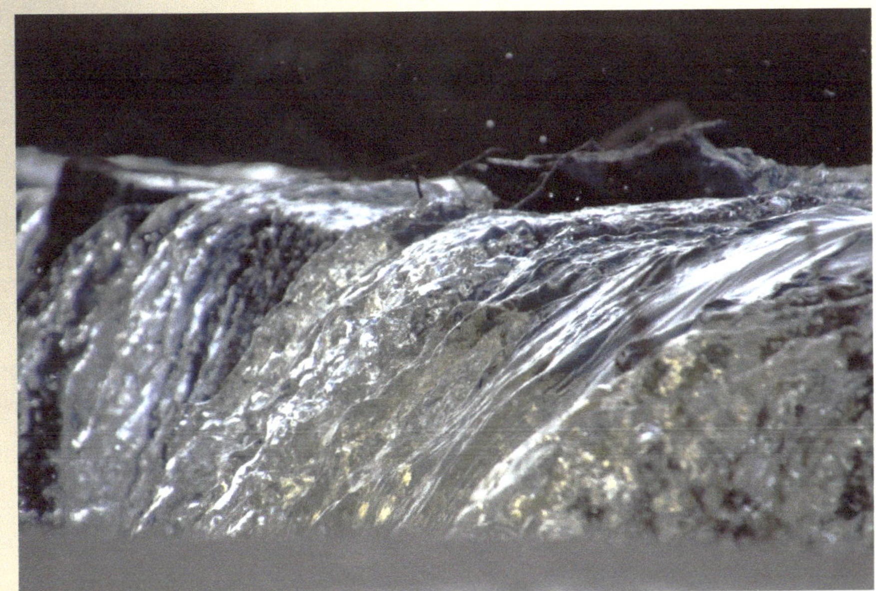
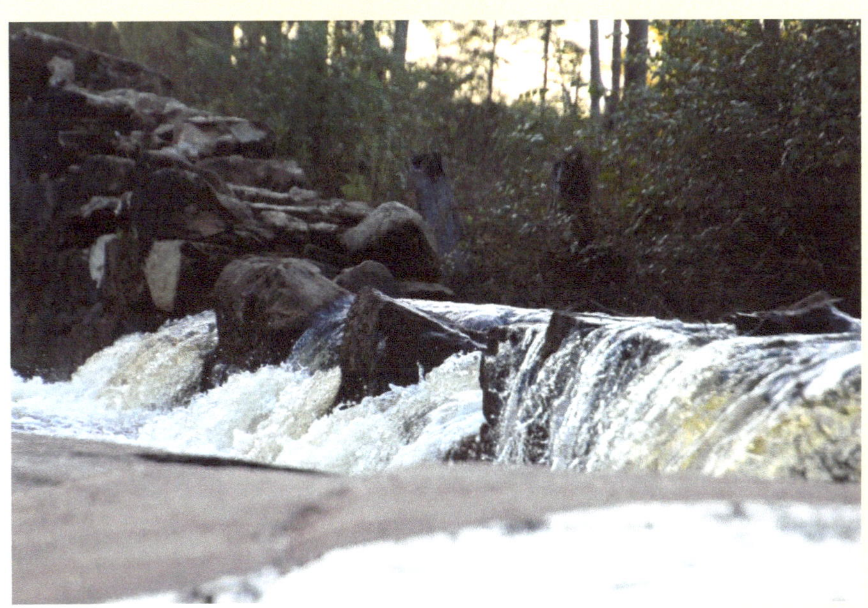
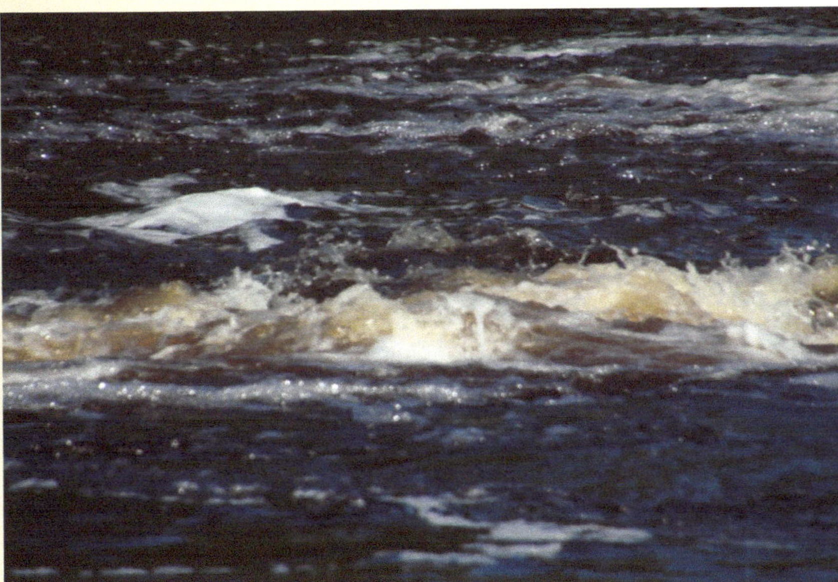
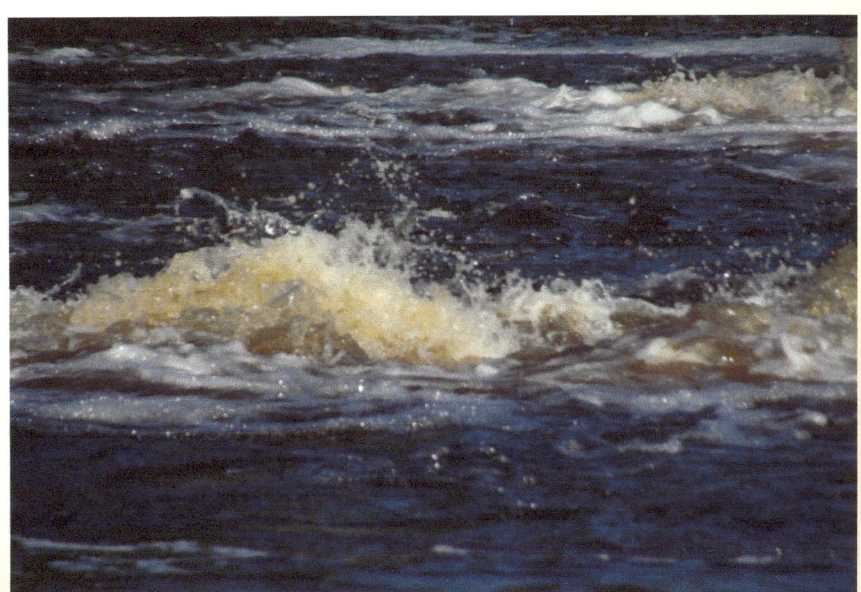

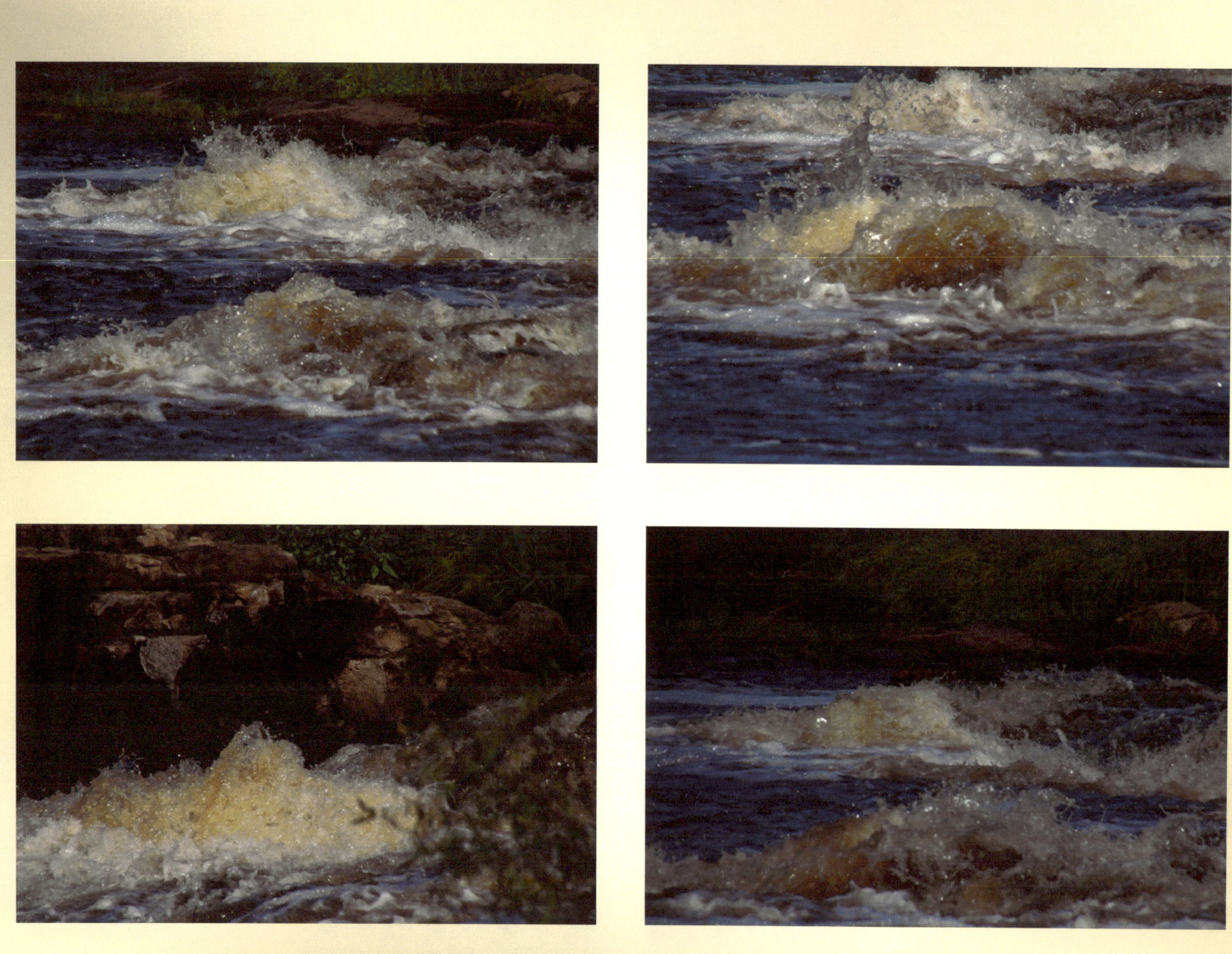

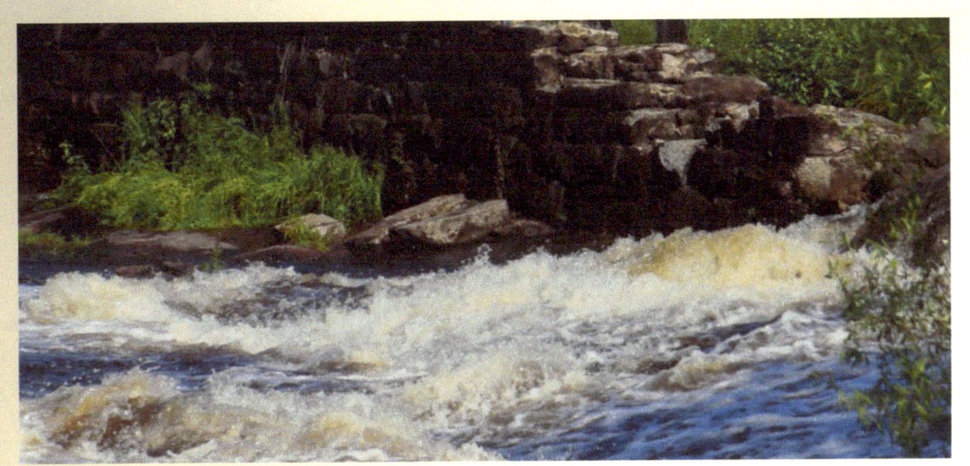
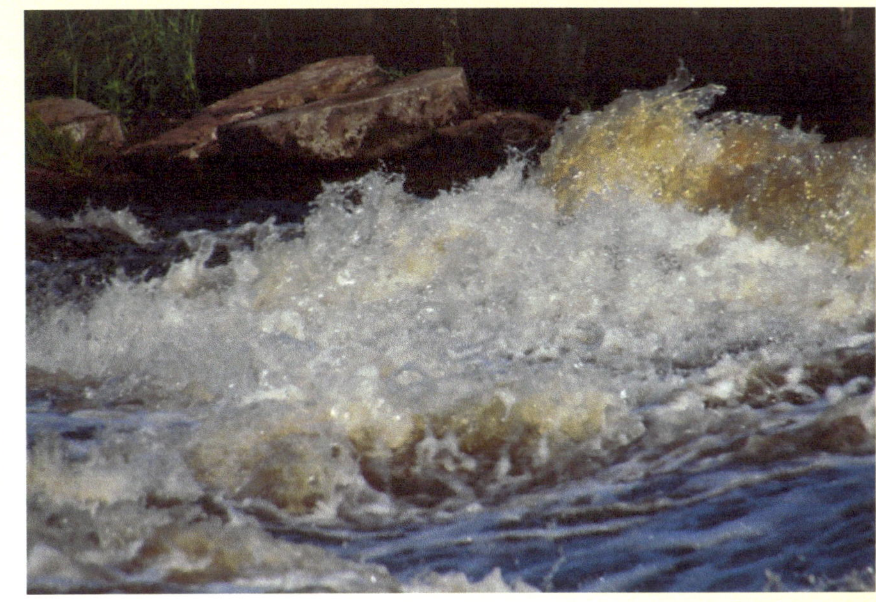
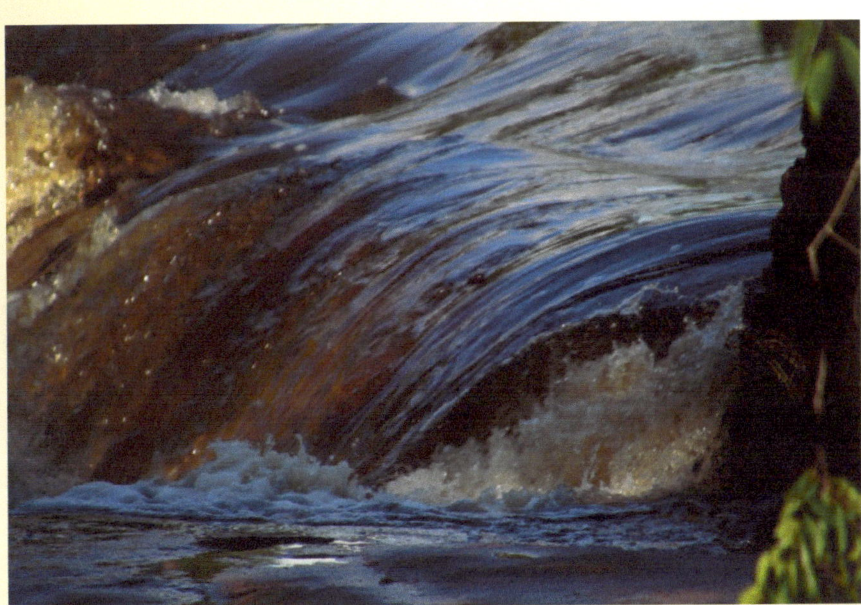
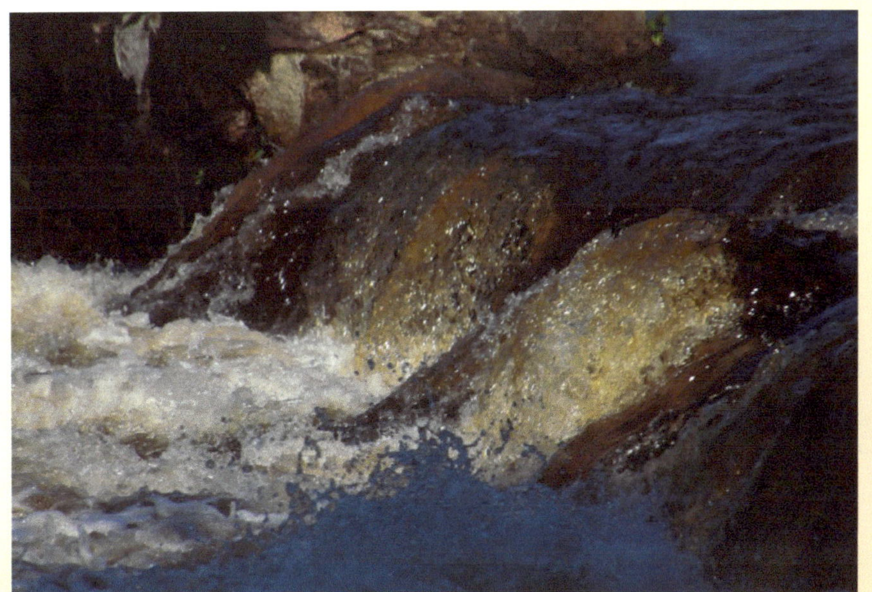

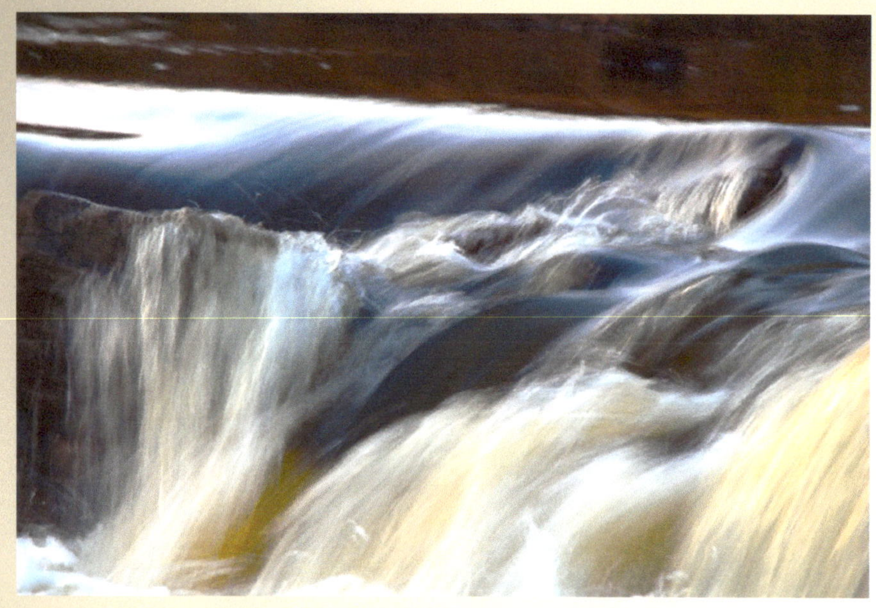
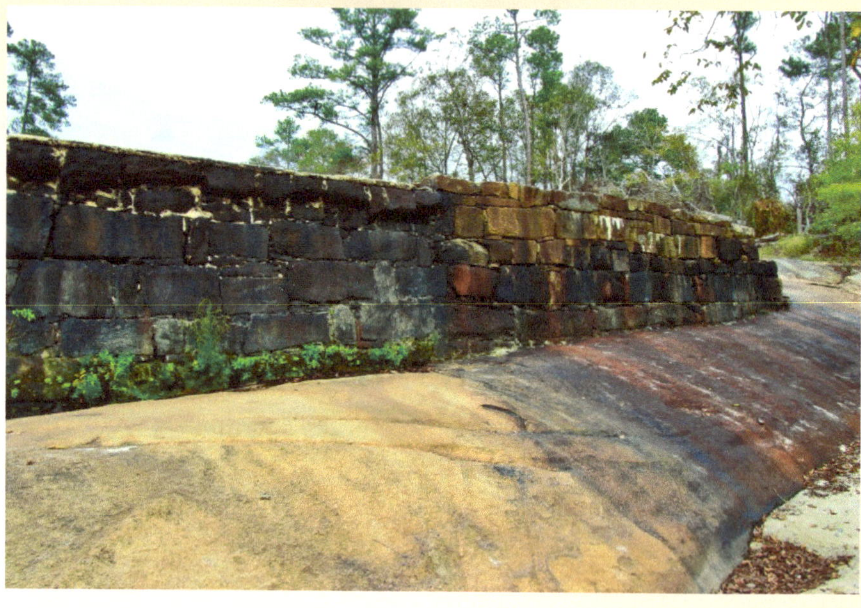
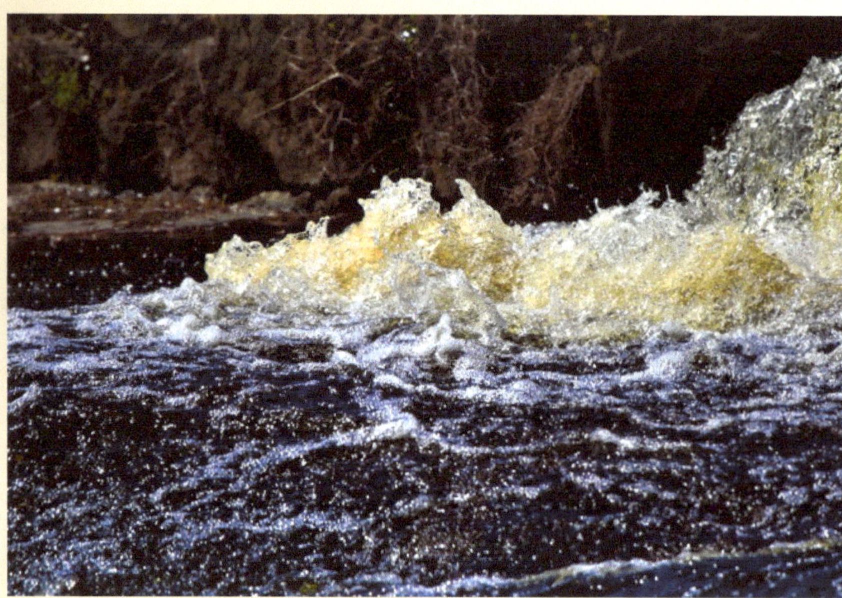
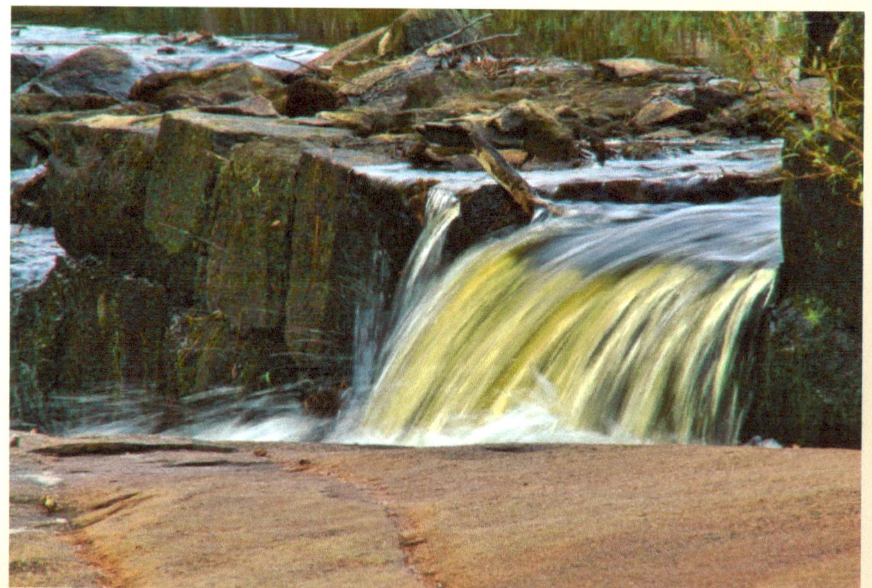

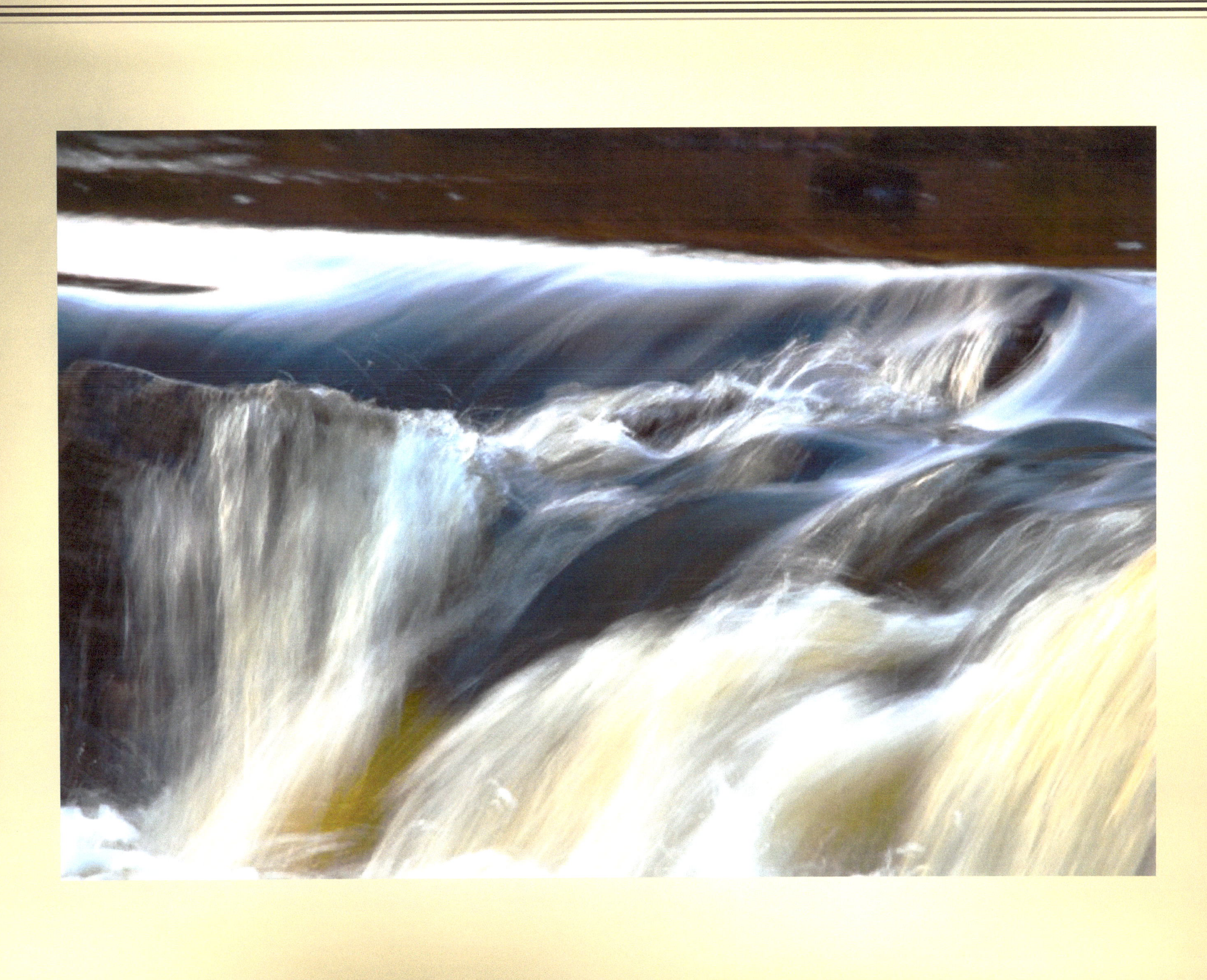

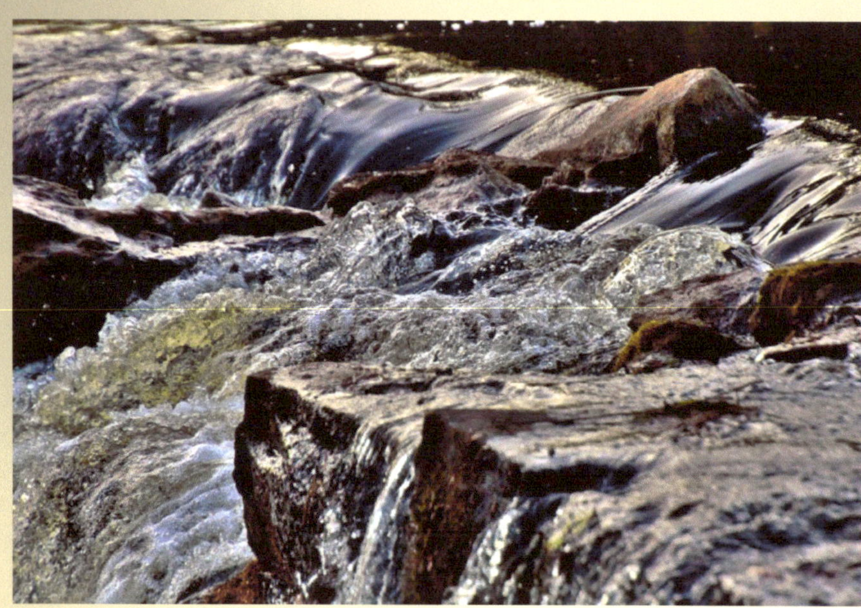
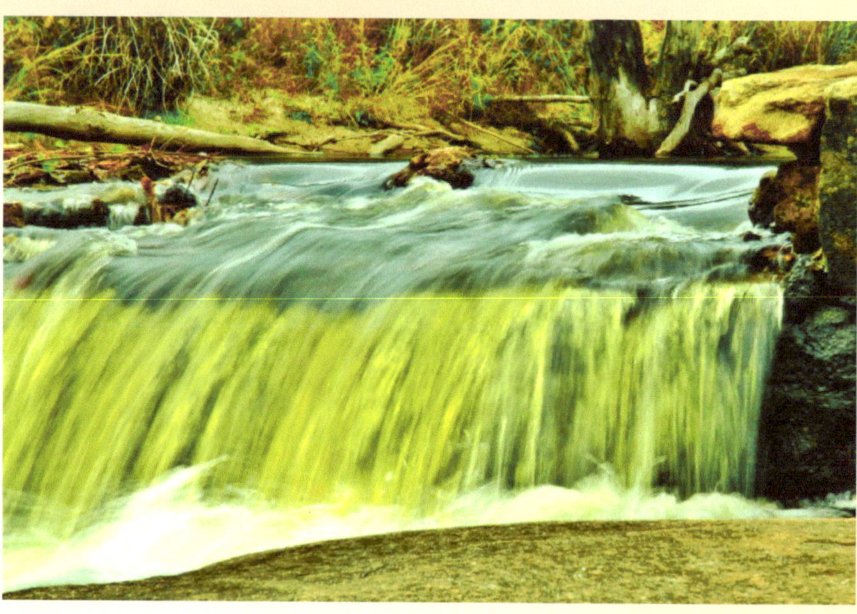
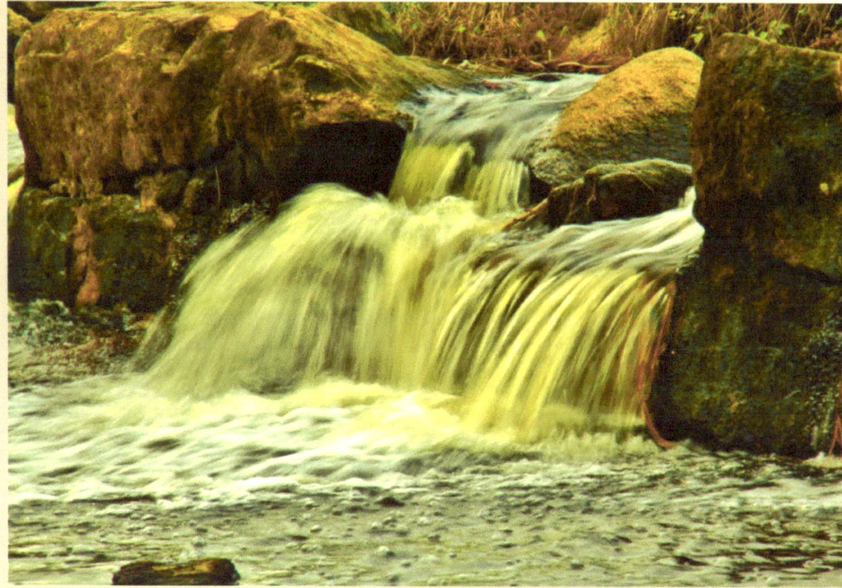
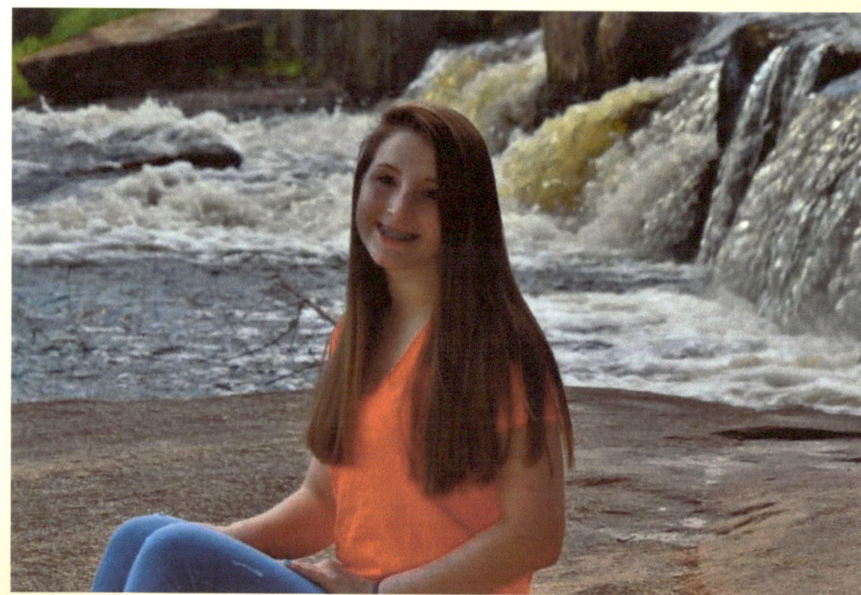

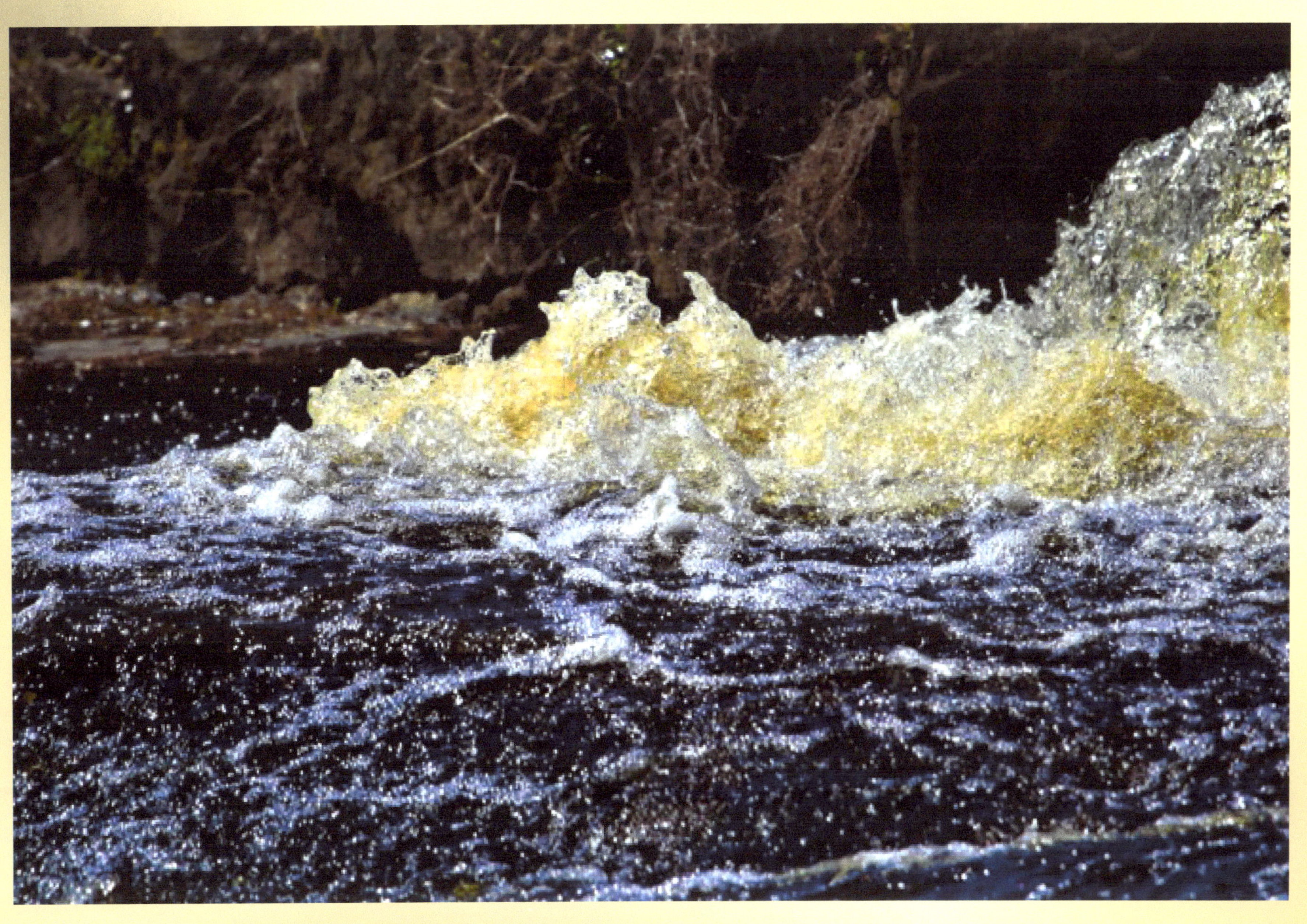

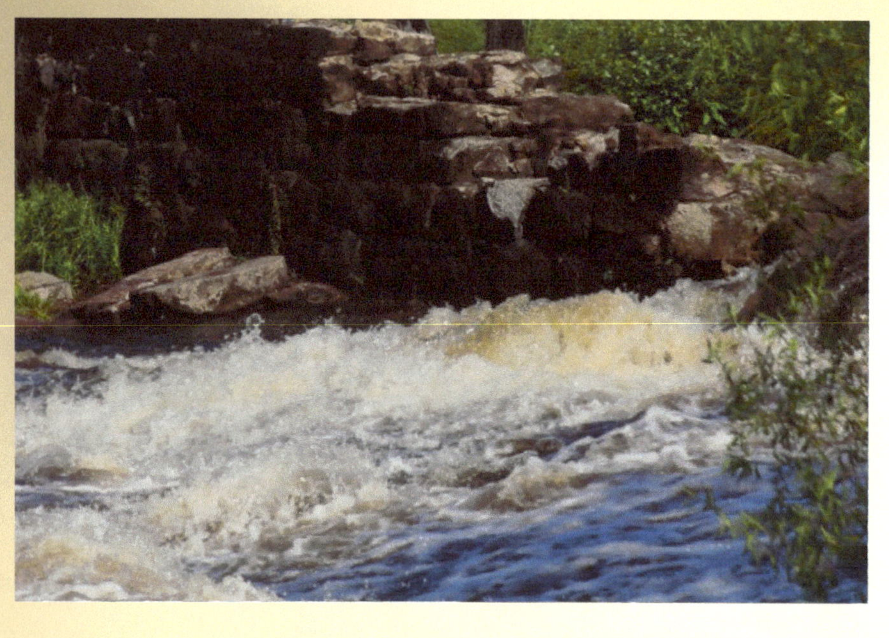
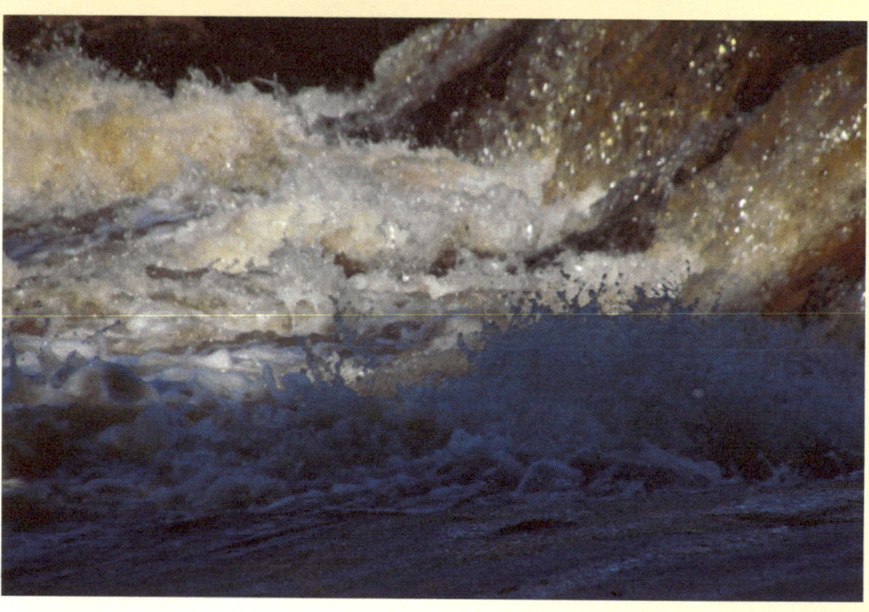
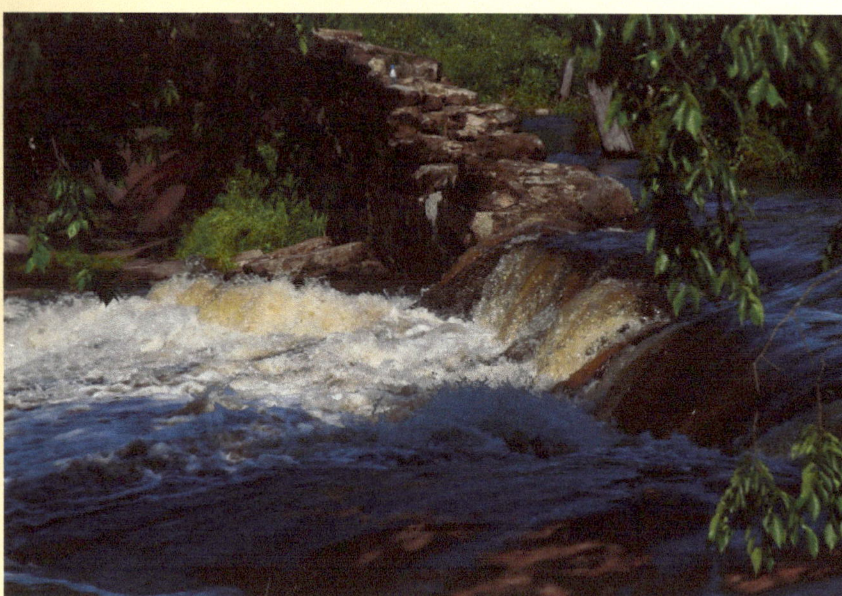
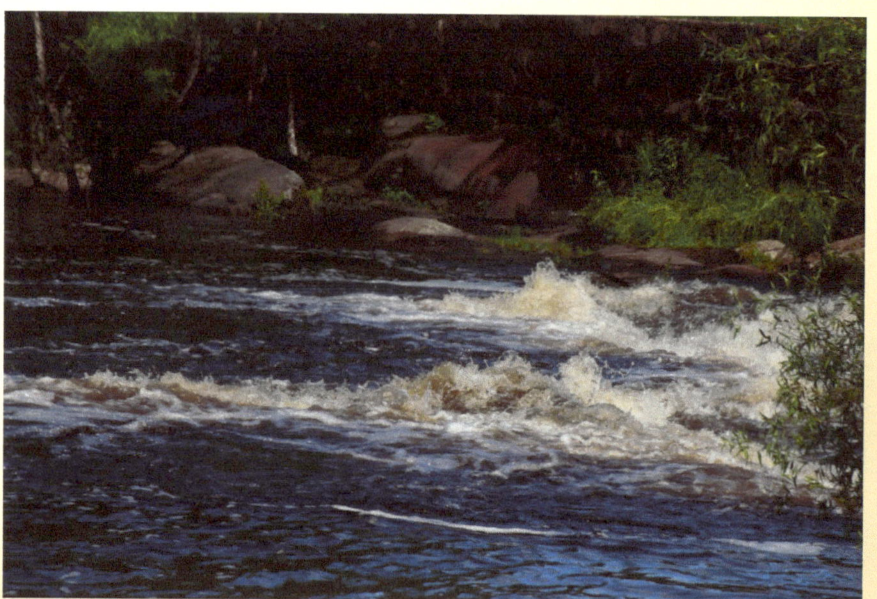

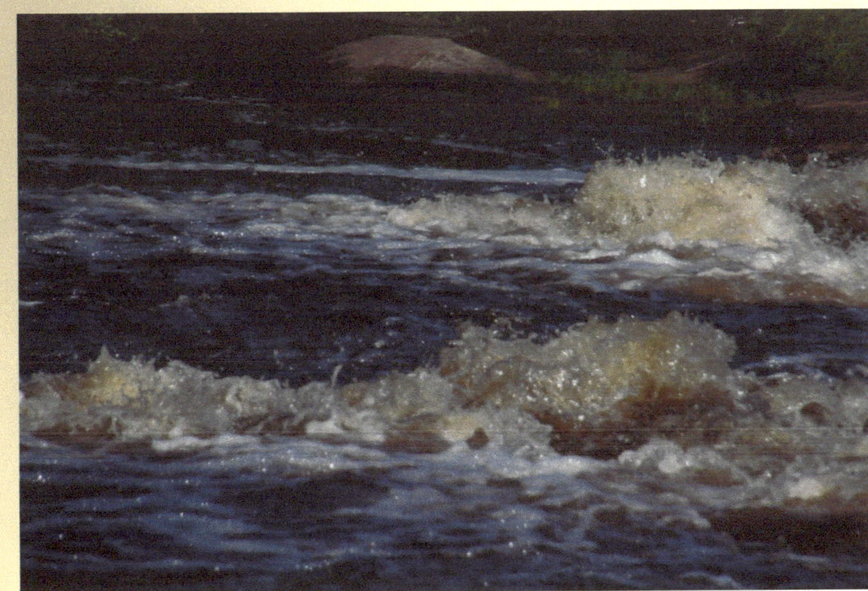
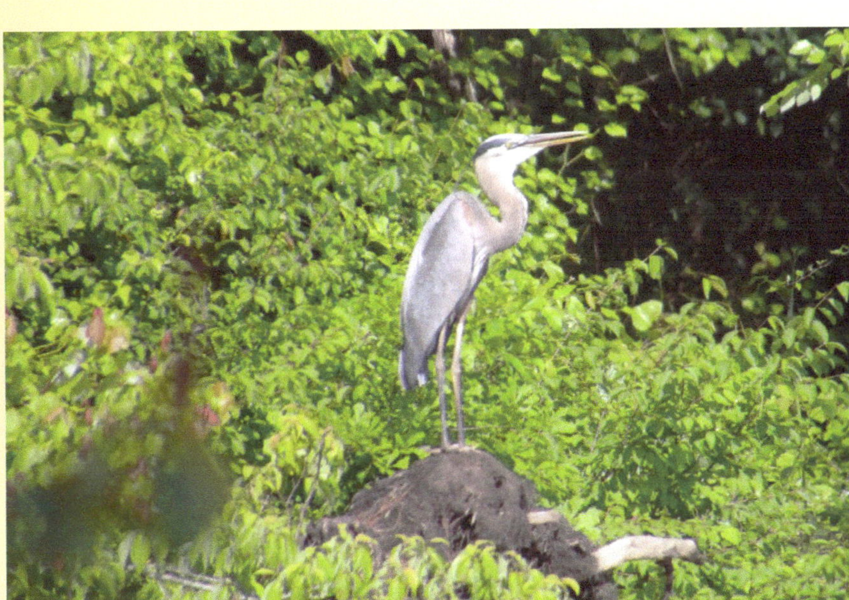
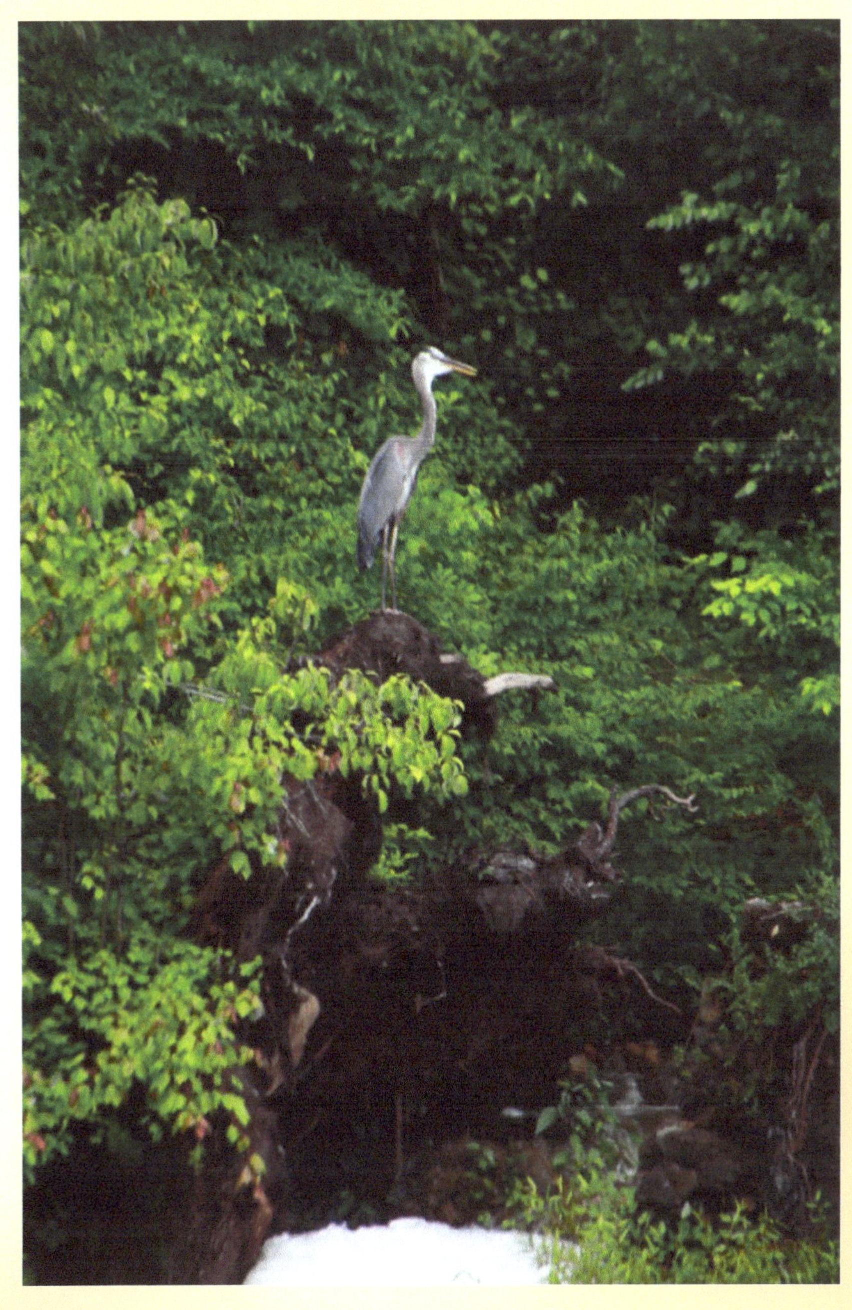

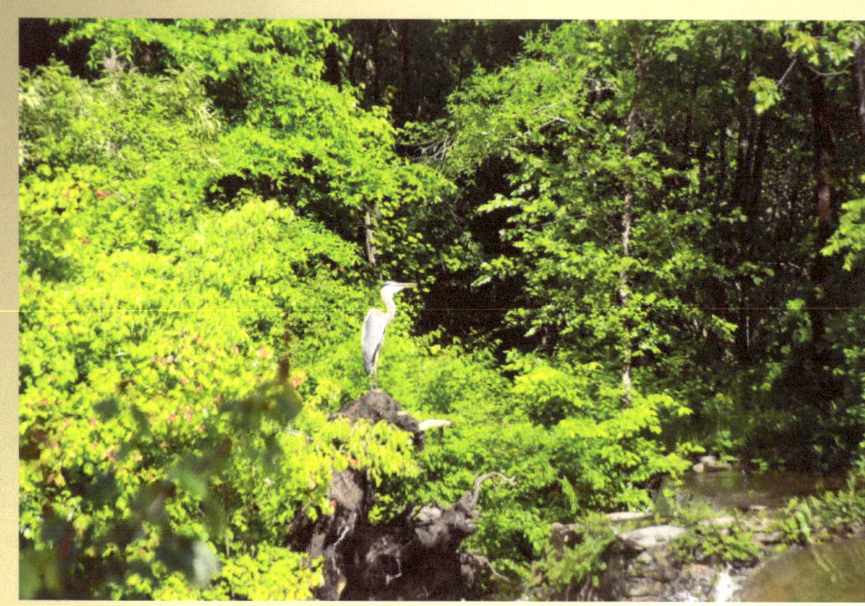

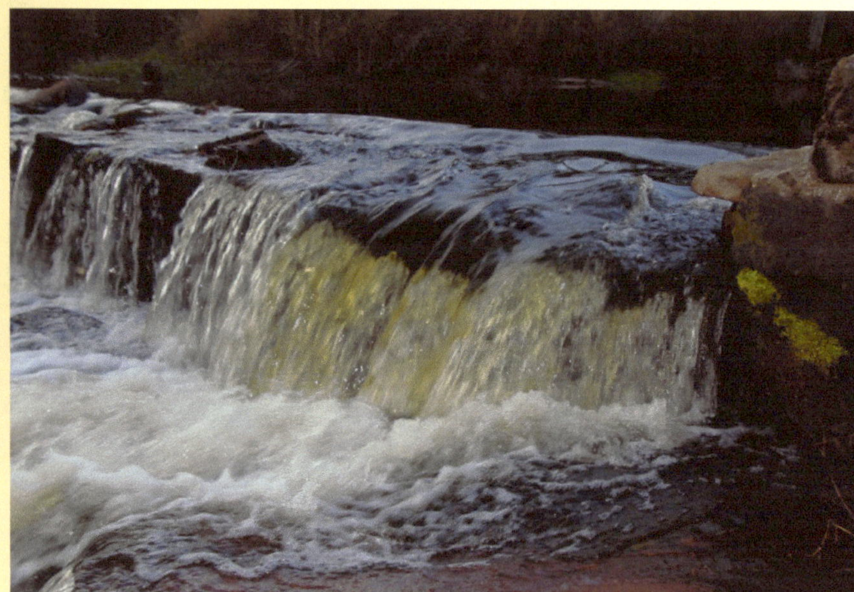

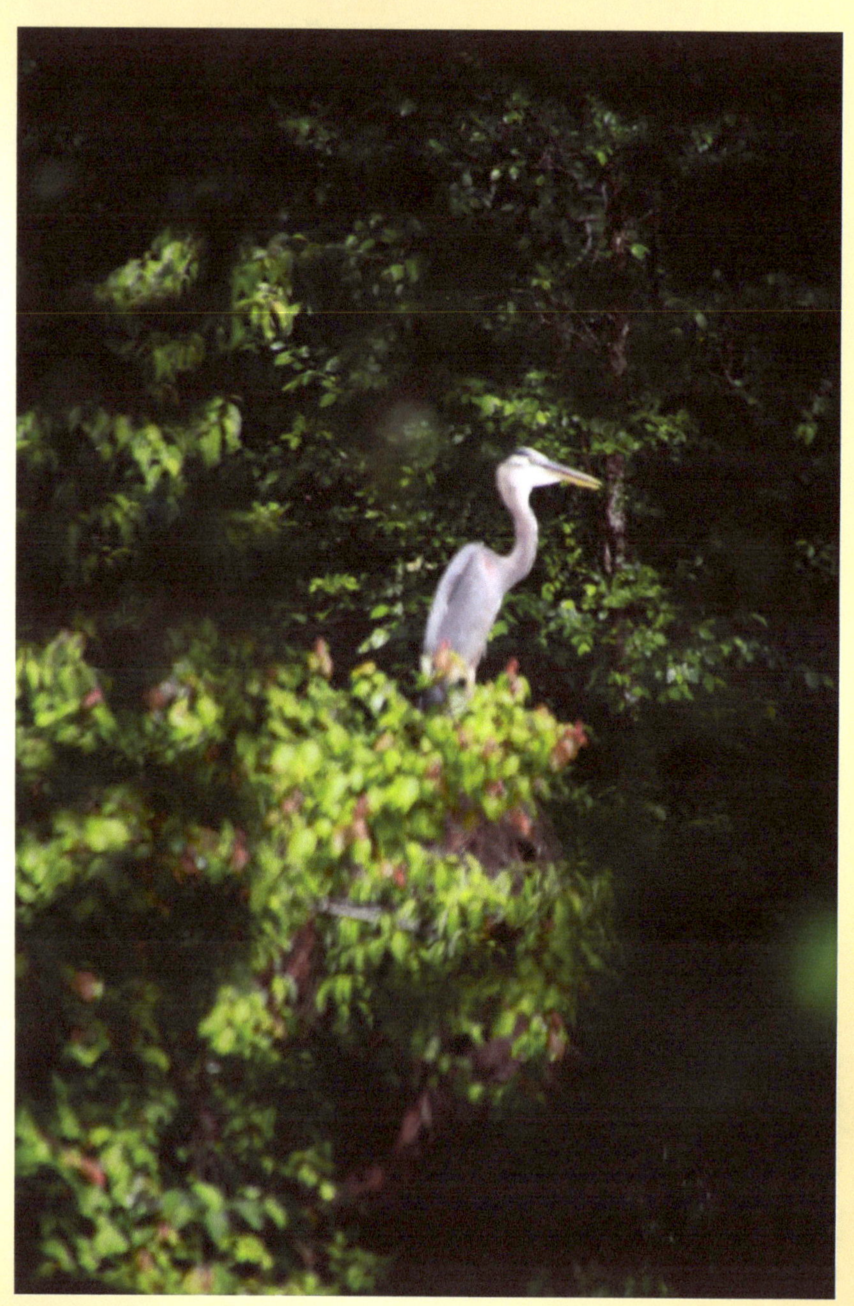

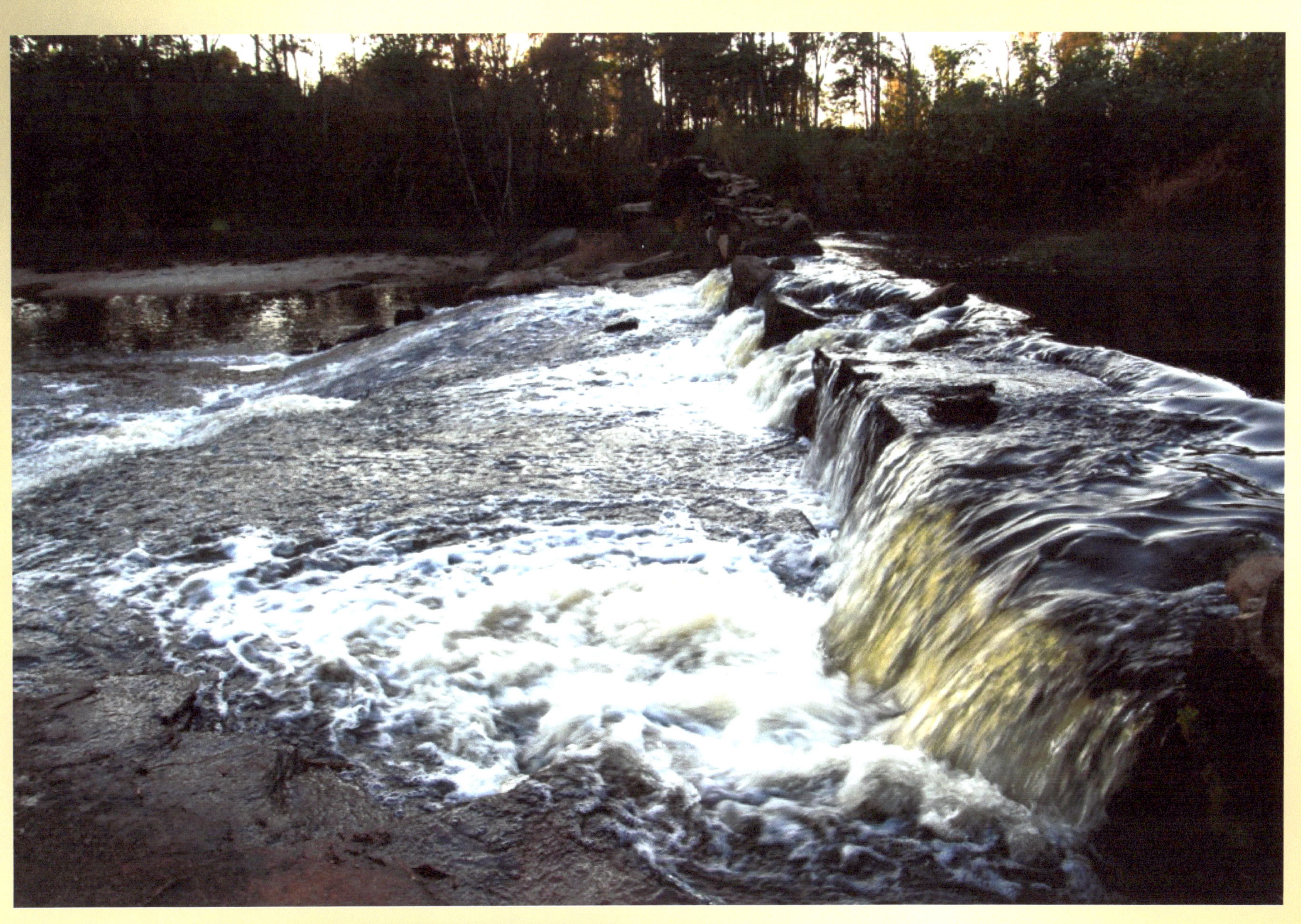

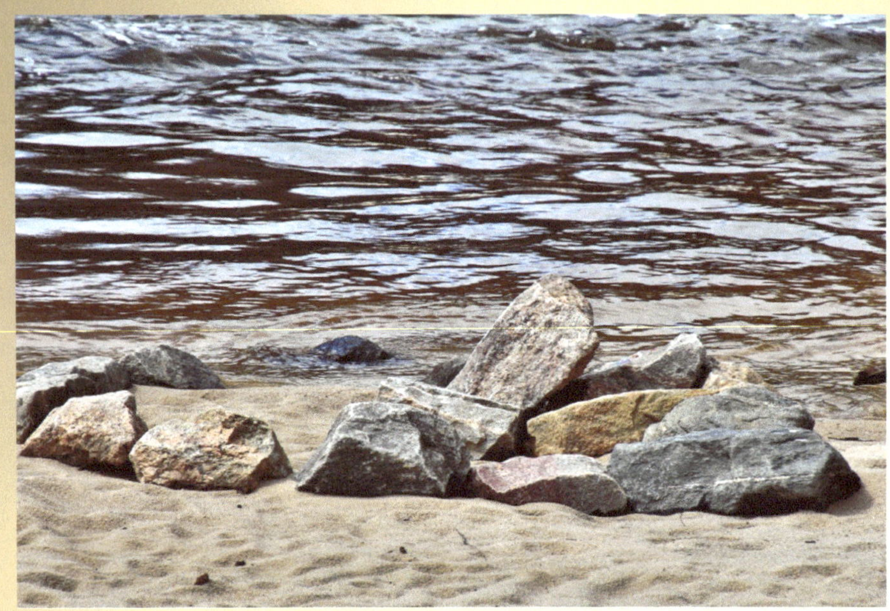

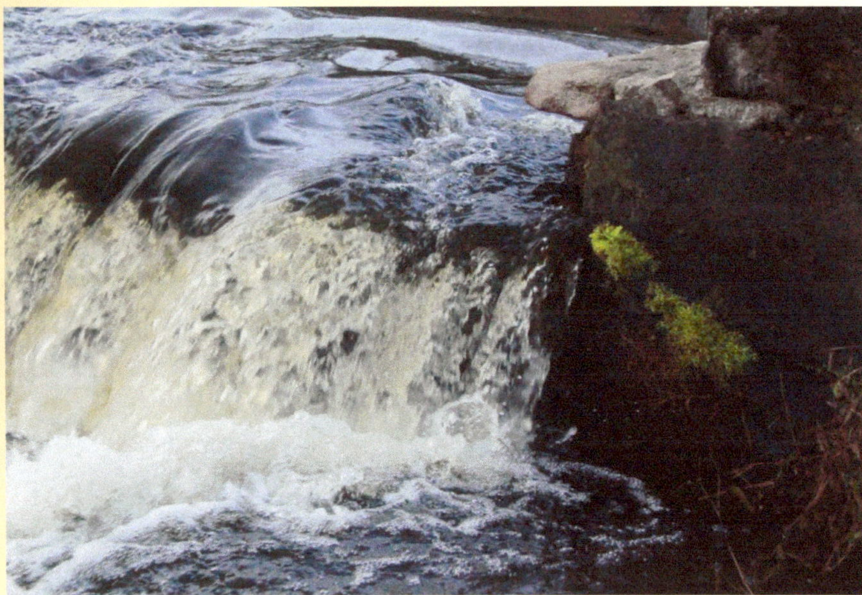

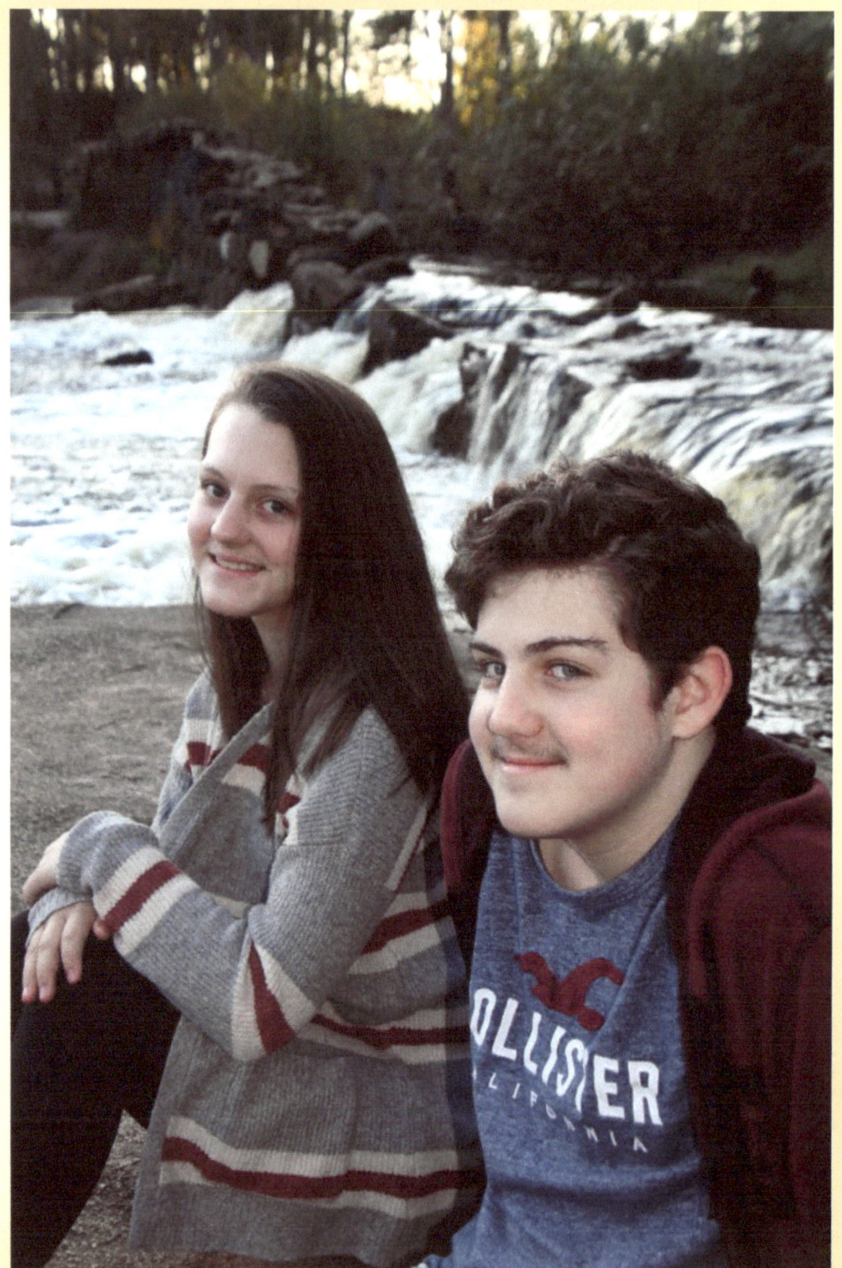

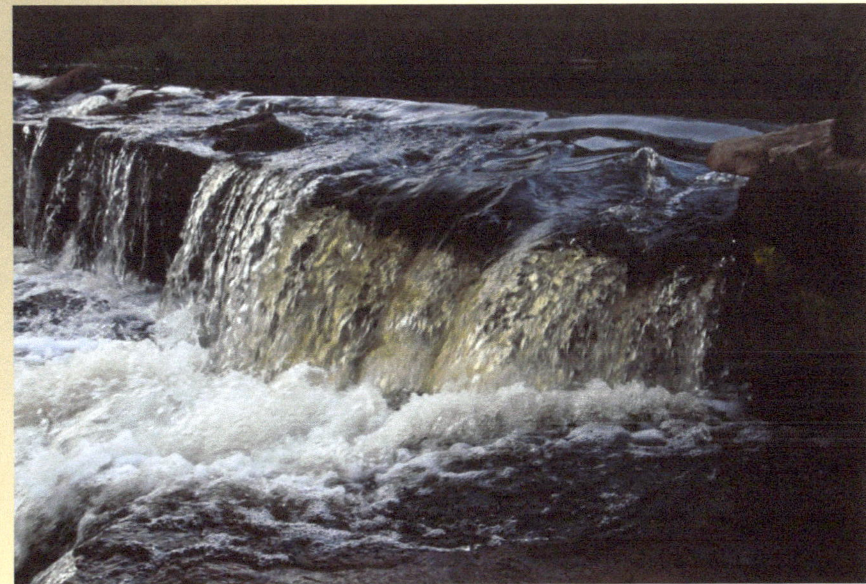
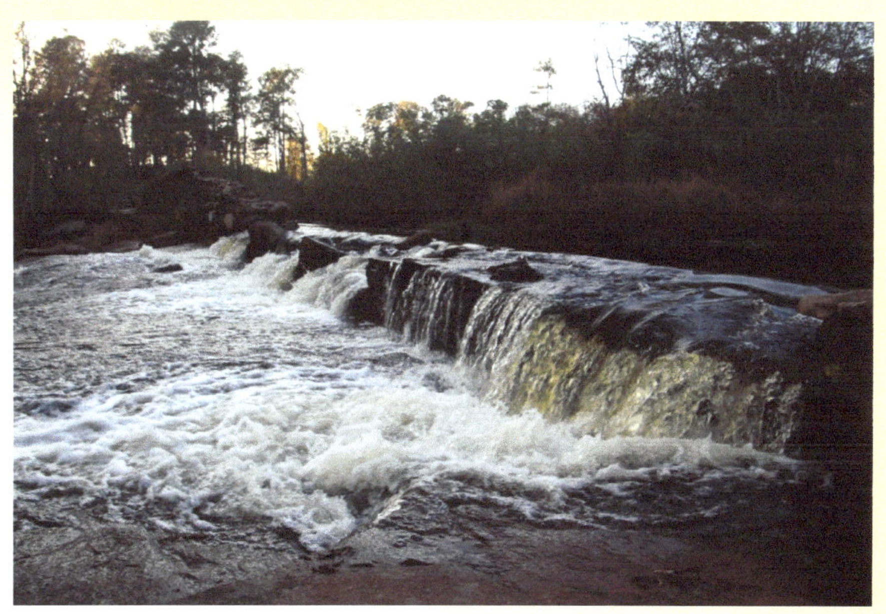
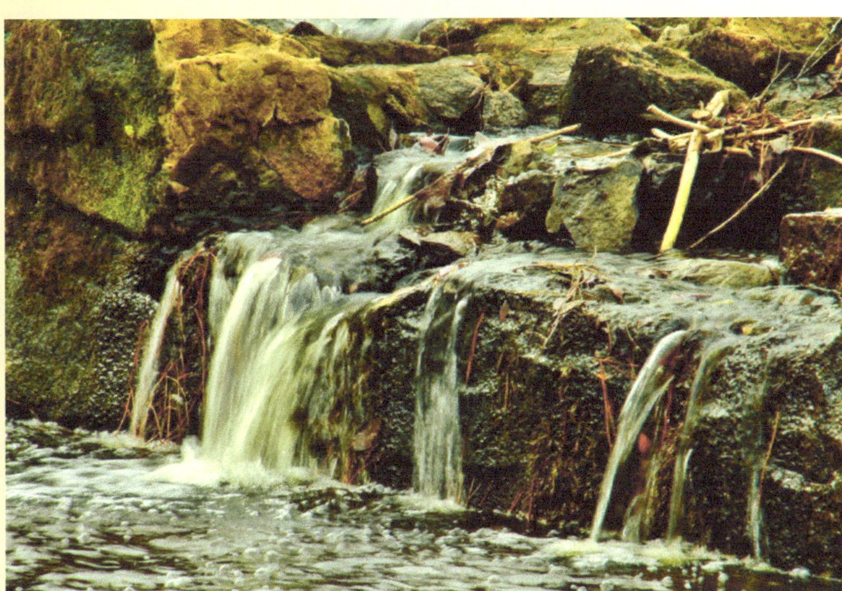
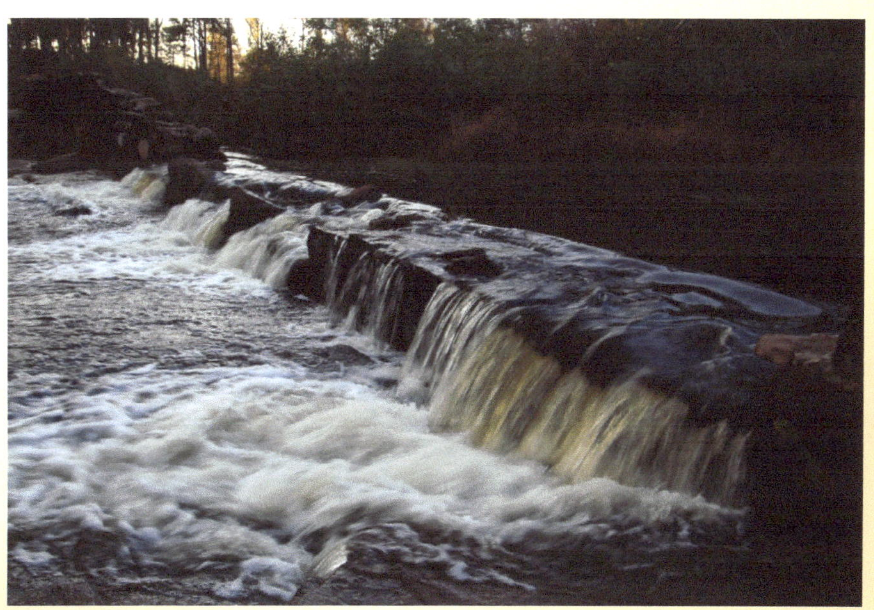

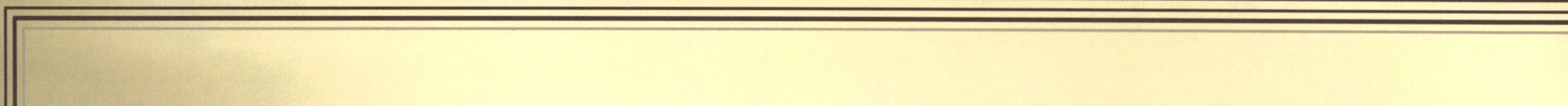

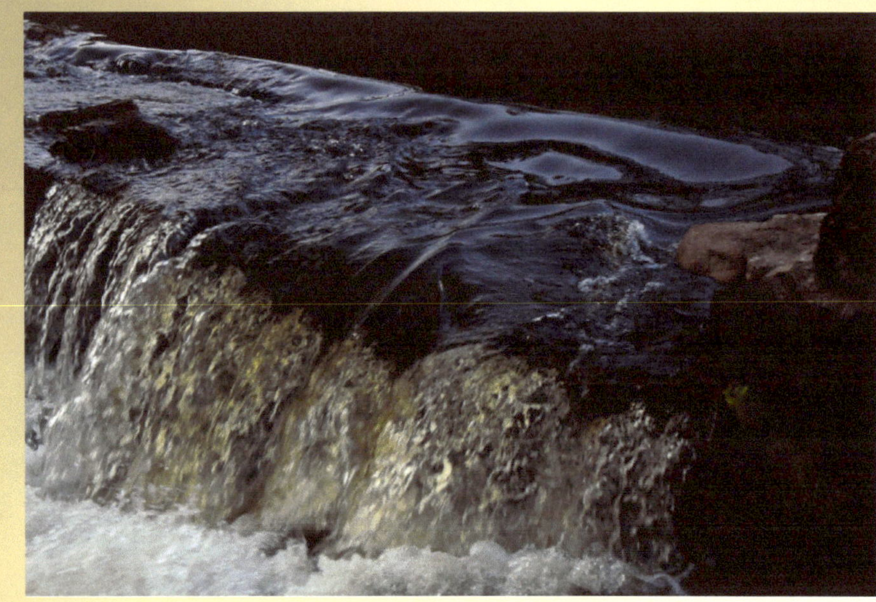

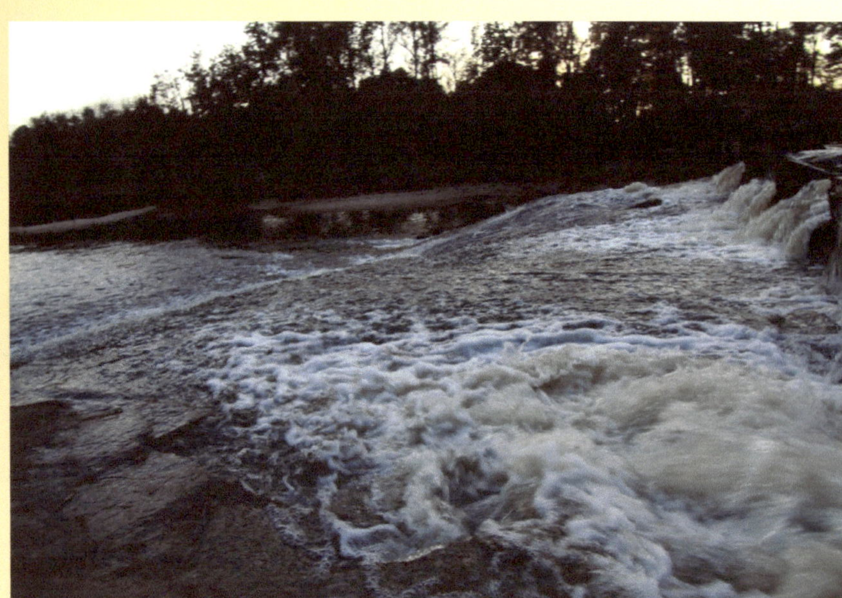

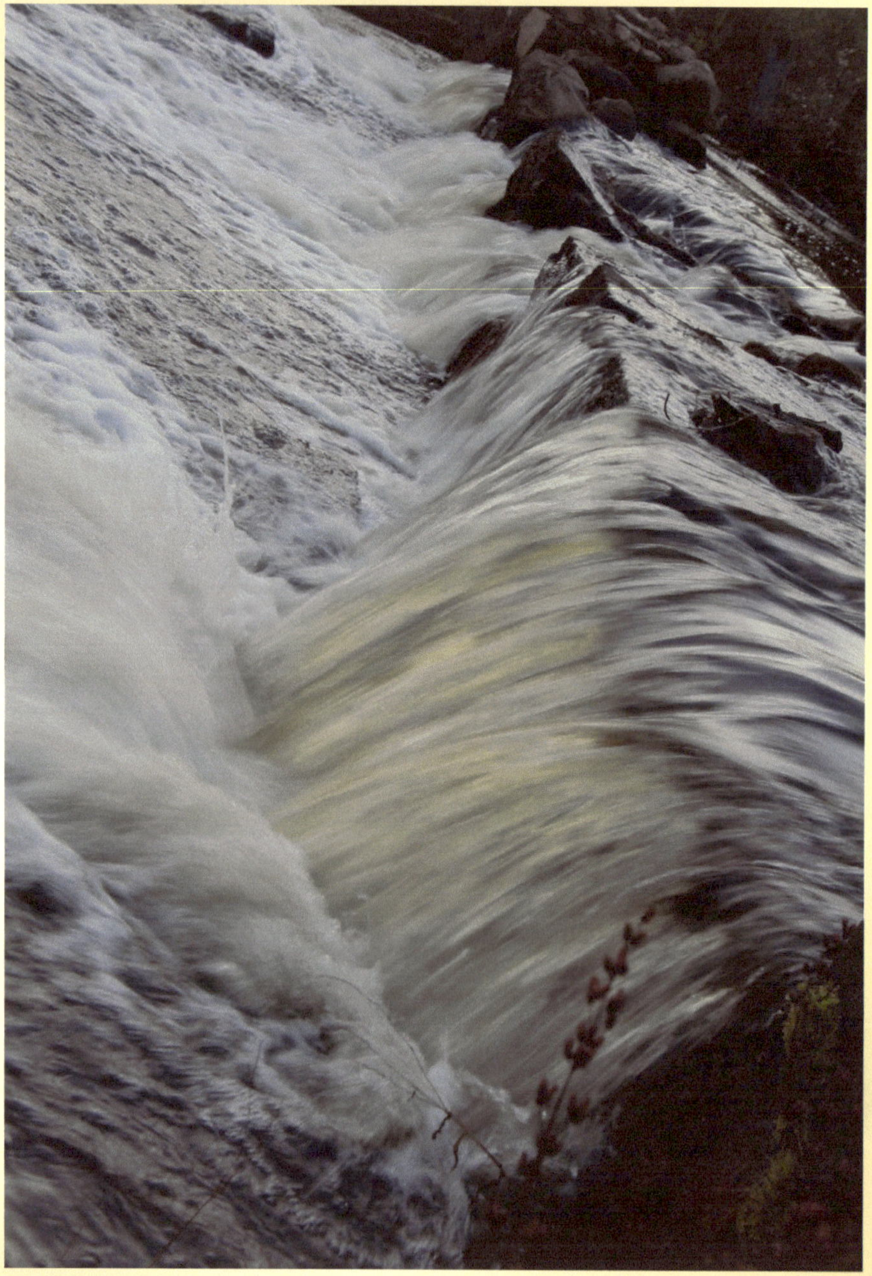

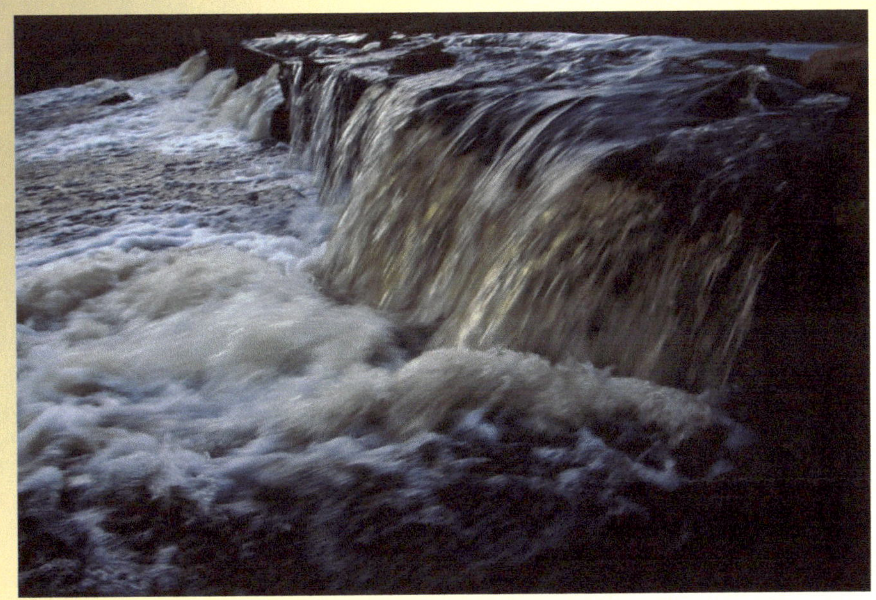
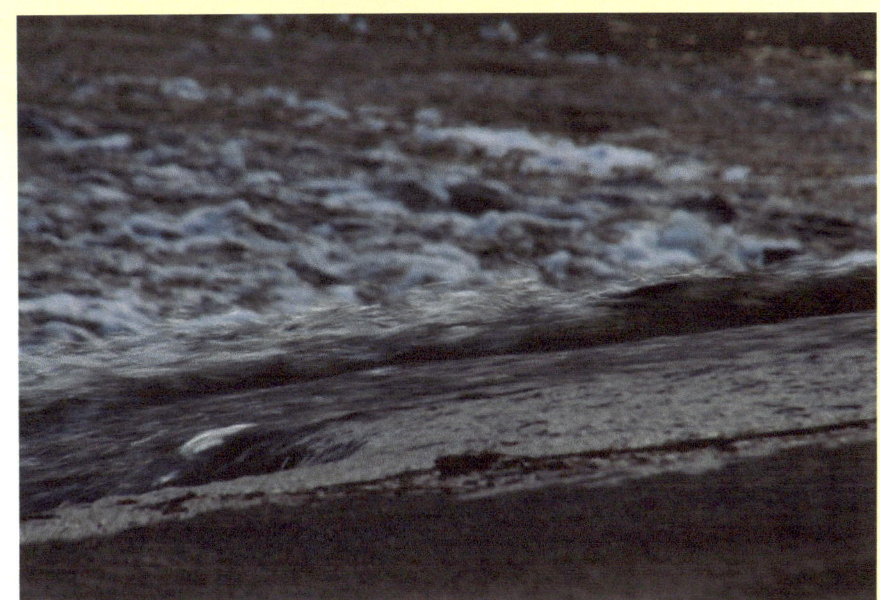
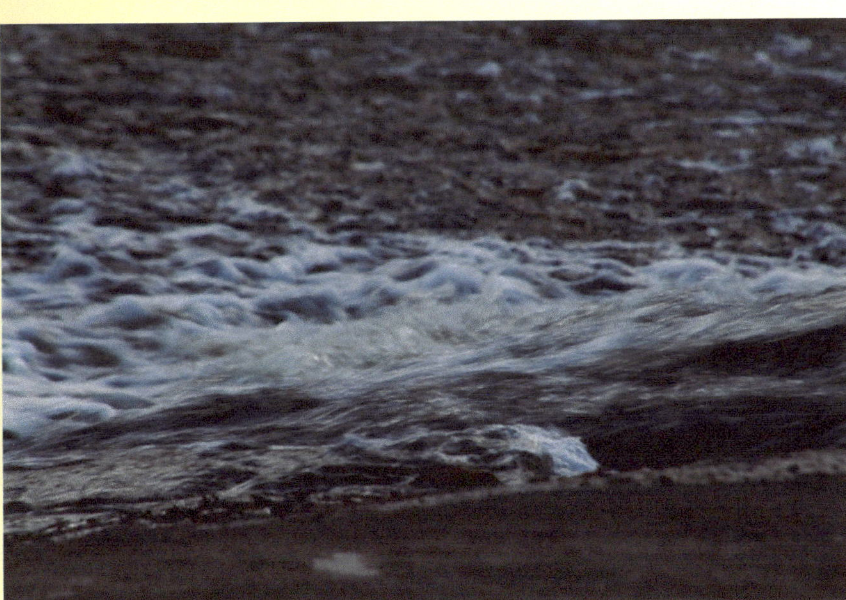
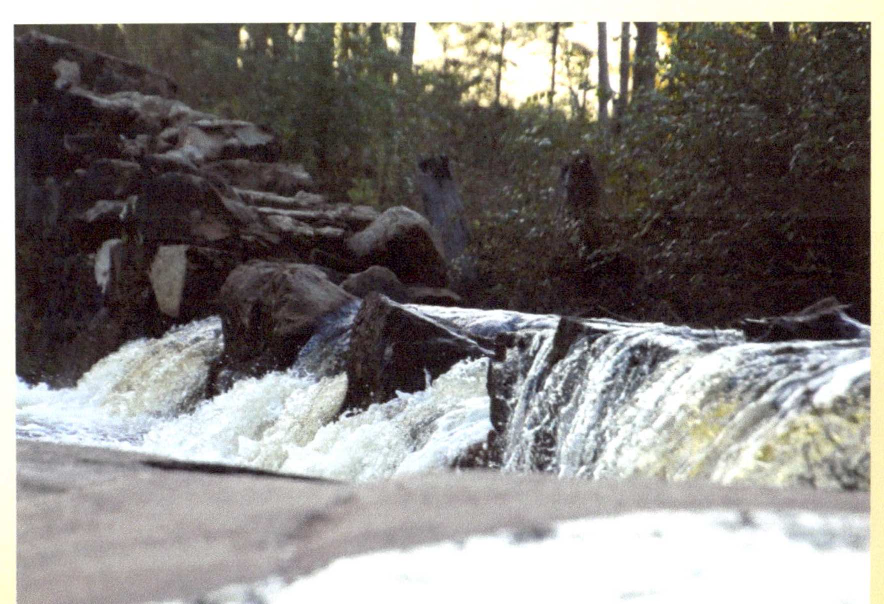

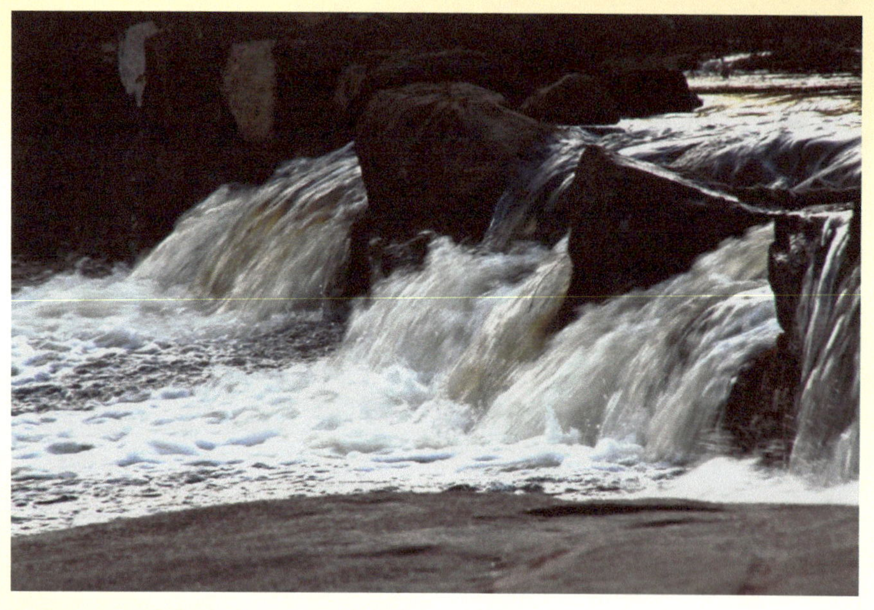

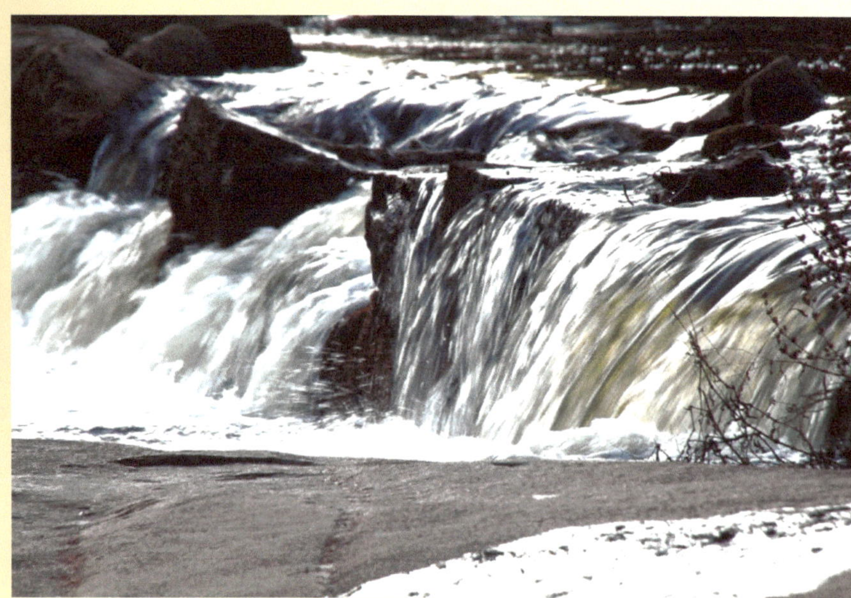

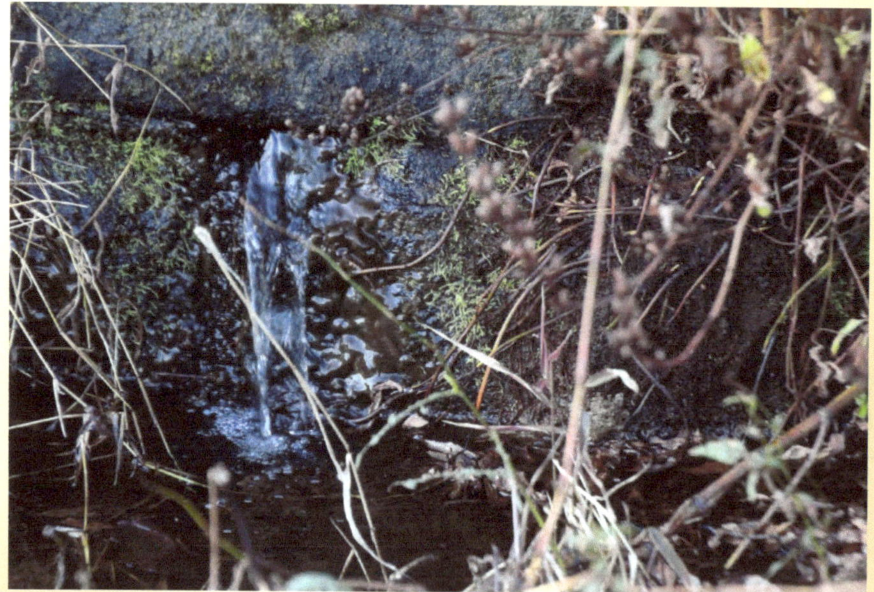

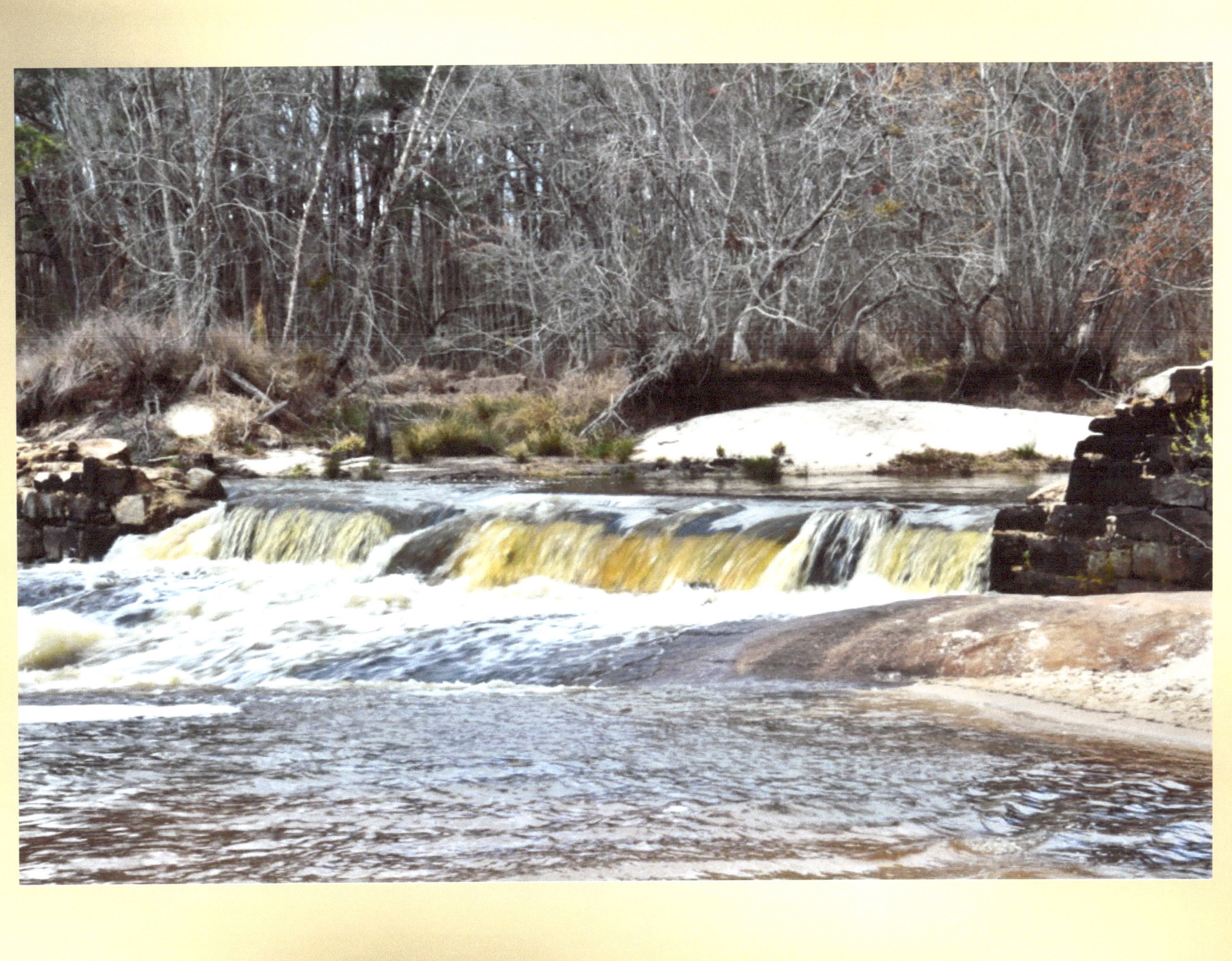

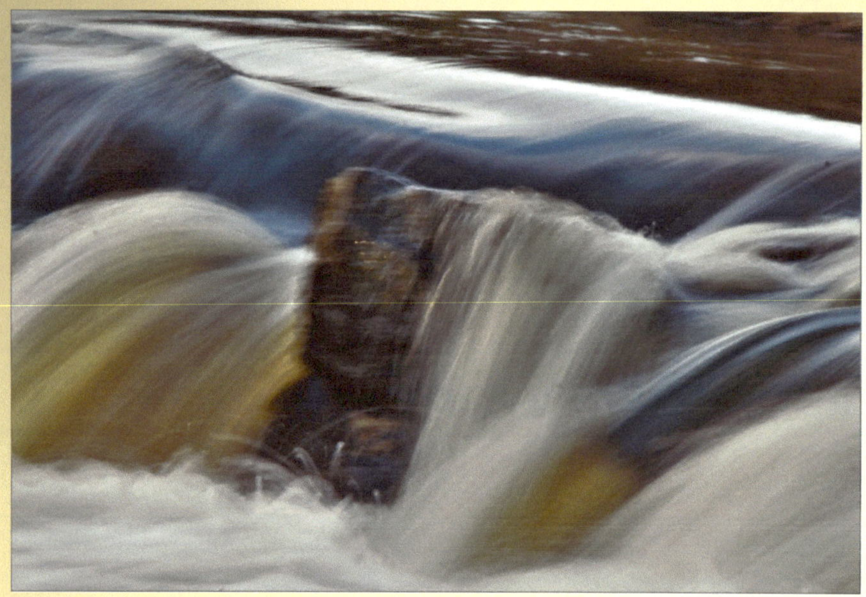
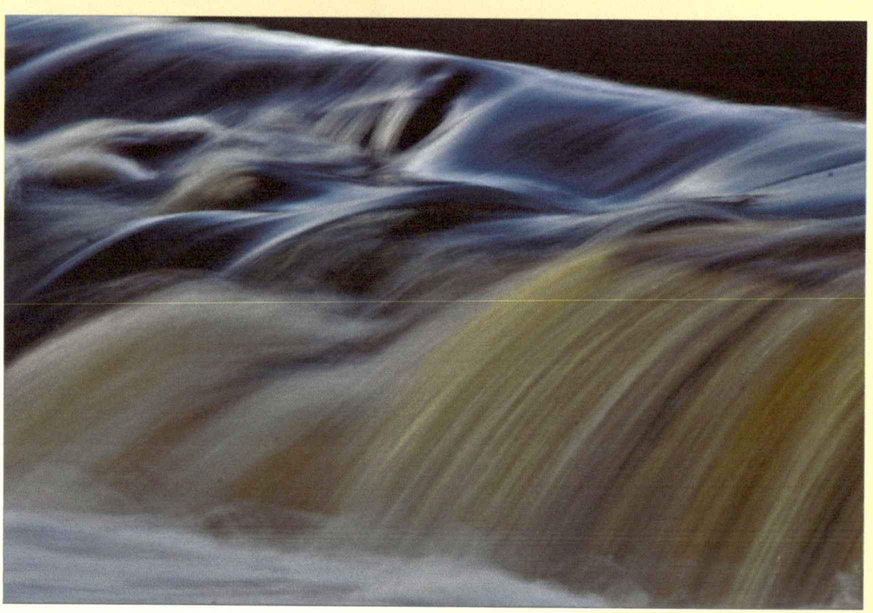
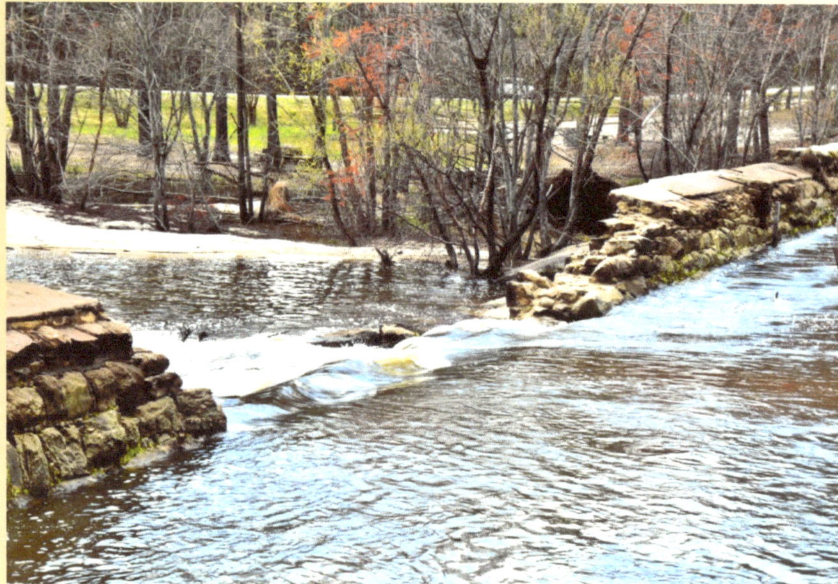
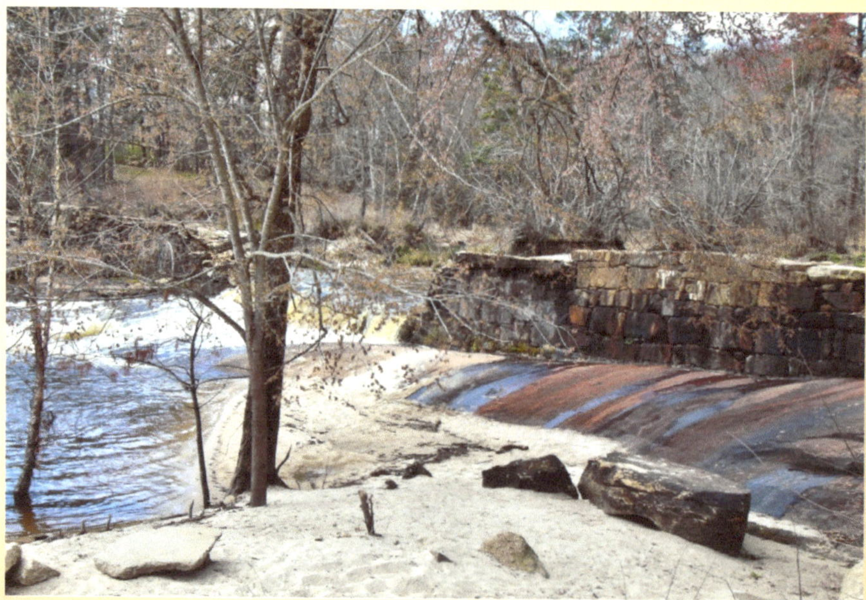

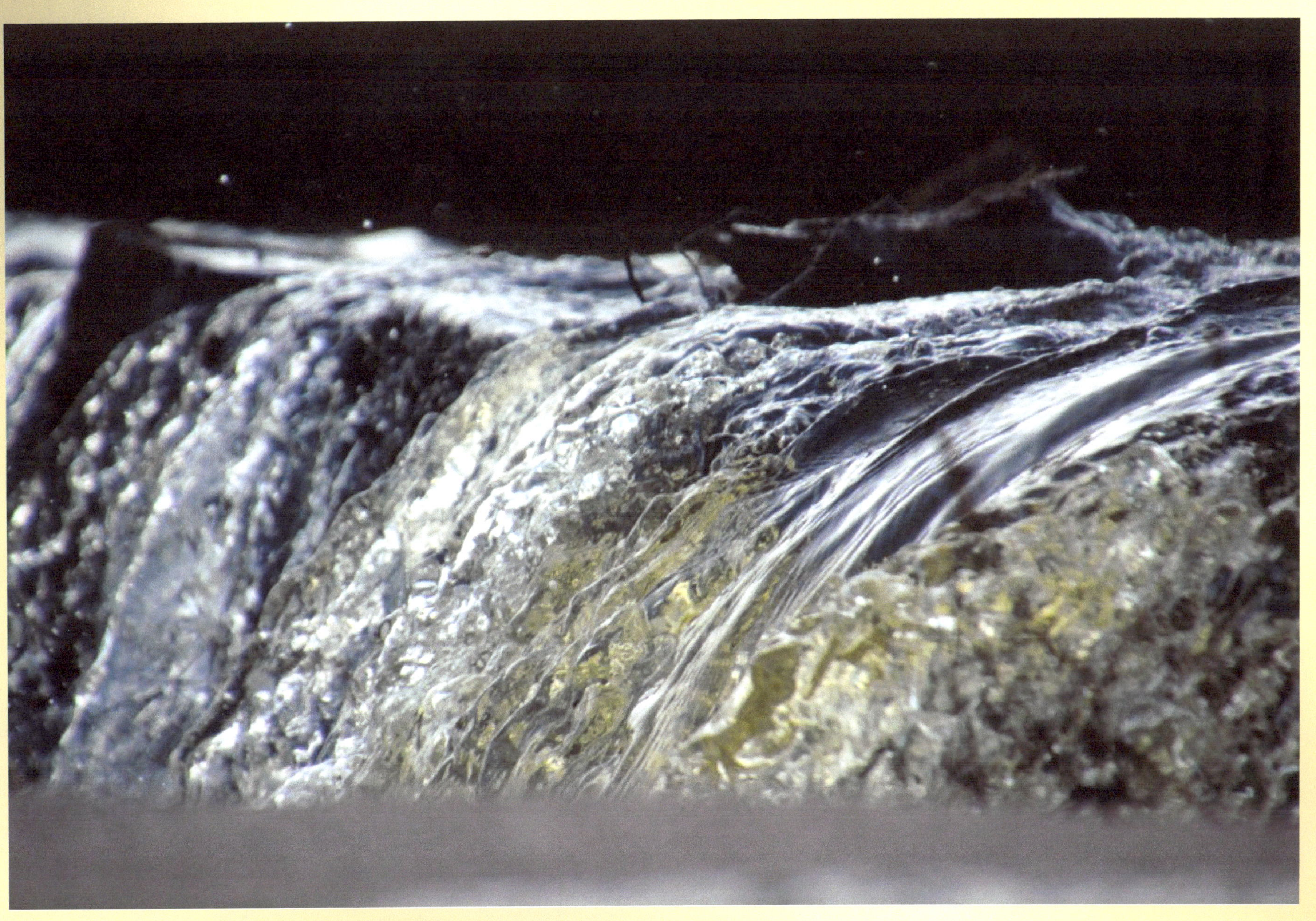

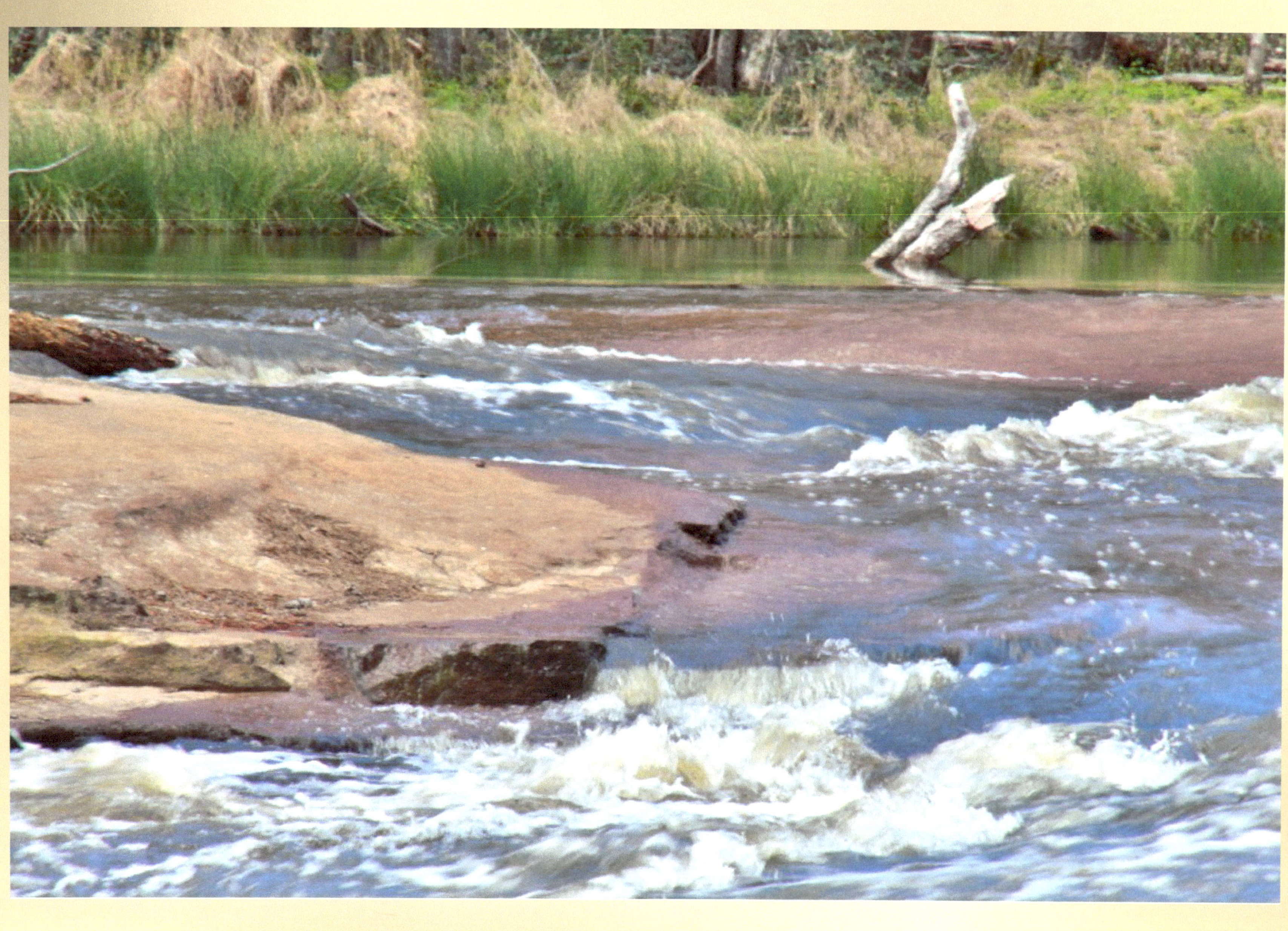

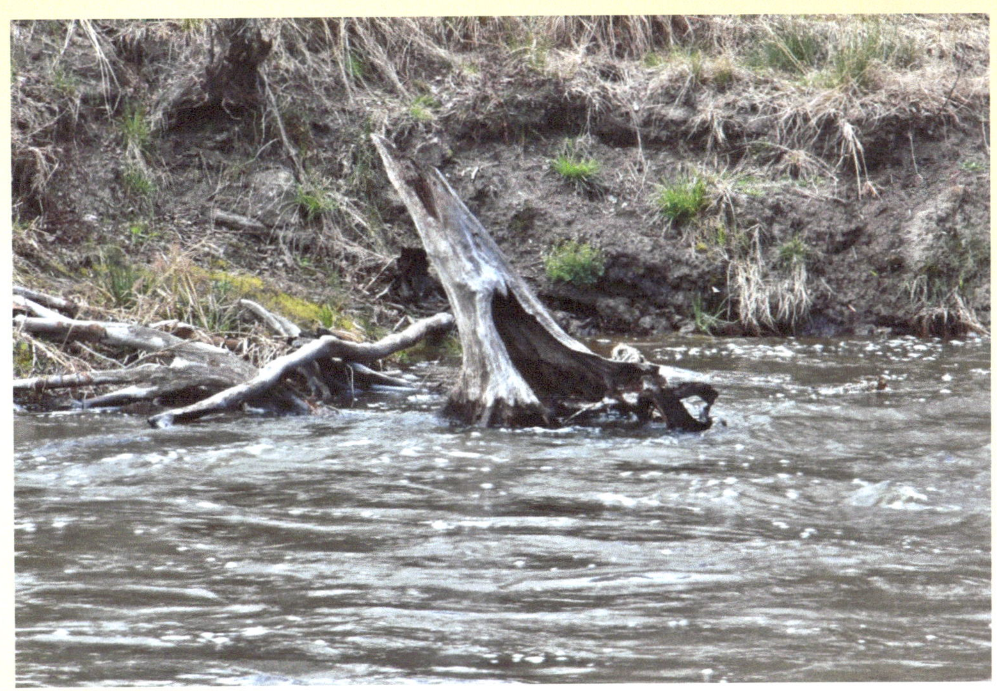

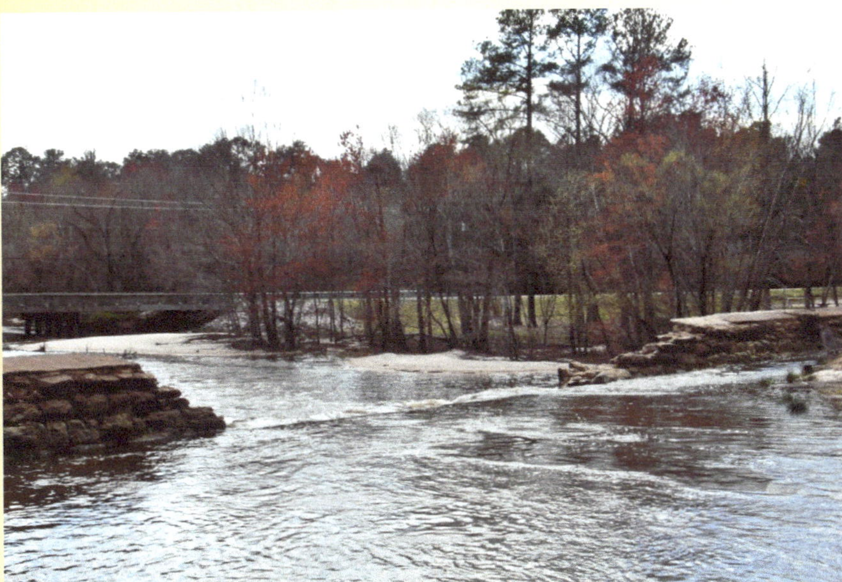

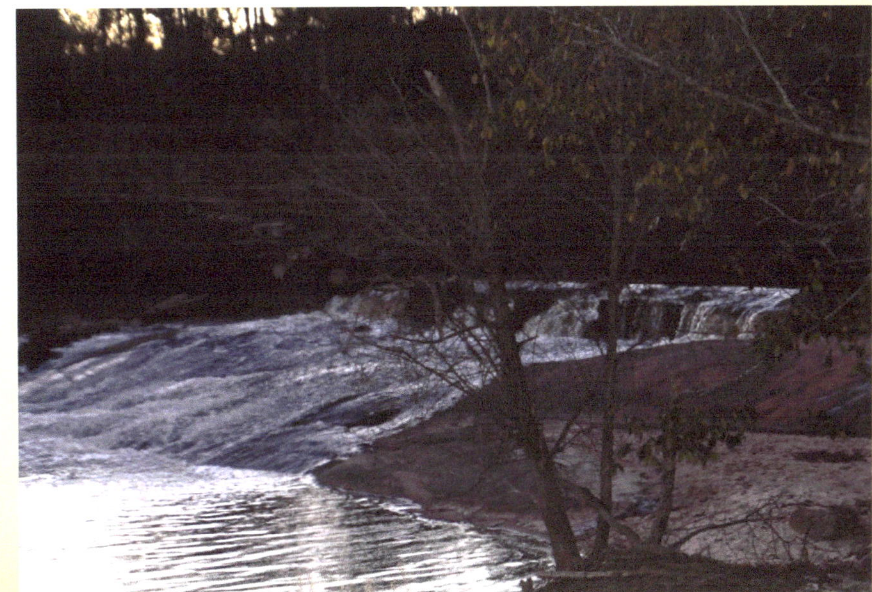

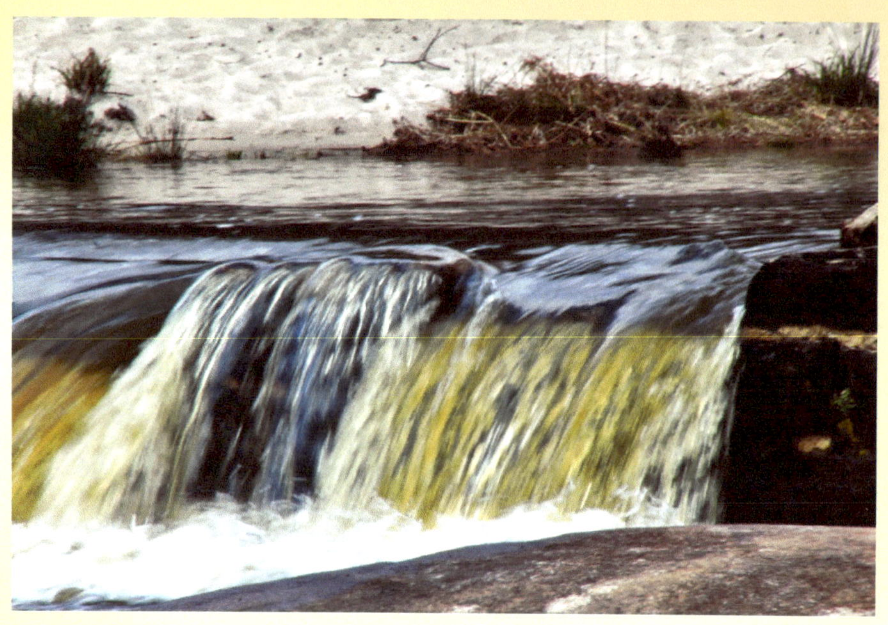

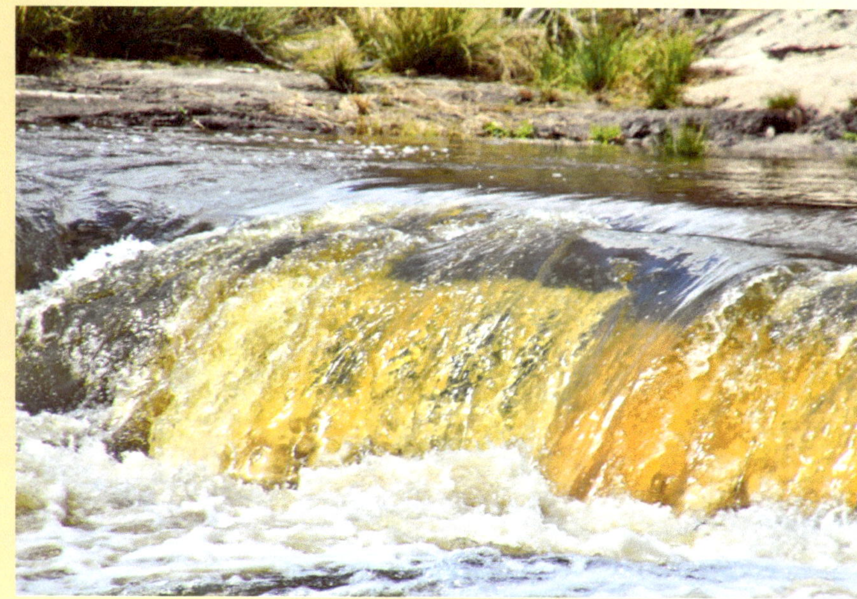

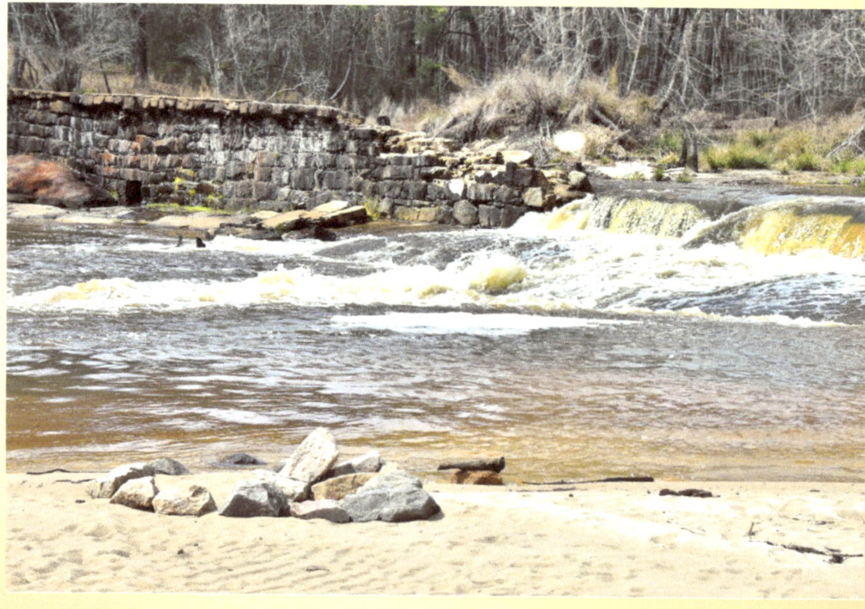

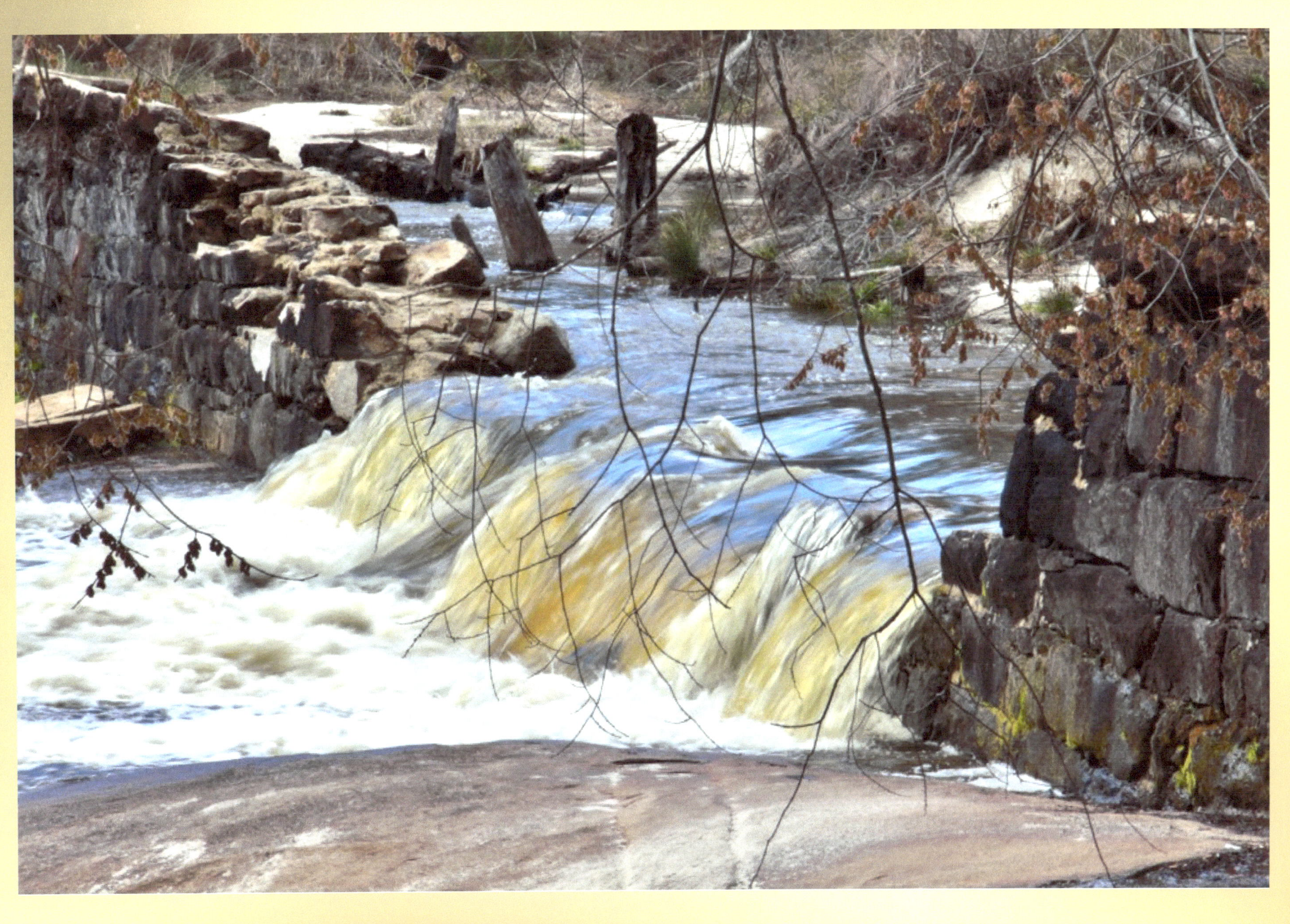

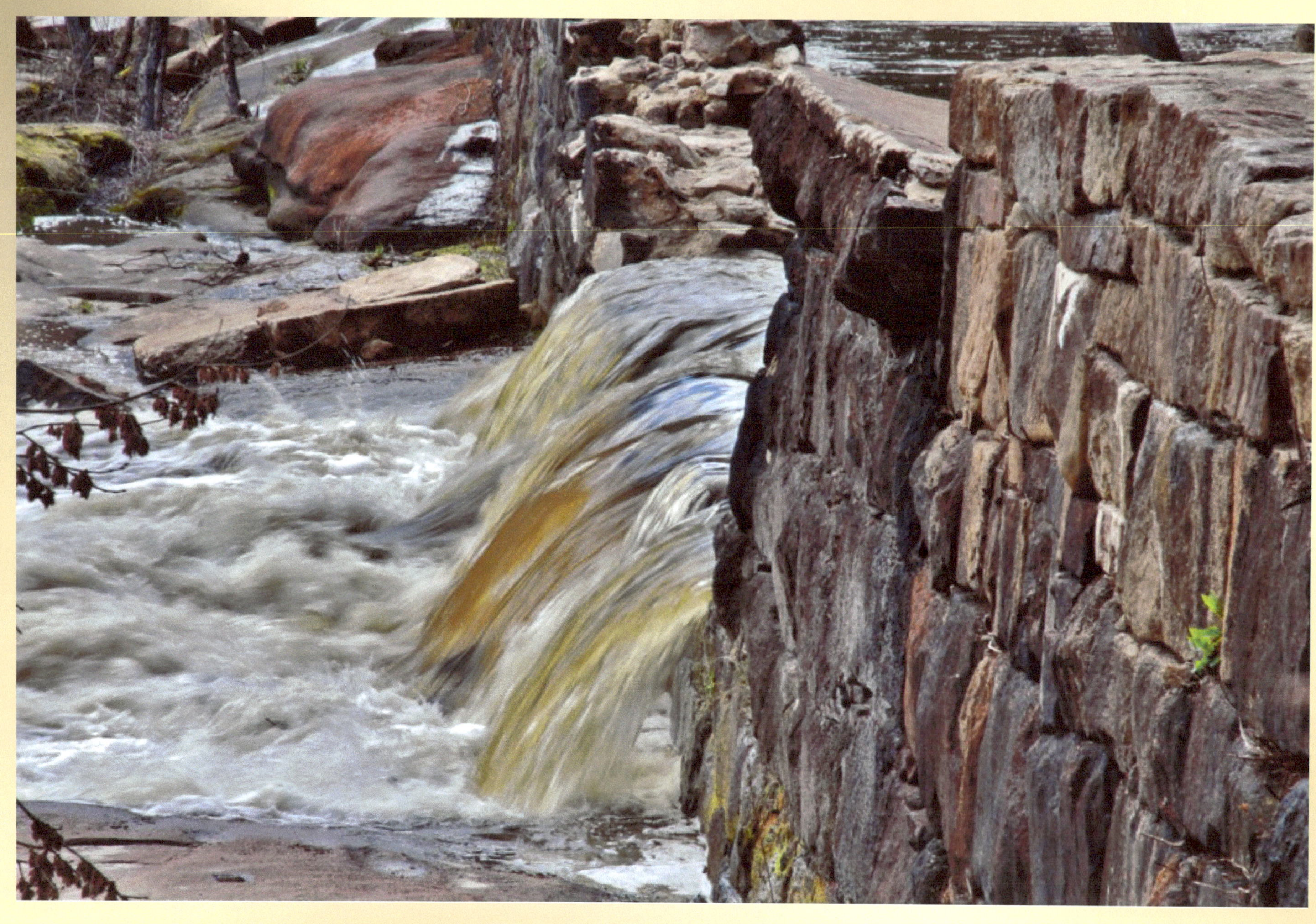

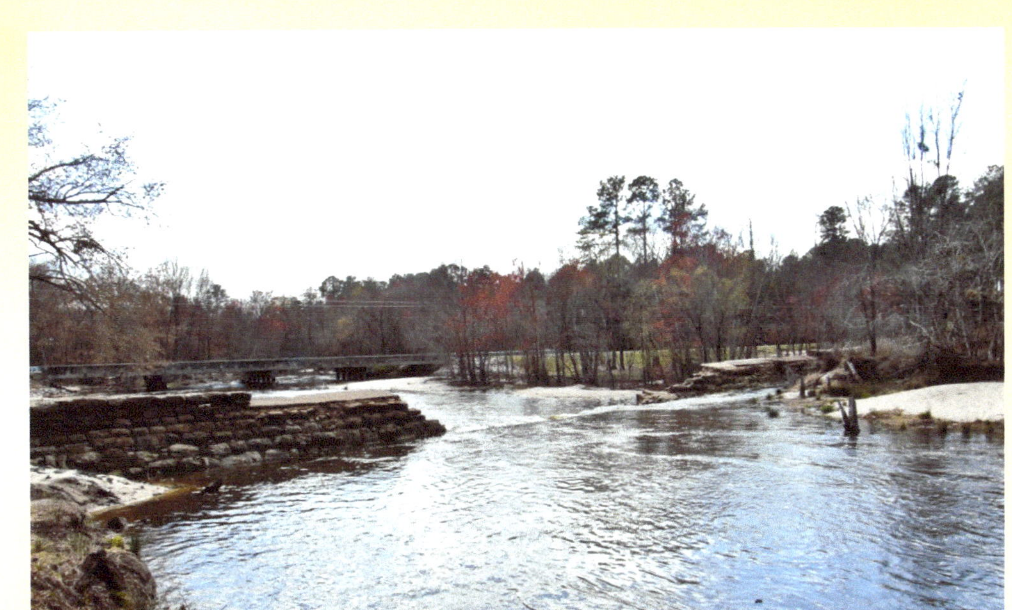

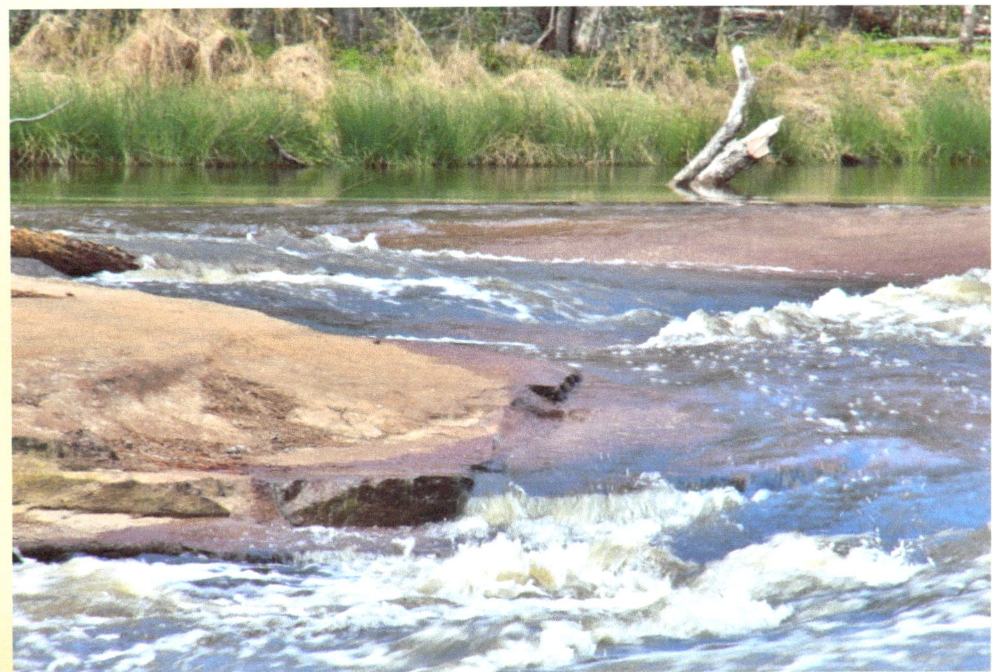

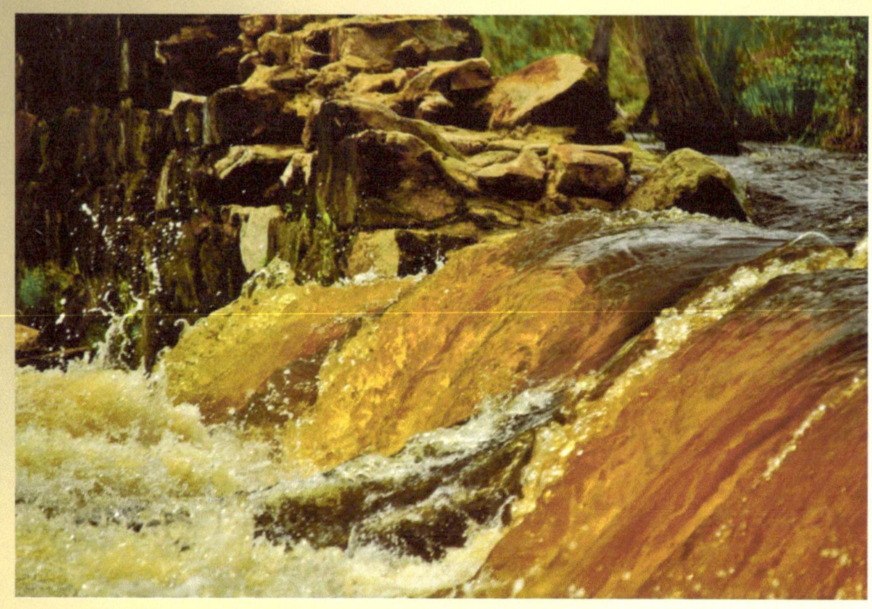
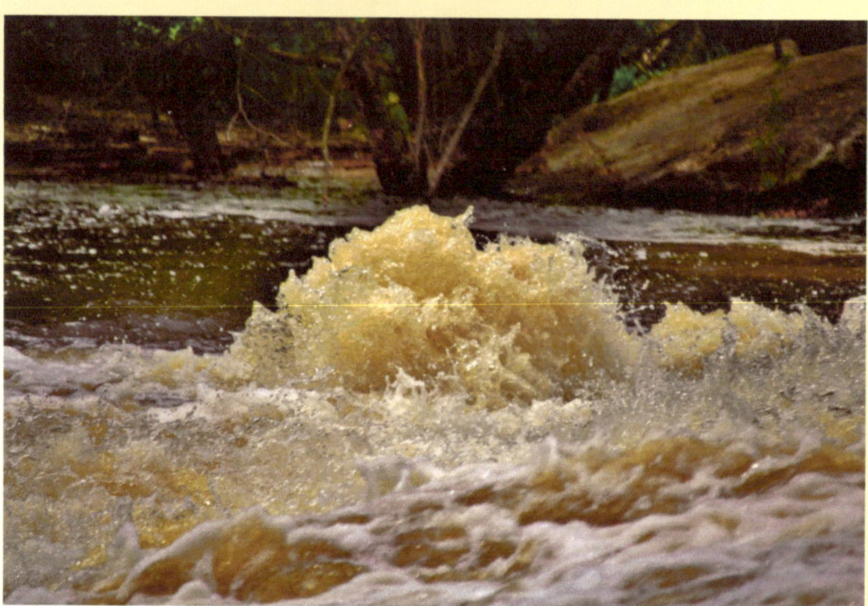
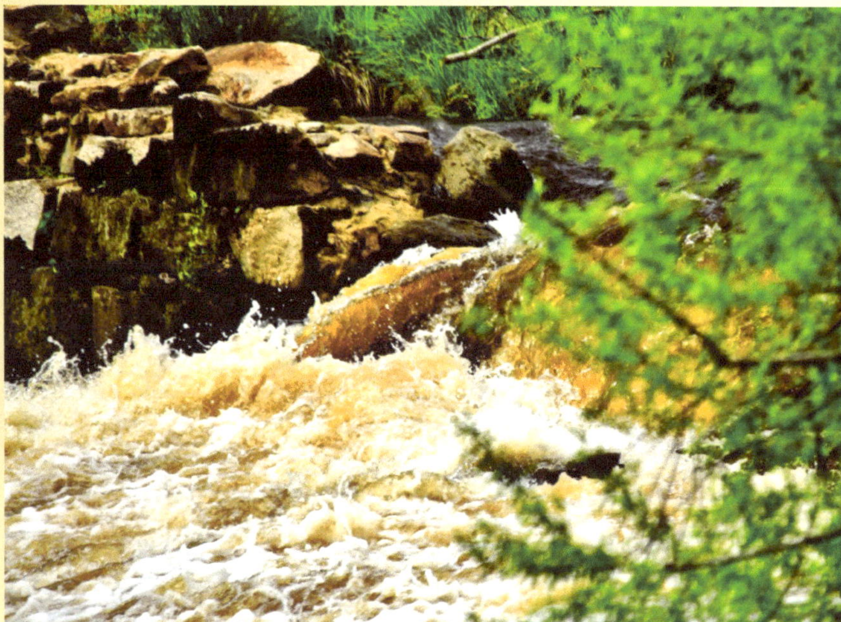
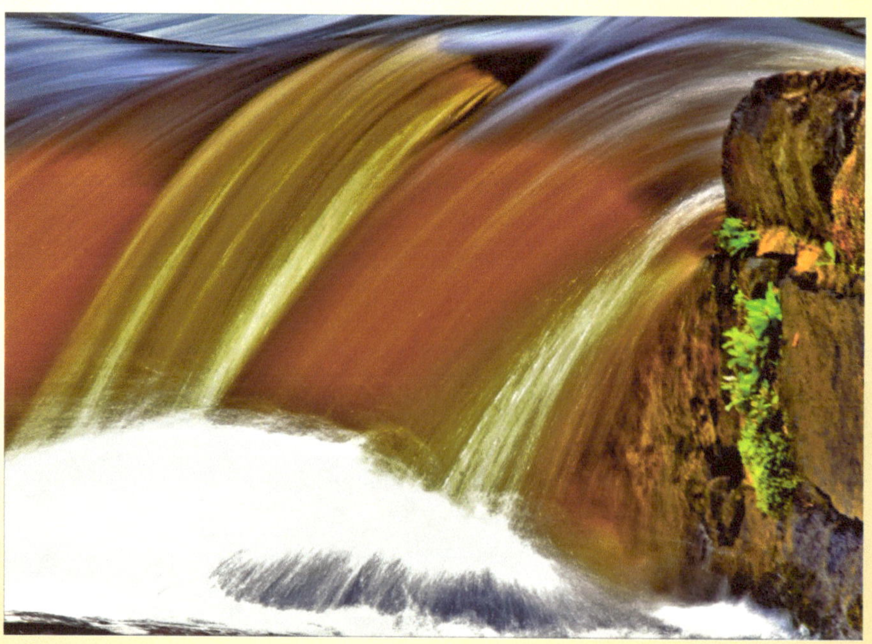

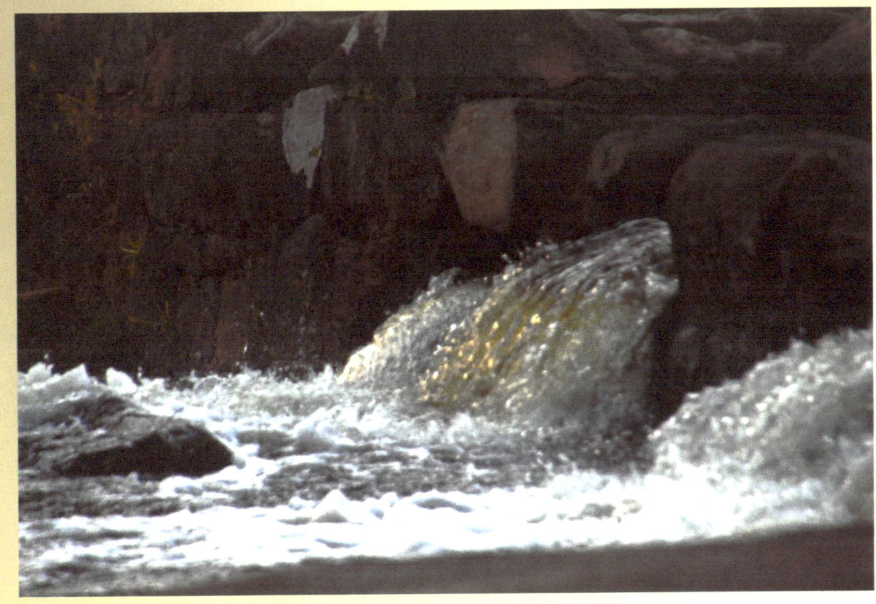

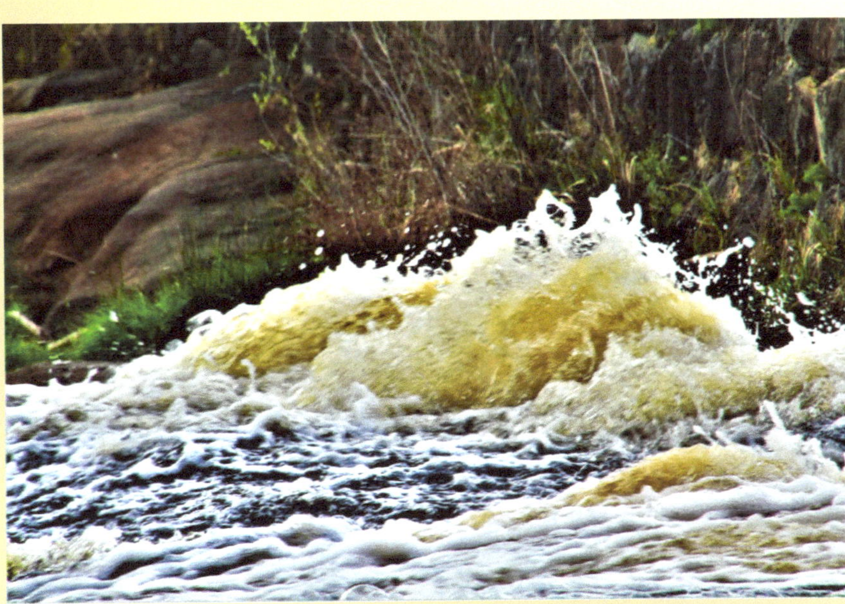

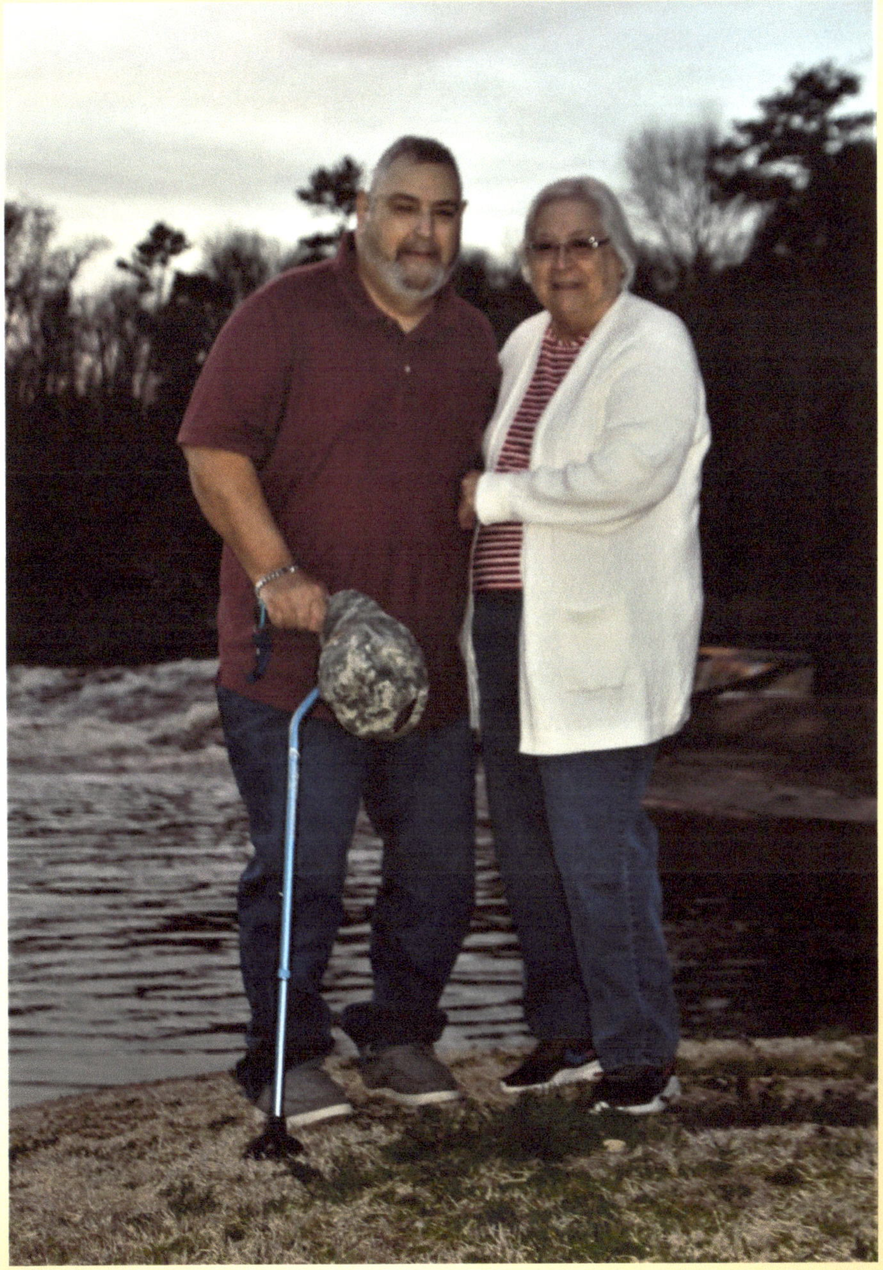

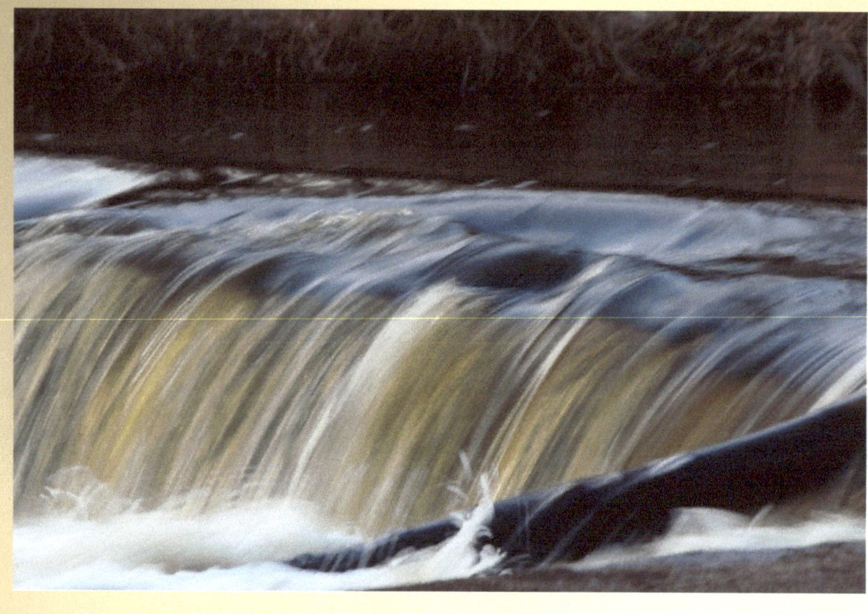
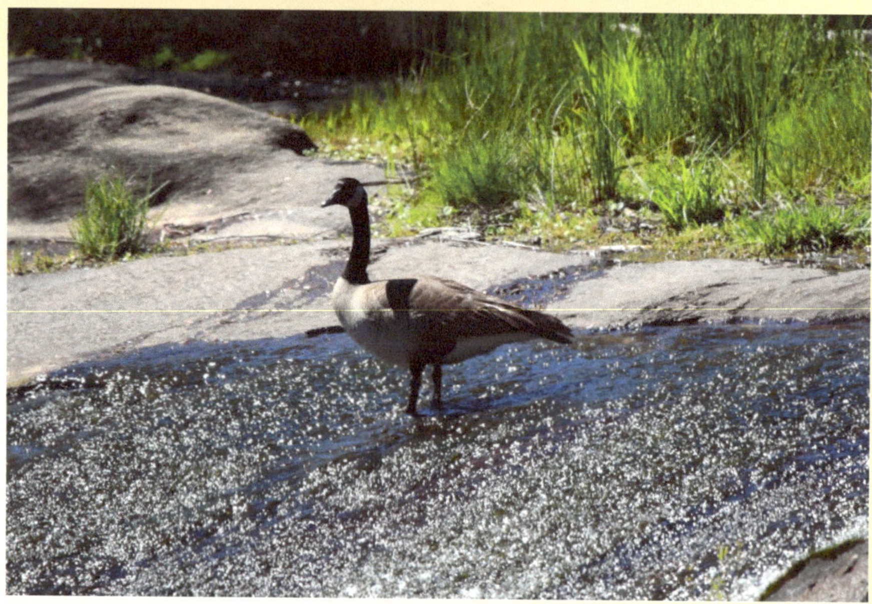
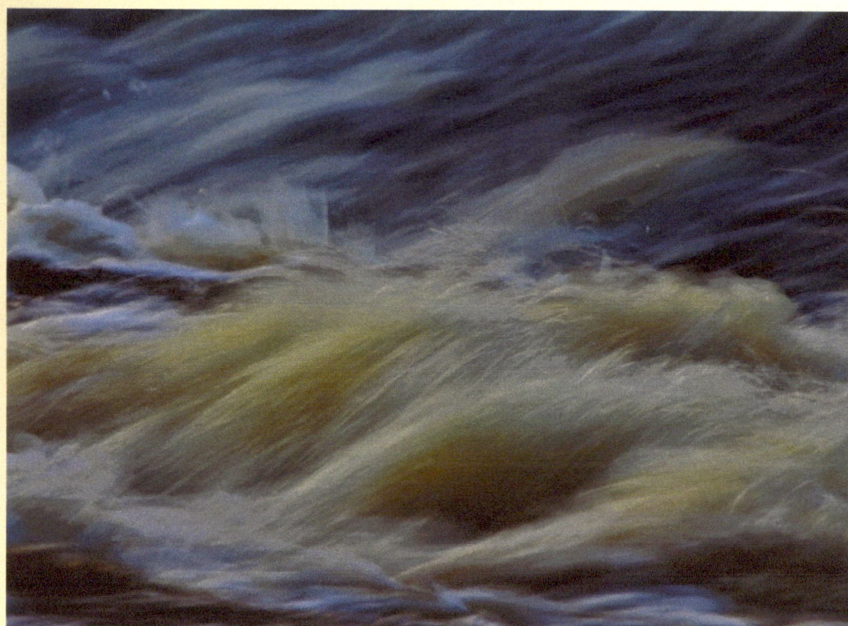
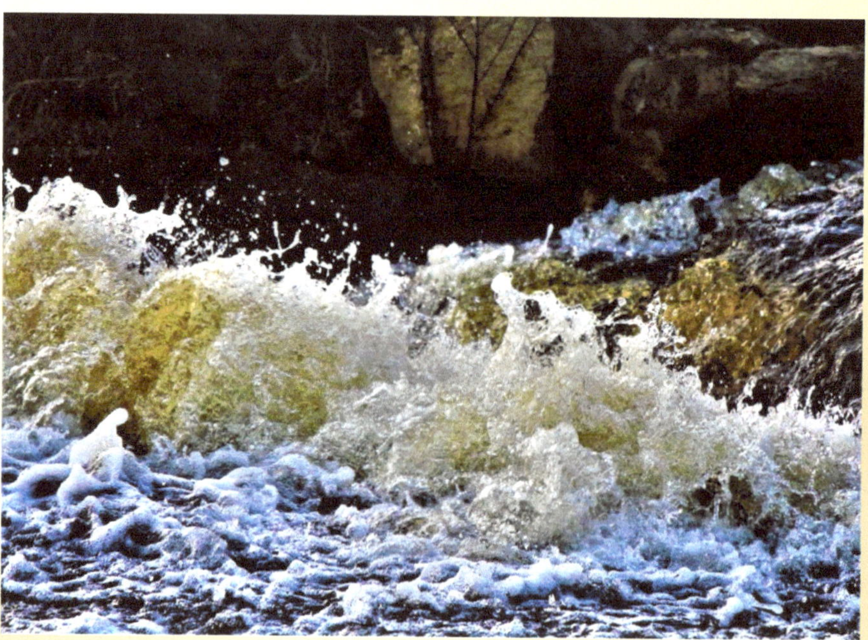

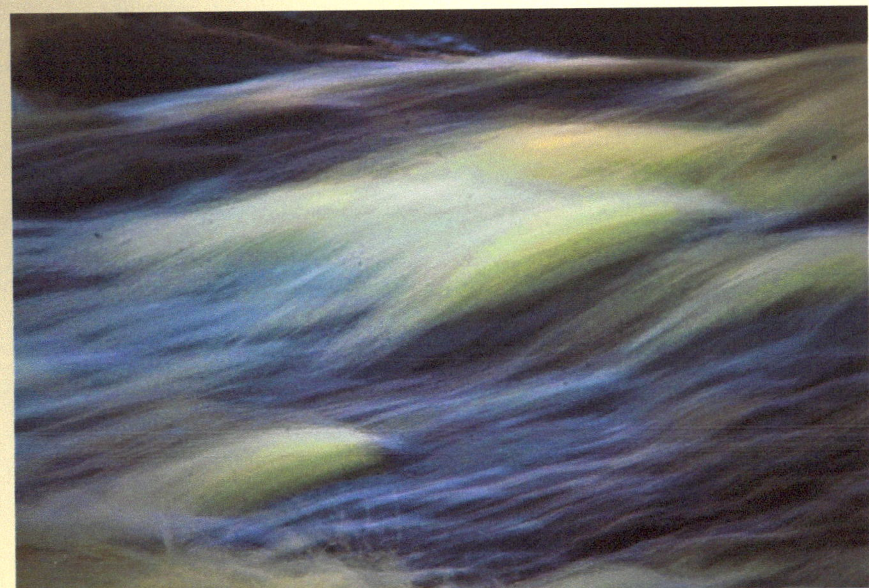

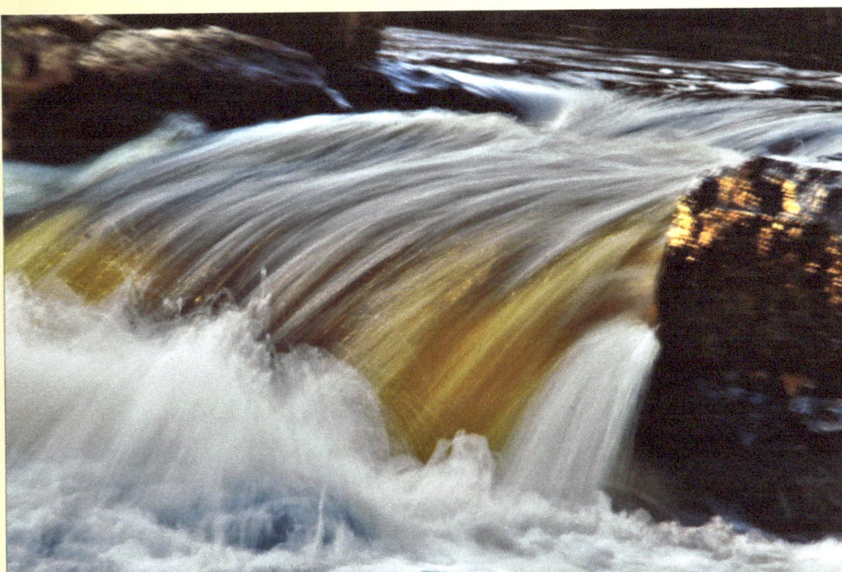

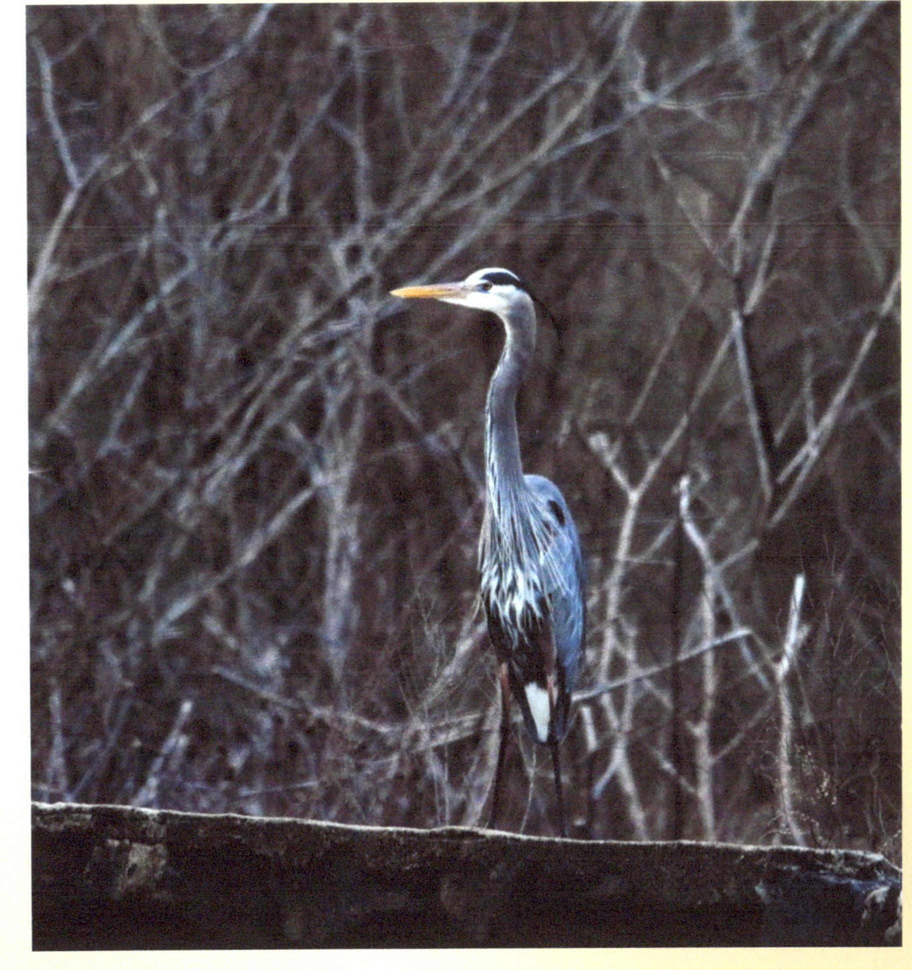

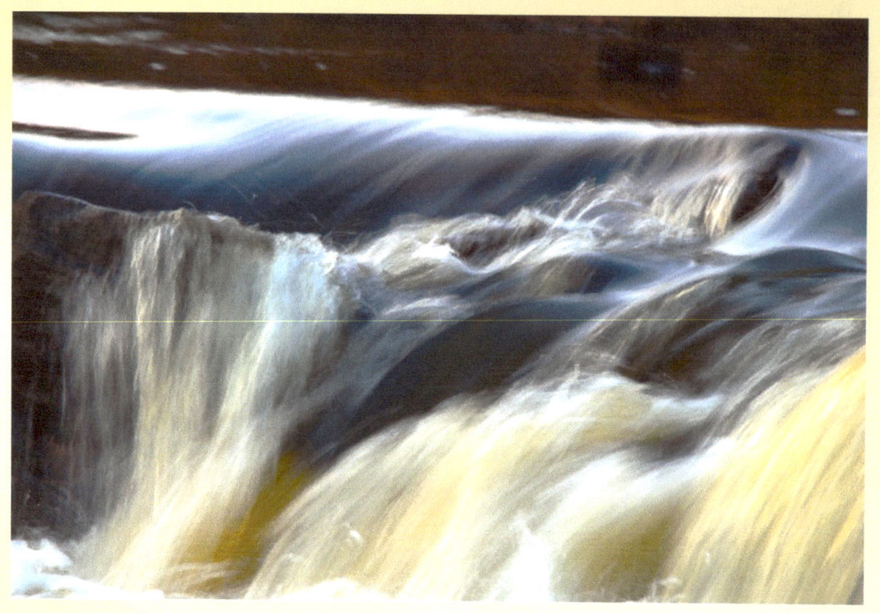

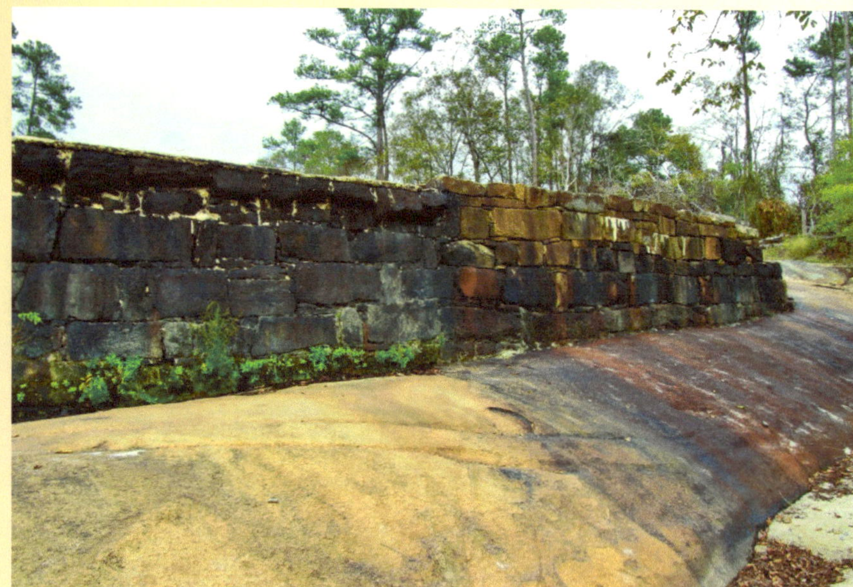

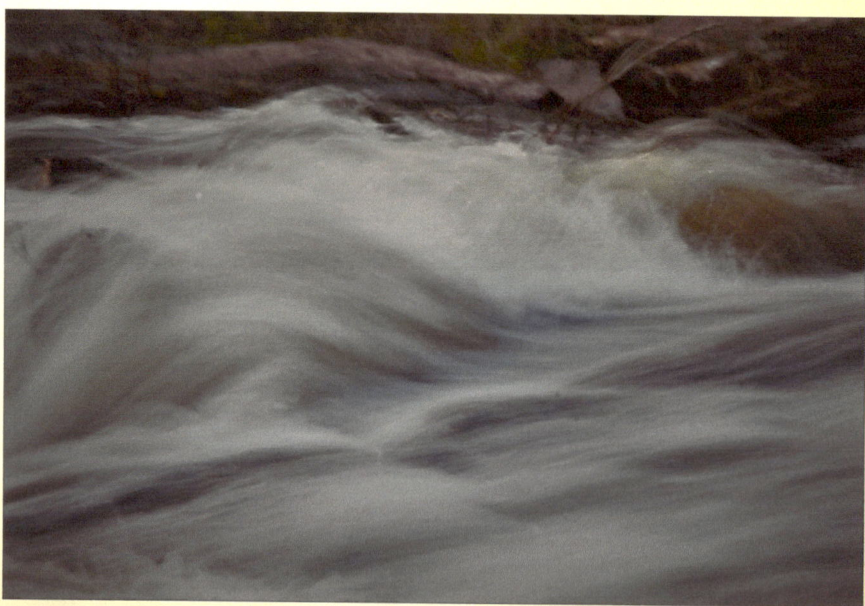

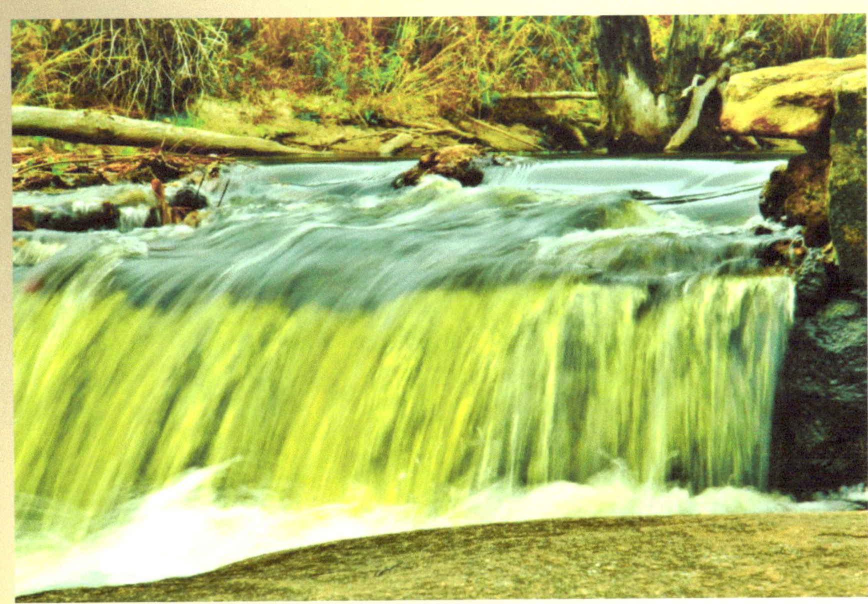
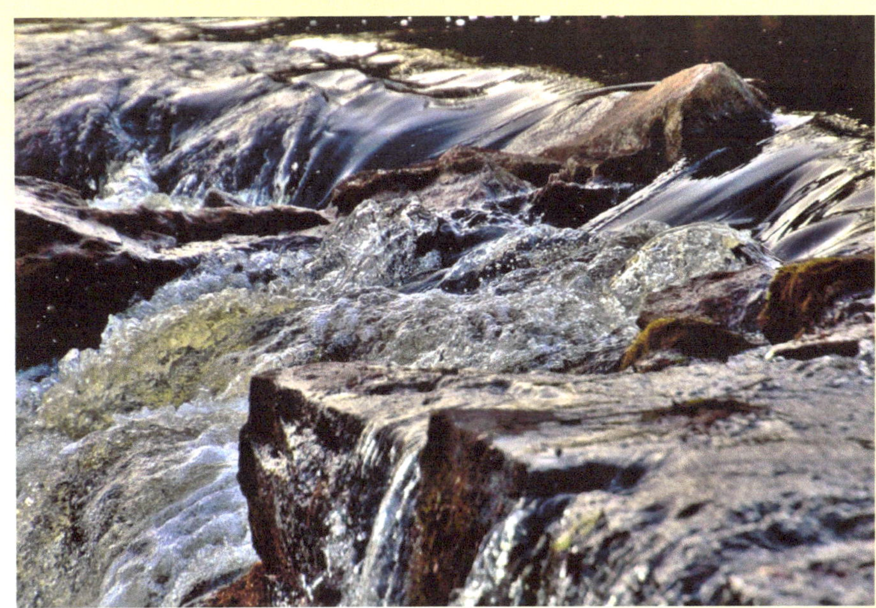
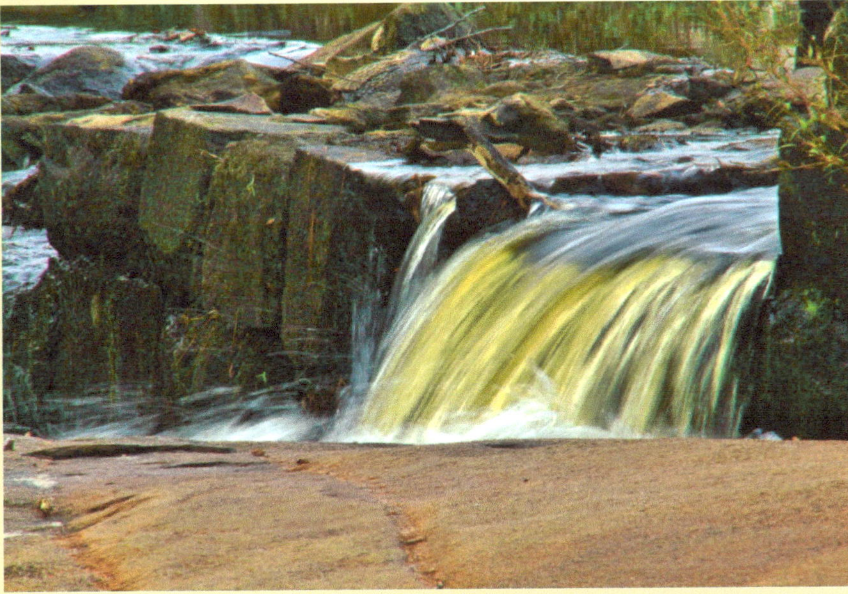
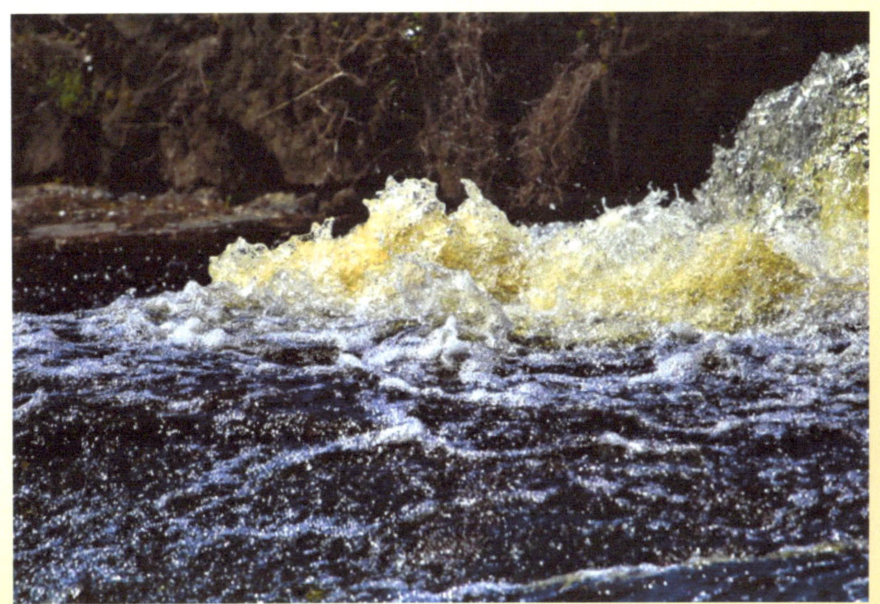

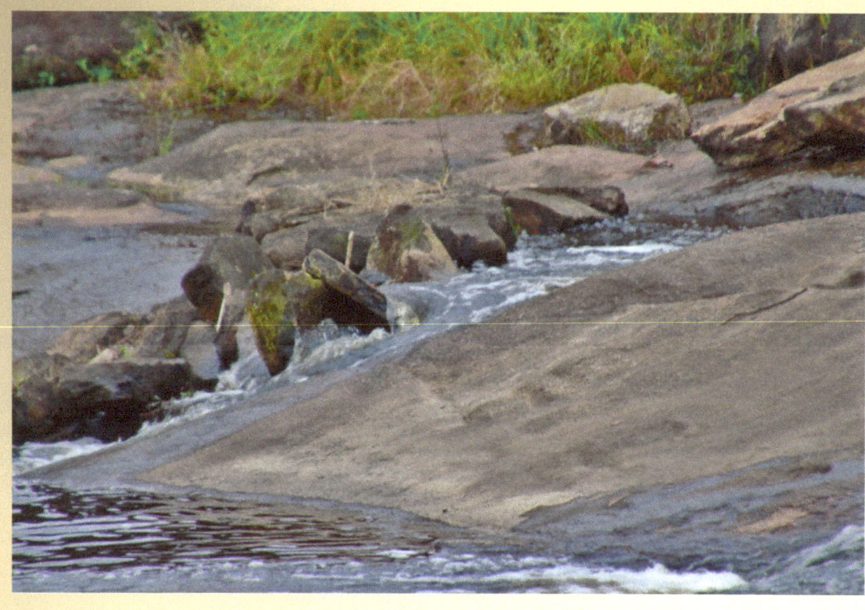
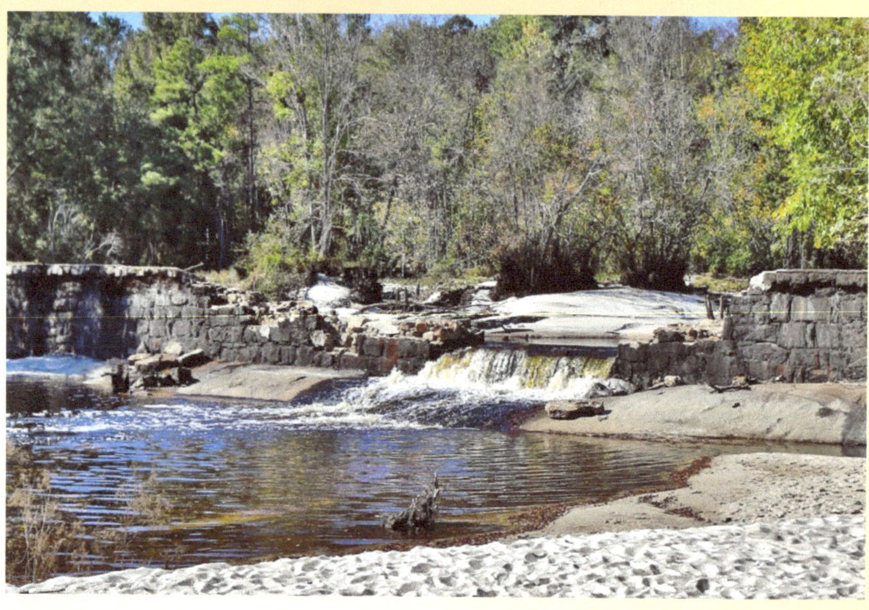
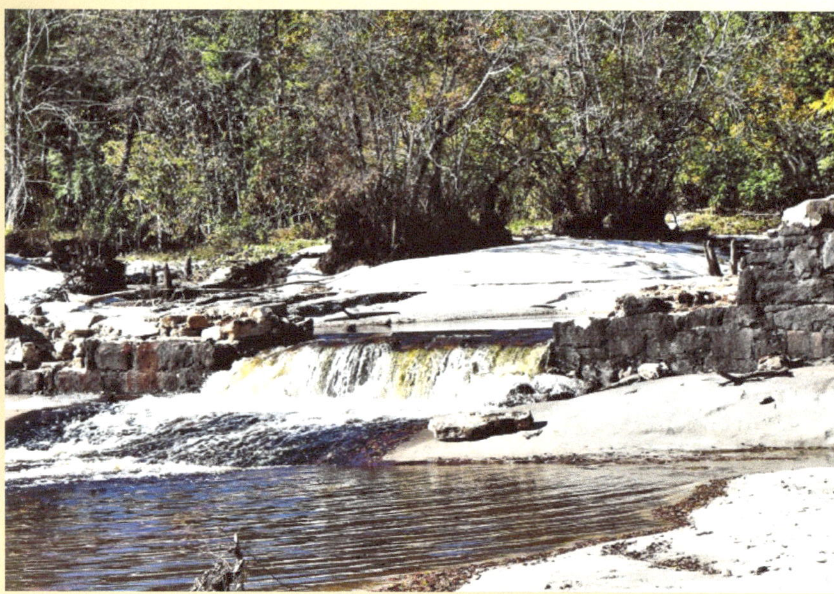
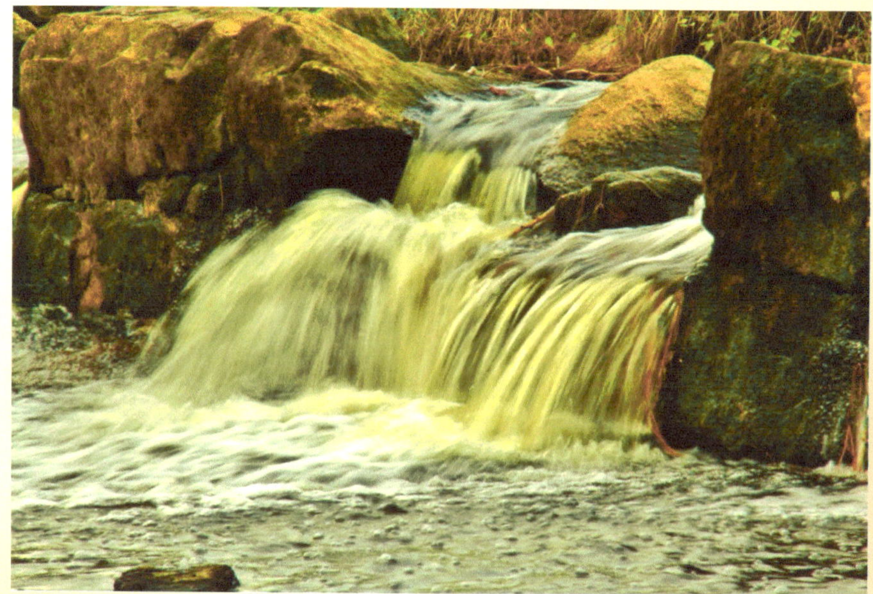

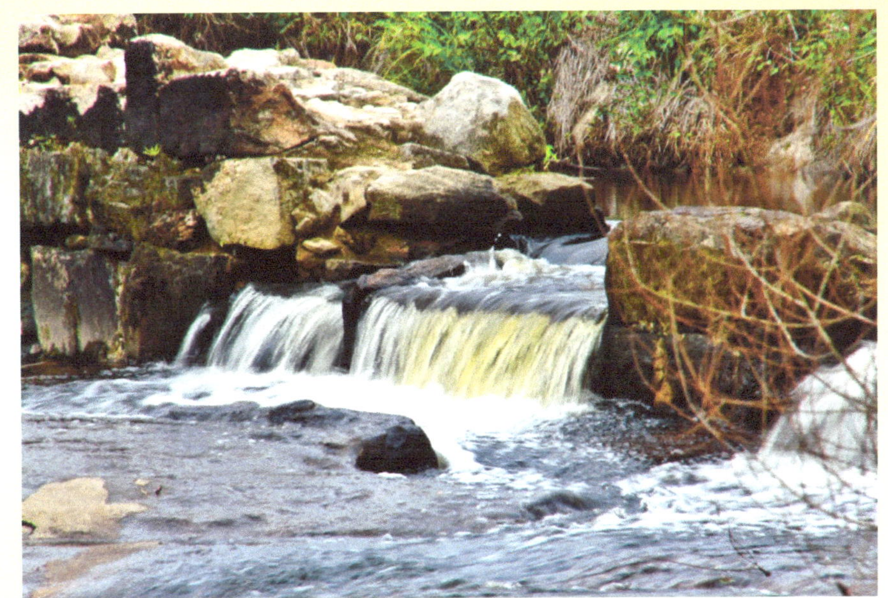

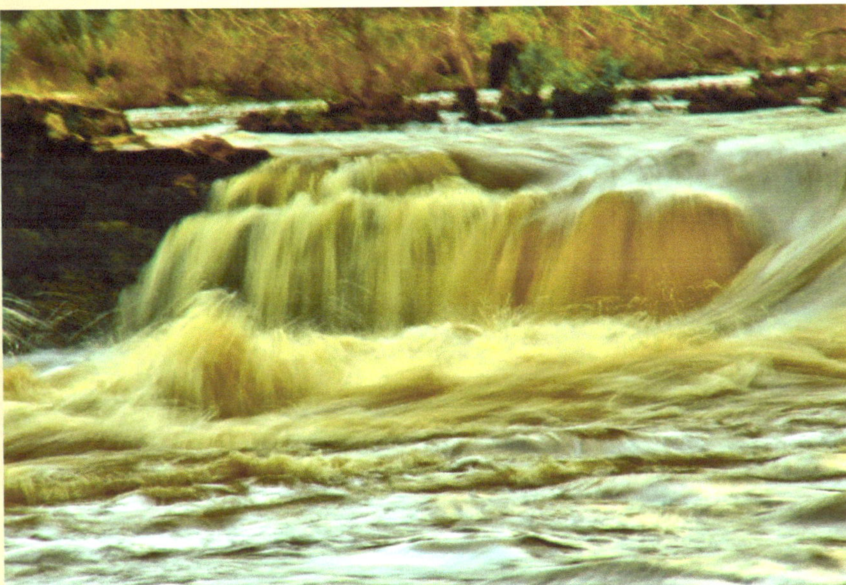

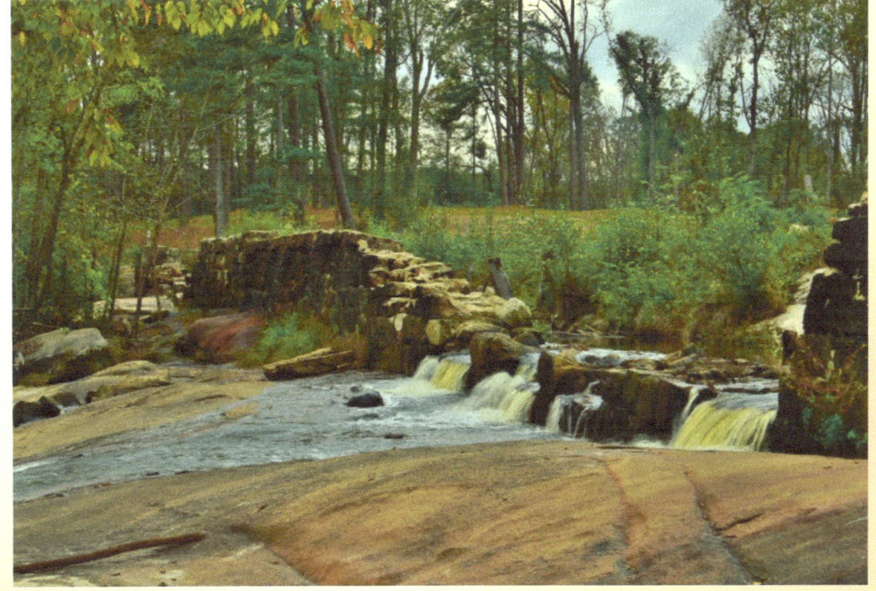

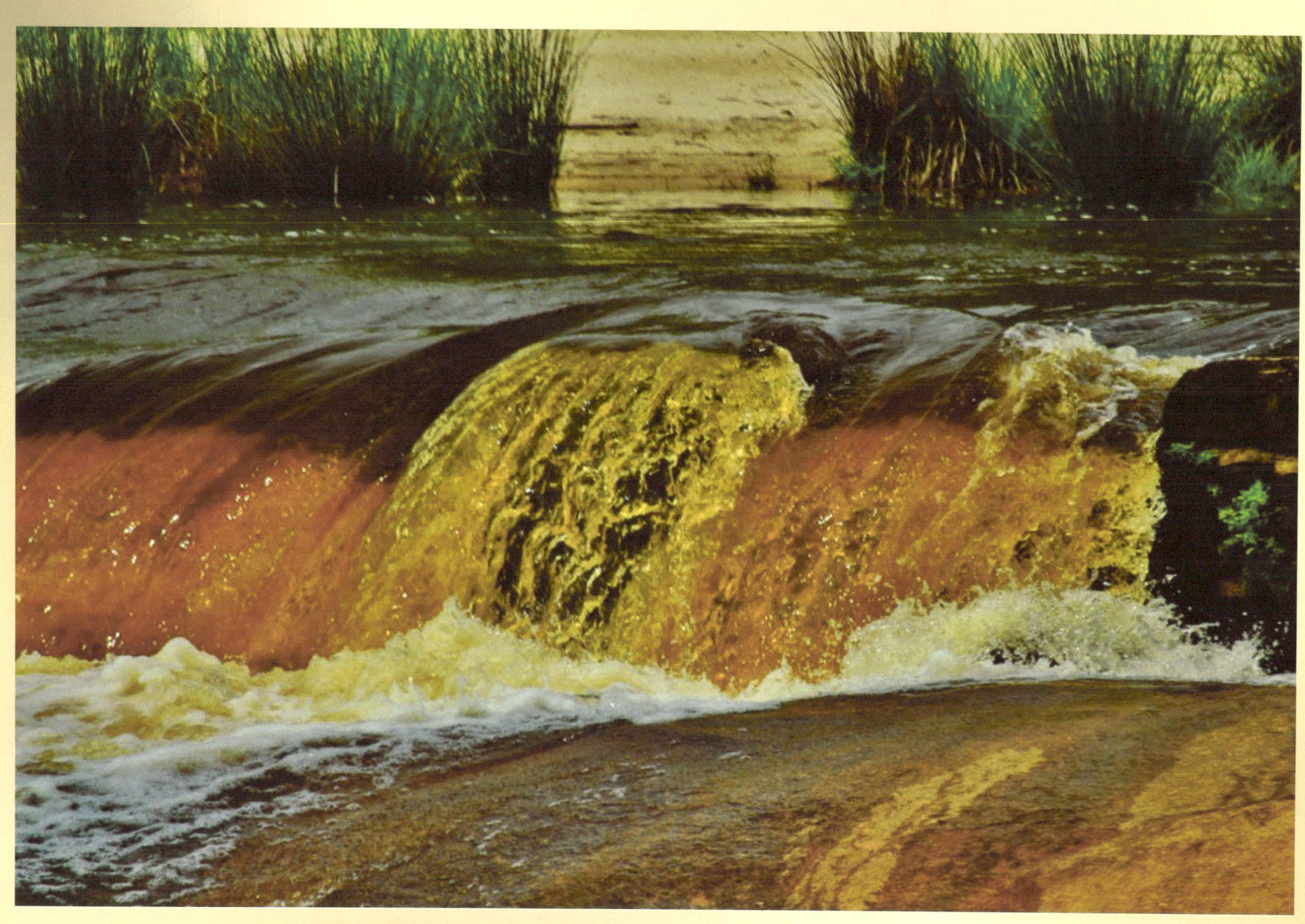

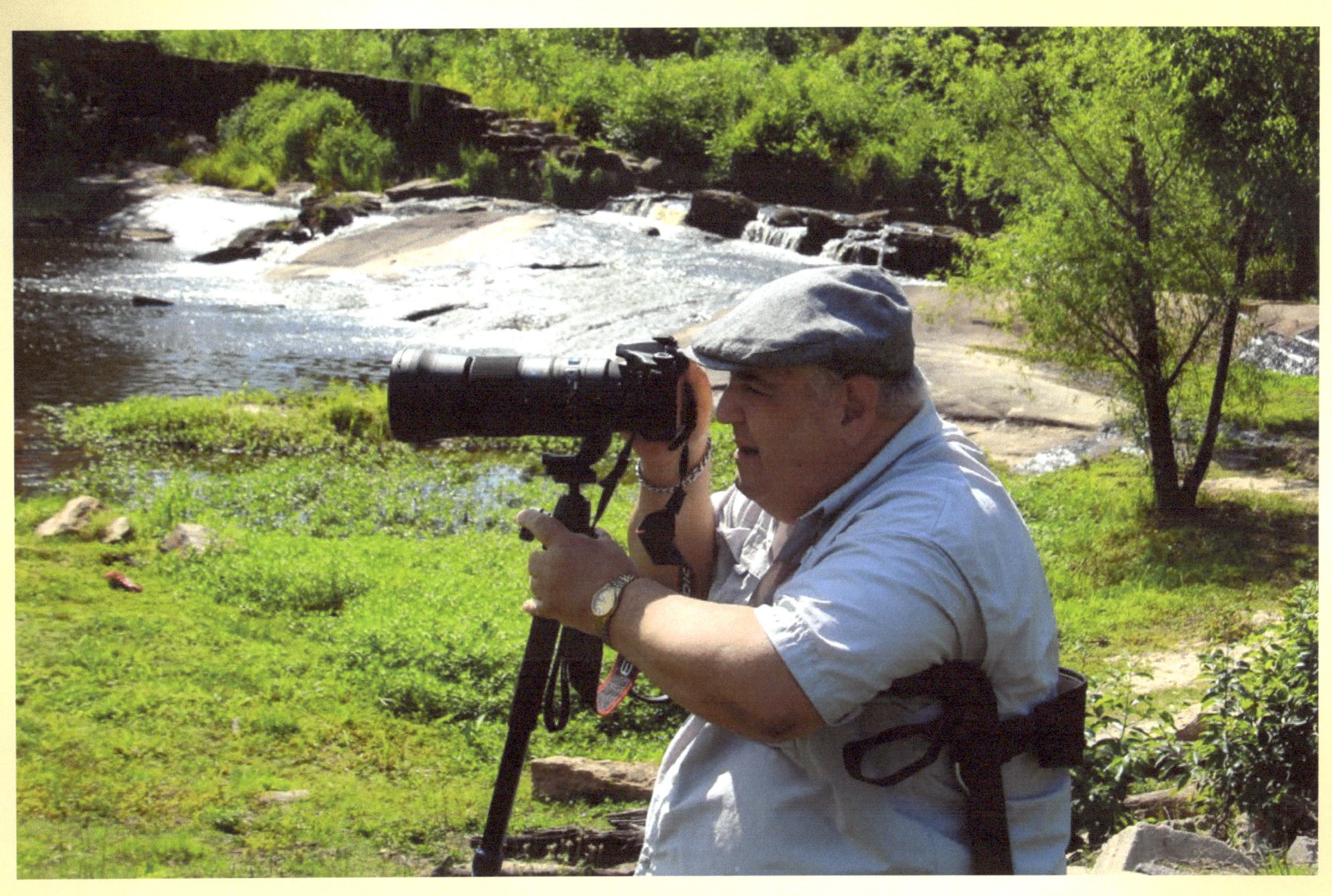

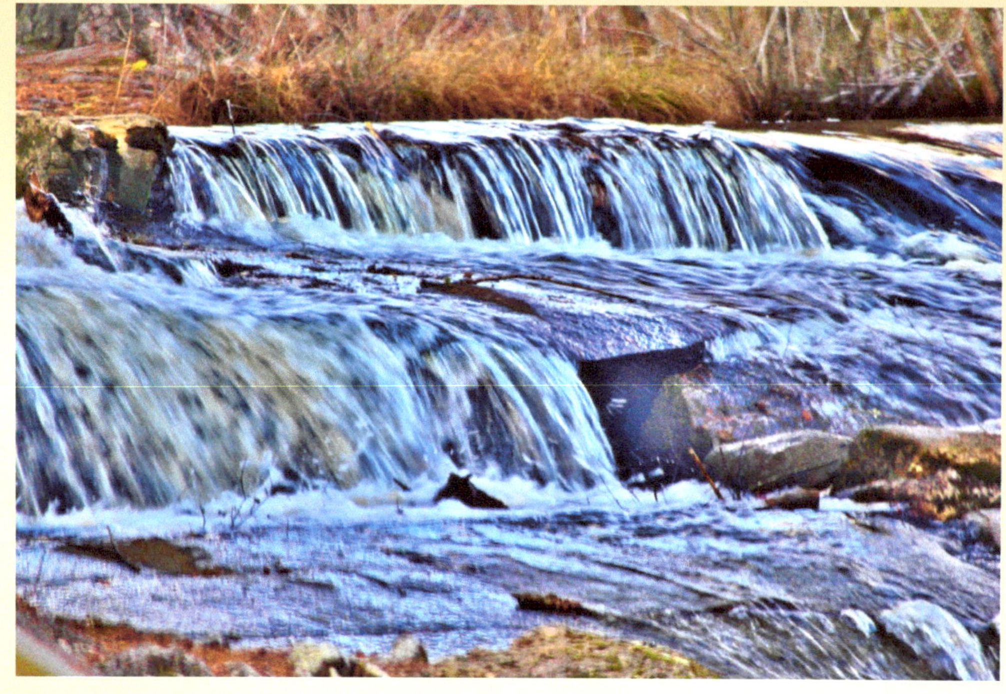

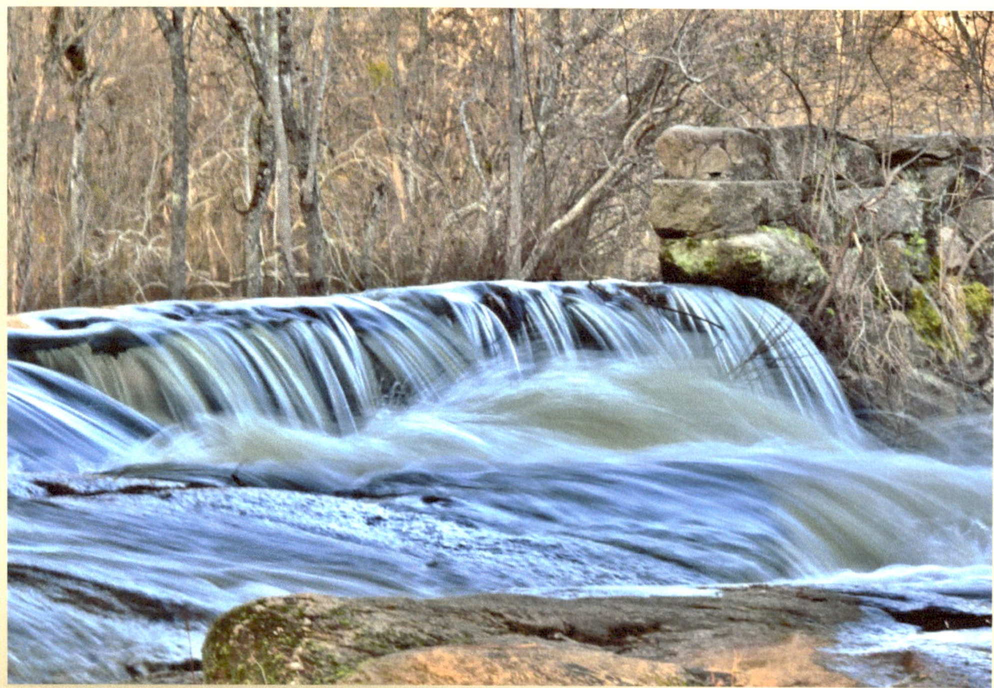

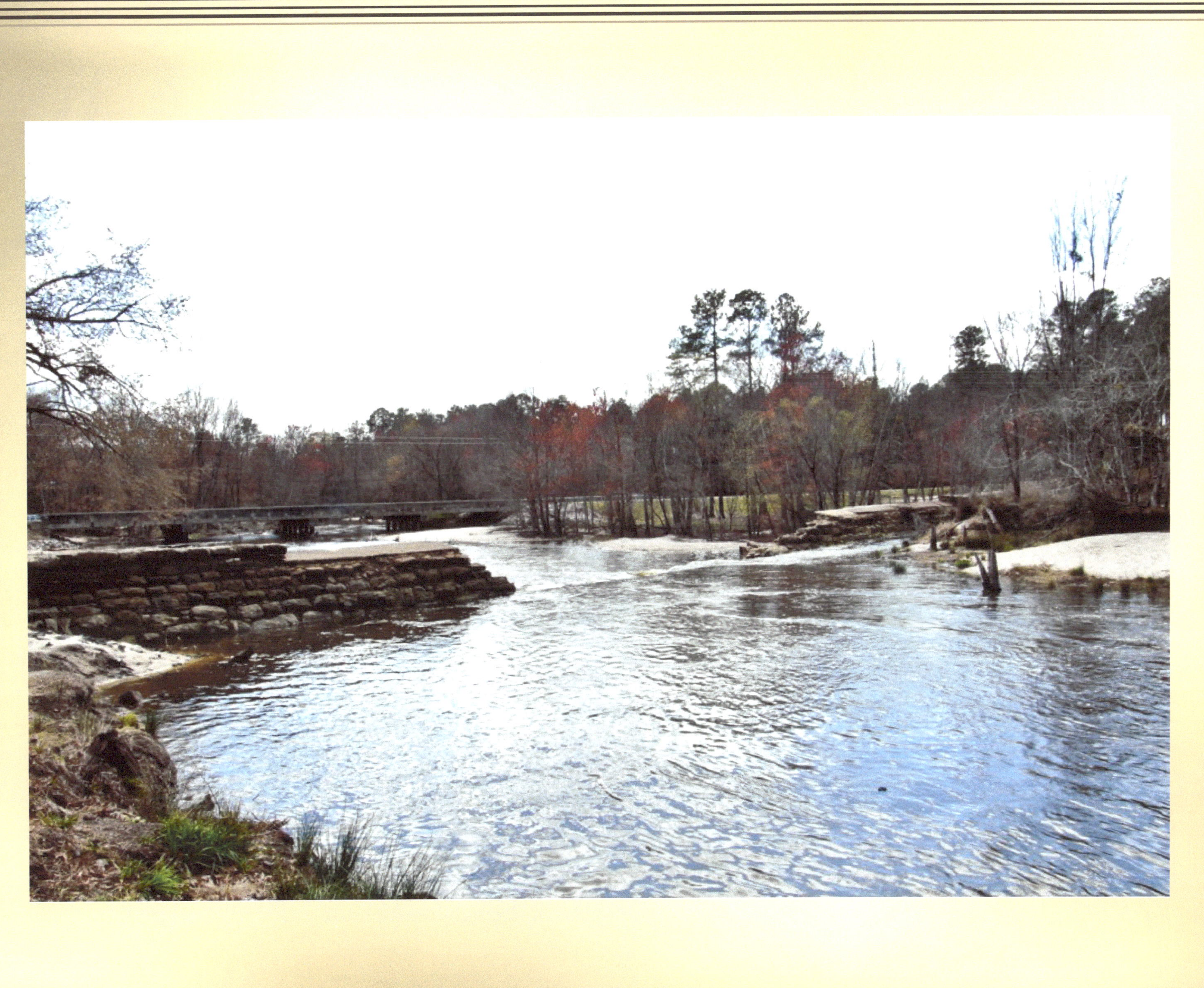

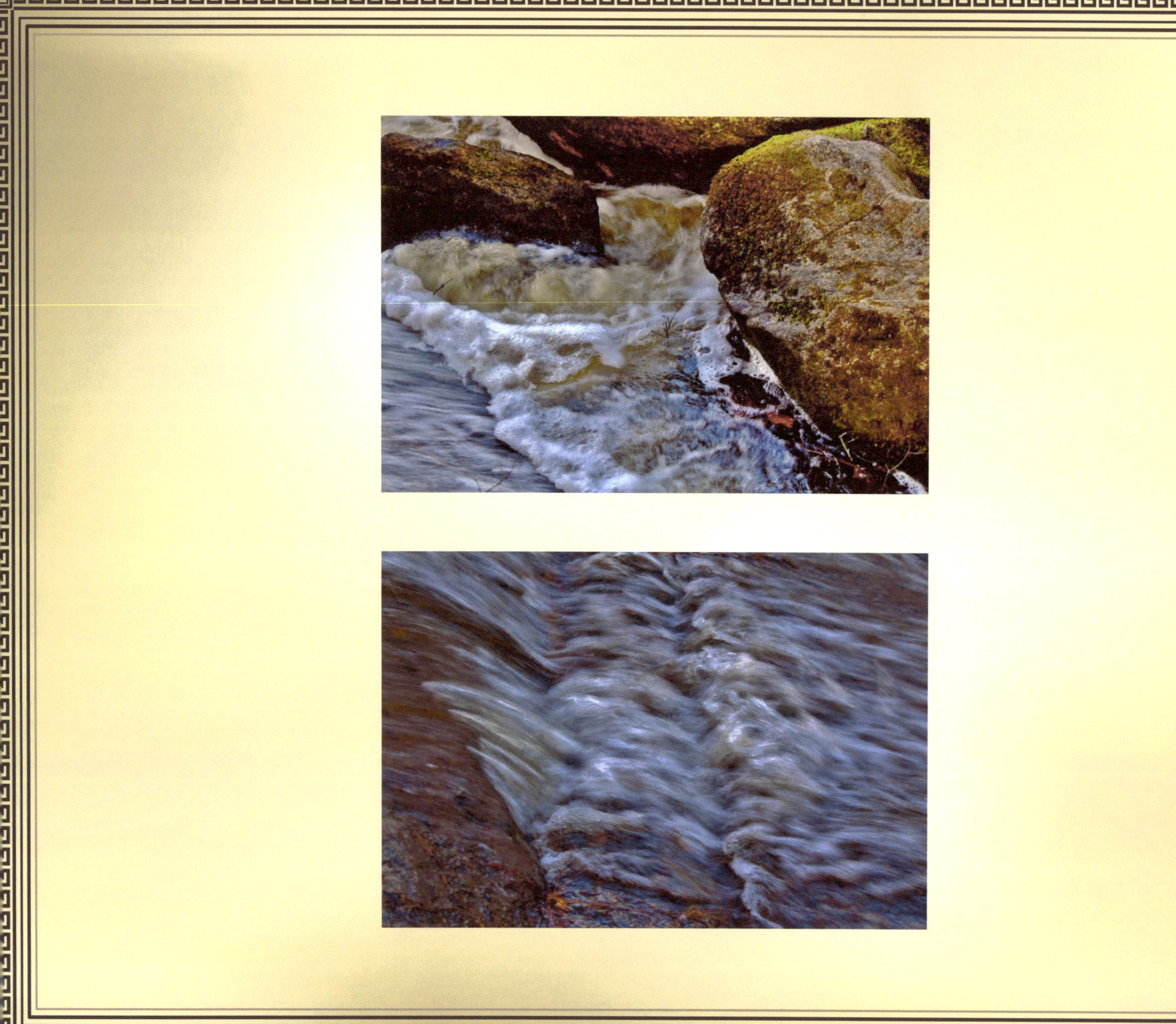

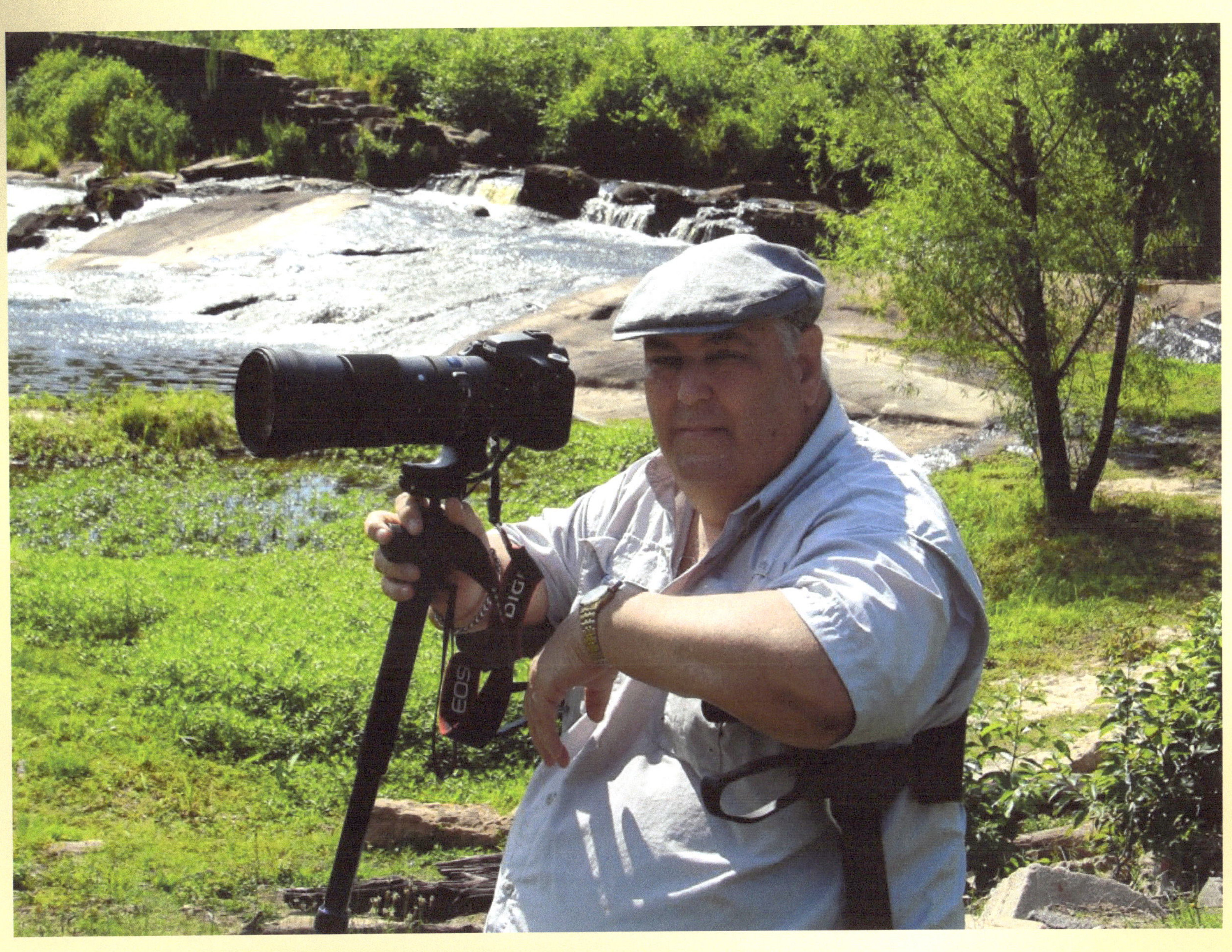

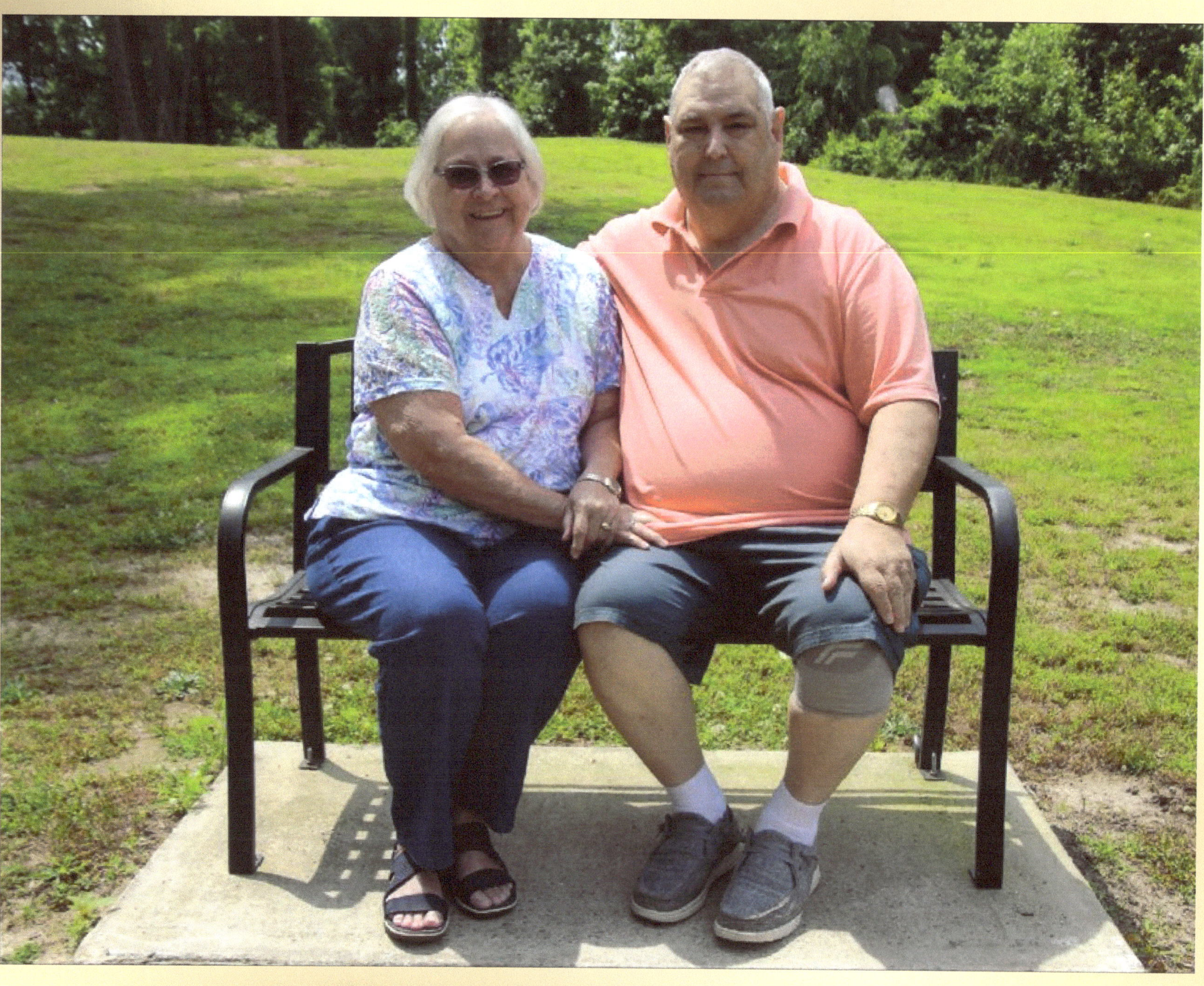

The Town of Zebulon Board of Commissioners adopted the Little River Park Site Specific Master Plan in November of 2022 following robust public engagement and outreach, and the adoption of the P&R Comprehensive Master Plan. The plan includes establishing paved and unpaved walking trails, open space, gardens, picnic shelters, restrooms, an amphitheater, fishing and viewing platforms, river restoration, and history exhibits. This park will bookend the Green Spine Greenway which will connect Little River Park, Downtown, and Five County Stadium. The Park will also serve as a trailhead for a planned greenway that will connect Zebulon and Wendell to the Little River Nature Preserve and other greenways in Wake County.

The Town of Zebulon was awarded a Parks and Recreation Trust Fund grant in August of 2023 to begin development of the Little River Park Site Specific Master Plan. The first phase of construction will expand access to the east side of the park, establish open space, develop paved and unpaved trails, provide shelters and restrooms, and create a natural classroom and native garden.

https://www.townofzebulon.org/sites/default/files/uploads/Parks/littleriverpark_park_program_plan_20...

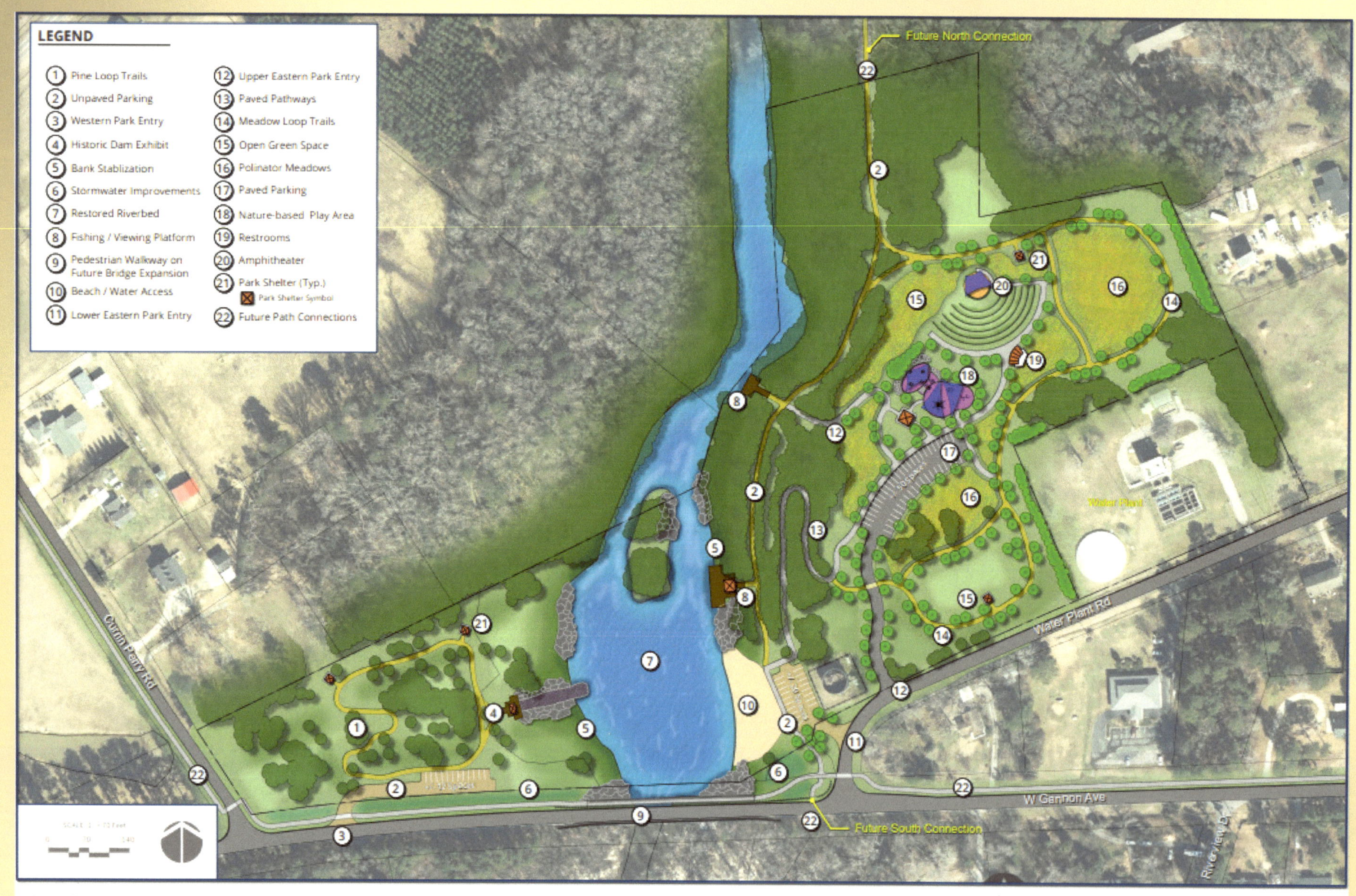

Little River Park Concept Plan